C.A. Weslager, Professor Emeritus of Brandywine College of Widener University is the foremost authority on the Delaware and Nanticoke Indians, as well as the 17th century Dutch, Swedish, and English settlements in the Delaware valley. His 20 previous books have received many citations including awards from the American Association of State and Local History.

Important places cited in text. Small lettering indicates names used in the
seventeenth century.

The Swedes and Dutch at New Castle

by C.A. Weslager

BART

NEW YORK

A MIDDLE ATLANTIC PRESS BOOK

First Middle Atlantic Press printing, October 1987

ISBN: 0-912608-50-1

Library of Congress Cataloging-in-Publication Data
Weslager, C. A. (Clinton Alfred)
    The Swedes and Dutch at New Castle.

    Includes index.
    1. New Castle (Del.)—History. 2. Swedish Americans—Delaware—New Castle—History—17th century. 3. Dutch Americans—Delaware—New Castle—History—17th century. 4. Delaware River Valley (N.Y.-Del. and N.J.)—History. 5. Swedish Americans—Delaware River Valley (N.Y.-Del. and N.J.)—History—17th century. 6. Dutch Americans—Delaware River Valley (N.Y.-Del. and N.J.)—History—17th century. I. Title.
    F174.N5W47 1987 975.1'1 87-11135

The Middle Atlantic Press, Inc.
848 Church Street
Wilmington, Delaware

Manufactured in the United States of America

TABLE OF CONTENTS

THE COVER DRAWING is the artist's impression of how the fort at New Castle may have appeared in the mid-seventeenth century after successive alterations by the Dutch and Swedish administrations. (Courtesy of the Historical Society of Delaware)

LIST OF ILLUSTRATIONS

GLOSSARY OF SELECT PLACE-NAMES USED IN TEXT

ALTENA, FORT

Dutch name for Fort Christina, used after Stuyvesant's 1655 invasion.

AMSTEL, FORT

Dutch fort at New Castle, first used in 1657 when the City of Amsterdam acquired New Castle and environs.

BEVERSREEDE, FORT

Fortified Dutch trading post on the Schuylkill River, built in 1648.

BOMBAY HOOK

Point of land where Delaware Bay ends and Delaware River begins, an English version of the Dutch name Boomptjes Hoeck ("Little-tree point").

CASIMIR, FORT

Dutch name for the fort at New Castle, built by Peter Stuyvesant in 1651.

CHRISTINA, FORT

Fort at present Wilmington, erected by the Swedes in 1638.

CHRISTINAHAMN

Village immediately north of Fort Christina, laid out in 1654–55 by Peter Lindeström on Governor Rising's orders.

ELFSBORG, FORT

Swedish fort on the Delaware River near Salem, New Jersey, erected by Governor Printz in 1643.

HOEREKILL

Dutch vernacular name for settlement at present Lewes, Delaware, which means Harlot's River; also called Swanendael.

MANHATTAN

Island at the mouth of the Hudson River, seat of the New Netherland.

MYGGENBORGH

"Mosquito Fort," name given by the Swedish garrison to Fort Elfsborg (see above) because of the prevalence of mosquitos.

NASSAU, FORT

Dutch fort at present Gloucester, New Jersey, erected in

	1626, and abandoned in 1655 after Fort Casimir was built.
NEW AMSTEL	Dutch name for New Castle, adopted in 1656 when the City of Amsterdam acquired Fort Casimir from the West India Company.
NEW AMSTERDAM	Principal Dutch settlement in the New Netherland on Manhattan Island, forerunner of present New York City.
NEW GOTHENBURG, FORT	Swedish Fort on Tinicum Island, Pennsylvania, built by Governor Printz in 1643.
PRINTZHOFF	Governor Printz's manse, erected on Tinicum Island in 1643–44 as his family residence.
SANTHOECK	Earliest Dutch name for New Castle.
TREFALDIGHET, FORT	Name given to Fort Casimir by the Swedish Governor Johan Rising in 1654 when he seized the stronghold from the Dutch.
TRINITY, FORT	English translation of Fort Trefaldighet, so named by Rising because he took the fort on Trinity Sunday.

PREFACE

NEW CASTLE'S HISTORY and architecture have been discussed in numerous articles, books, and papers, although a comprehensive history of the old Delaware town still remains to be written. The most commendable effort to date is *New Castle on the Delaware* by Jeannette Eckman (1882–1972), sponsored and published by the New Castle Historical Society. It was first published in 1936 and updated in later additions. Miss Eckman was a competent researcher and I knew her very well and admired her work. But her book was limited in size to less than 200 pages, and since it was intended as both a history and a tourist guide, her historical treatment was necessarily terse. Her appended chronology "Years and Events" summarized events from 1609 to the date of publication and it was not within the purview of her book to treat any of the entries in depth. Dr. John A. Munroe elaborated on some of these events in his informative volume *Colonial Delaware, A History* (KTO Press, 1978), but his focus was on the state, and the book doesn't purport to be a history of the town.

In this little book I have narrowed my scope to one phase of the story of New Castle, the early Dutch and Swedish period which ended with the English conquest of 1664. This delimitation permits me to treat the subject in depth, and, I hope, definitively. I have had the advantage of translations of Swedish and Dutch documents that have become available in recent years which permit new or revised interpretations of certain events in New Castle's early history. It is now evident that the Swedes and Finns had more influence than has generally been recognized, and the town's role in Delaware valley seventeenth century history must be seen in a broader context than "a little old Dutch town." As in my previous books, I have tried to write an account that historians will accept as a worthwhile contribution, but at the same time I have tried to reach general readers, including intelligent young adults, with a book that will provide information and reading enjoyment. For this reason my supporting documentation is placed at the end of the book to avoid distracting footnotes, but it is available for those who may want to check the source material.

Unless otherwise indicated, the dates used in the text correspond with those found in the contemporary references. In the seventeenth century the Dutch used the Gregorian system, or the new style calendar, which was ten days ahead of the Julian, or old style calendar that the Swedes and English continued to use. I have followed a style of capitalizing Company when reference is made to the Dutch West India Company, and City when references are made to the City of Amsterdam in chapters dealing with the City's colony.

The reader may find some of the family names confusing, and a brief explanation seems in order. Some Dutch proper names were formed by adding the suffix "zoon" or "zen," meaning "son," to a Christian name, and this was often abbreviated in writing to z, se, sen, or simply s. Willem, who was a son of Johan or Jan, might be identified as Willem Janszoon, Willem Janssen, Willem Jansen, Willem Janz, or Willem Jans.

He may have used different spellings at different times for his own name, or his name may appear one way in a certain document and in another way in another document. Sometimes a person's name was spelled in different ways in the same document.

In Swedish names Anders a son of Sven might be called Anders Svensson. Olla, a son of Anders Svensson could be known as Olla Andersson, and the patronymic could become a family surname. Under English influence Andersson became Anderson, and some individuals appended an alias to their names. One of the Johan Anderssons added Stalkofta ("steel jacket") to his name for the purpose of distinguishing himself from other Johan Anderssons. This evolved into a family name recorded as Staelcop or Stalcup-Stalcop. On at least one occasion John Andersson Stalcup's son reverted to the old system and referred to himself as John Johnson.

Kock, which means "cook" in Swedish, became a family name which Peter Larsson appended to his name to distinguish himself from other Larssons, i.e., Peter Larsson Kock. A prominent Swedish colonist named Lasse Cock continued to use the new surname substituting a C for a K.

At the time of a transition from a patronymic system to the American system of giving fixed surnames, Swedish names were often very confusing. Spelling by both Dutch and Swedes was also careless and inconsistent which is an aggravating problem for both the genealogist and historian, and the situation was worsened by the large number of illiterate persons who were dependent upon different scribes to record their names. Even the names of literate persons became garbled. A barber-surgeon who wrote his name Tymen Stiddem is variously referred to as Stidden, Stiddens, Stodden, Tiddens, and even Diddens!

In dealing with the name problem, I have adopted the style followed by Dr. Charles T. Gehring in transcribing entries found in primary sources; namely, I spell the name as it was given at a particular time and place, even though I may again spell it differently as it appears in another document. The possibility may exist that two different individuals are involved, and it could be a case of causing mistaken identity if a standardized spelling is arbitrarily used. Some exceptions have been made in the case of a few prominent persons. The form Peter Stuyvesant is consistently used in the text, even though he sometimes signed his Christian name Pieter (the Dutch form), Petrus (the Latin equivalent), and he sometimes spelled his surname Stuivjesant. Another exception is Peter Lindeström who sometimes wrote his surname Lindheström and his Christian name as Pehr, Per, or Petter. The Swedish governor's surname is consistently spelled Johan Rising, although it appears in some records as Risingh, and Stuyvesant spelled it Rysingh.

Another bewildering issue are the references to the Swedish daler and to Dutch guilders or florins. Readers are naturally curious about the equivalent value of this specie in terms of American dollars. One historian writing in 1908 believed that the seventeenth century guilder had the same buying power as forty cents in American money as of 1908. In 1965, a later historian wrote that the seventeenth century guilder had the buying power of about $10.50 in 1965 American money.

There is no practical way to support such speculations since a common, acceptable monetary standard is lacking to evaluate purchasing power. Even if money value could be translated into a select commodity it would be impossible to arrive at an equation having validity. How can one estimate what a TV set or an automobile would be worth in terms of bushels of wheat, corn—or any other common denominator—at a time when such products did not exist? What measure of monetary value could be placed on a seventeenth-century silver scabbard? It does not have any utilitarian value in America today, but as a rare antique its inflated museum value would be grossly disproportionate to its original value in Holland or Sweden as a functional artifact. Subsistence allowances in terms of the daler or guilder given to executives of the West India Company or the New Sweden Company have no relative basis for value comparisons with today's cost of living, which includes electricity, central heating, and indoor plumbing. Many of us have wrestled with this subject and we have not yet been able to equate seventeenth-century specie quantitatively with inflated dollars, marks, francs, or shillings. The reader's question, "How much would such-and-such amount be in American money?" must remain unanswered.

The cooperation extended by the staffs of the Albany Institute of History and Art, the Historical Society of Delaware, the Hockessin Public Library, the New York Historical Society, the New York State Library, the Pennsylvania Historical Society, and the Winterthur Museum Library is gratefully acknowledged.

I am also deeply grateful to my two colleagues, Peter S. Craig and Dr. Richard H. Hulan for their invaluable assistance. Both are specialists in their own right in the Swedish and Finnish occupations, and I have obtained their advice and critical comments on numerous topics relating to New Sweden, its people, and events.

I am also indebted for information or assistance to J.J. Alexander, Dr. Barbara Benson, Mary Childs Black, Roy Blankenship, Dr. Charles T. Gehring, Dr. Herbert C. Kraft, Dr. John A. Munroe, James A. Rementer, Judith A. Roberts, Hugh G. Ryan, Jr., and Dr. Andrew C. Twaddle. I am grateful to my granddaughter, Doctor-in-prospecto, Peggy A. Tatnall, for typing my manuscript and correcting it on her word processor.

C.A.W.

Brandywine College of
Widener University

1. THE SANTHOECK AND THE COMPANY

"A DAY IN Old New Castle" is celebrated once a year on the third Saturday in May. Delawareans, as well as visitors from near and far, make the rounds on foot in the closely-built area between the Strand and Fourth Street, bounded by Harmony Street and Delaware Avenue. The main attractions are the more than two-score public buildings, churches, and private houses. Many of these homes are open to the public on this special day, and for a moderate fee, visitors can see the interiors and the fine mantels, panelling, staircases, fireplaces, and beautiful period furniture owned and in daily use by the residents. Together the structures represent typical early American architecture, not reconstructions but the real thing, which is still being lived in. "History, adventure, and romance are written in the doorways and roof lines, in the broad chimneys, and in glimpses of spacious rear gardens," one historian wrote.

The residents love their old homes and take pride in welcoming appreciative visitors and in giving the day's proceeds to a fund for renovating and preserving the historic churches. There is no

1

question that the eighteenth and nineteenth century architecture is an authentic continuity with the past, but New Castle's history goes back many years before the oldest of these old houses was originally built. The true colonial vintage has been maintained, as few communities have, but there is a rare flavor in the earlier period that the visitor seldom ever tastes. This takes us back before Governor William Keith chartered the city of New Castle, before the first assembly met, before the old courthouse was built, and long before William Penn's arrival on October 27, 1682.

To begin at the beginning with the Lenape Indians, one of their names for the place where the town now stands was Quinamkot. It was not unusual for the Indians to have more than one name for the same place, and a second native name, Tamakonck, meant "place of the beaver." It is variously spelled in early documents, e.g., Tamicongh, Tomguncke, Tamecongh, Tamakock, and Camecouck. Since the Lenape had no system of reading or writing, and could not spell their words, it was difficult for Europeans to put down exactly what they heard when they addressed themselves to recording native sounds.

Tamakonck (in its various spellings) was a common Algonkian place-name; the modern town of Tamaqua in Schuylkill County, Pennsylvania derives its name from the Lenape word for a nearby stream. It was also an Indian personal name—Tamaqua, a Lenape chief during the French and Indian War, was called King Beaver by the English.[1] The Lenape had then become known as the Delaware Indians, a name given them by Anglo-Americans after the main river in their homeland derived from Lord de la Warre.

No one knows why New Castle was called "place of the beaver," but there may have been beaver colonies in two nearby creeks. One north of the town became known to the English as "ye Little or Town Creeke," and the second immediately south of the town is named Tamaconck on a 1654–55 Swedish map.[2] It is among Delaware's "lost creeks," but may possibly have been the "Mill Creek" shown on the New Castle map on p. 21 of Beers 1868 *Atlas of Delaware*.

The second name, Quinamkot, would be equally mystifying if a definitive name for the locale were not given in an Indian deed dated July 13, 1651. Therein, a Dutch scribe noted that land was purchased from a Lenape chief "at a place named the Santhoeck, otherwise called Quinamkot by the Indians."[3]

Santhoeck is given in other seventeenth-century accounts as Zand Hook, Sanhoeck, Sand-Hoek, Sandhock, Sandhuk, and in other forms. The first element is readily translatable as "sand," but the suffix "hoeck" has several possible Dutch meanings. Used in a topographical sense it did not refer to something bent and sharp like a fishhook. Hoeck was used to describe a blunted cape or headland, or a projecting corner extending into the water; in other words, a point. Professor A. R. Dunlap, an outstanding scholar of Delaware place-names, translated Santhoeck as a "long sandy point."[4] The word Sandhook, frequently used in the historical literature does not convey the true Dutch seventeenth-century meaning also reflected in the Lenape word Quinamkot, which can be translated as "a sandy area that is long." Thus Dutch and Indian names are practically synonymous.

Although the Santhoeck was never described in full detail in contemporary Dutch accounts, nor its measurements given, certain assumptions about its appearance can be made from brief passages in early Dutch, Swedish, and English sources. It was an unusual topographical feature, a tapered earthen promontory apparently covered with a sandy mantle; the front bank facing the river arose vertically from a narrow beach where the water was deep enough for large sailing vessels to anchor. There were other hoecks along the west bank of the Delaware River north of the Santhoeck, such as those referred to as Paerd Hook, Crane Hook, Tridie Hoeck, etc. All provided some sort of anchorage for sailing craft, but none had the characteristics of a natural pier where vessels could lighter their cargoes without the use of smaller landing craft. The ebb and flow of the tides and severe wind and rain storms over a succession of years eroded the Santhoeck. Alexander B. Cooper, a New Castle resident, wrote in 1905 that to his personal knowledge some thirty or forty feet of fastland at what was then called Front or Water Street had been "swept away by the erosion of tides within the last forty years."[5]

Nothing remains today of the point that gave the Santhoeck its name, but it is generally believed it was north of the end of present Chestnut Street (originally Thwart Street) and is now submerged in the waters of the river. Prior to the opening of the Delaware Memorial Bridge in 1951 this general area was the location of a slip of the New Castle ferry to New Jersey where automobiles often waited in long lines to cross the river.

Before the arrival of Europeans, the Lenape may have landed their dugout log canoes on the narrow beach when they paddled down the river on hunting or fishing trips. There is no historical or archeological evidence of an Indian village at the Santhoeck, but the writer has found arrowheads and other stone artifacts plowed up in the farm fields north and south of New Castle: evidence that it was Indian hunting territory. The Indians also trapped beavers, otters, muskrats, and other fur-bearing animals along the tributaries of the Lenape Wihittuck ("River of the Lenape"), their name for the Delaware, which the Dutch called the South River.* Dutch names for Delaware Bay were New Port May and Godyn's Bay.

There was a kind of primeval sameness along the flat shoreline of the Delaware with its low vegetation and marshes and backdrop of hardwood forests. The shoreline was indented with

---

*Seventeenth-century Dutch and Swedish accounts cited in this book refer to the South River inasmuch as the name Delaware River had not yet been applied to the stream. To avoid confusion, Delaware River has been used as a synonym for South River except in direct contemporary quotations.

the mouths of many tributaries, some skirted by marshland such as Lewes Creek, Broadkill, St. Jones Creek, Slaughter Creek, Mispillion, Cedar Creek, Murderkill, Blackbird, Drawyers, Duck Creek, and others. The Santhoeck with its higher elevation stood out in sharp relief in the landscape. It was such a conspicuous feature that the first Dutch mariners who explored the South River (in contrast to the North or Hudson River) could not have overlooked it. But it was no easy task to sail in safety so far up the uncharted stream.

A Dutch skipper wrote in 1633 after turning the prow of his vessel upstream from the present Lewes, "It is full of shoals between which are channels, from six to seven fathoms deep, but the deepest channel is on the west side." That was the side on which the Santhoeck was located, and he cautioned helmsmen sailing north from Cape Henlopen to be sure "to run in then [go] northwest along the west shore, and you will be out of danger of the banks, and keep [to] the west side where you should keep sounding . . ."[6] It was essential to keep measuring the depth of the water with a leaded line because many vessels foundered in the bay and river. To a ship's captain moving cautiously up the river, taking soundings to avoid the shoals that could ground the sturdiest craft without warning, the unexpected appearance of the Santhoeck was a welcome finger beckoning him to come ashore where the water was deep enough for safe anchorage.

A Dutch visitor viewing the Santhoeck in 1679 described it briefly as follows as he stood on the shore looking out at the river:

> . . . a point which extends out with a sandy beach affording a good landing place, better than is to be found elsewhere on that account. It lies a little above the bay where the river bends and runs south from there, so that you can see the river southerly, the greater portion of it, which presents a beautiful view in perspective, and enables you

to see from a distance the ships which come out of the great bay and sail up the river.[7]

The first navigator to enter Delaware Bay was an experienced English sea captain in Dutch employ named Henry Hudson. Hudson anchored his vessel the *Half Moon* opposite Cape Henlopen on August 28, 1609, but he refused to take the risk of sailing up the river because of the shoals. Hudson's first mate Robert Juet noted in the logbook that "hee that will thoroughly Discover this great Bay, must have a small Pinasse [pinnace] that must draw but four of five fotte [foot of] water to sound before him."[8] Hudson's "discovery" of the bay, even though he reversed the course of his vessel before entering the Delaware River, was the basis for the Dutch claim to ownership of the territory.

About seven years later, a Dutch navigator named Cornelis Hendricksen came into Delaware Bay in a yacht called the *Onrust* (*Restless*). Hendricksen believed that his little craft could safely navigate the river without stranding on the shoals and he headed upstream. He could not have missed seeing the Santhoeck as he sailed as far north as the Schuylkill and back south again to the bay and the open ocean. There is no evidence that he landed at the Santhoeck. His mission was not to find suitable landing places or potential Dutch town sites, but to learn whether the Delaware River valley held promise for commercial opportunities that would benefit the Dutch merchants who employed him.

On August 16, 1616, after his return to Holland, Hendricksen reported to his employers that he found a bay and three rivers in the latitude of from 38 to 40 degrees, presumably the Delaware, Christina, and Schuylkill, although he did not give them any names. He may have been unaware that Hudson "found" the same bay seven years before, or if he knew about it, he was reluctant to give credit to someone else. Hendricksen said the climate was temperate; the woods were full of trees, including oaks, hickories, and pines, which he knew would interest shipbuilders in Holland where trees were scarce; he had seen bucks, does, turkeys, and partridges; and he had traded with the native inhabitants for "Sables, Furs, Robes, and other skins." Accompanying his report he submitted a "Figurative Map" showing the yet unnamed Delaware River as he thought its course to be, although the map has numerous inaccuracies. There is no reference to the Santhoeck on this first known map of the Delaware River drainage system.[9]

The encouraging news that furs were plentiful in the Delaware River valley awakened the interest of Dutch merchants, who formed small companies and dispatched a number of vessels to barter with the Indians; individual merchants also engaged in the fur trade.[10] Although these early Dutch traders established commercial relations with the native tribes, and limited geographical information was obtained about the New World during their voyages, aggressive exploitation of the fur trade did not occur until after the formation of the Dutch West India Company in 1621. The Company's vast financial resources permitted full development of the Indian trade in a territory already known as the New Netherland, which included southern Connecticut, New York State, New Jersey, parts of eastern Pennsylvania, and all of the state of Delaware. How the Company was structured and what action it took to attain its objectives are relevant to the first settlement made at the Santhoeck; the directors shaped the destiny of the New Netherland, and New Castle had its genesis in the West India Company.

The States General, the "parliament" or ruling body of the government of the Dutch provinces, which were known in the aggregate as the United Netherlands, supported the formation of the Dutch West India Company.* The States General owned

---

*In the present text the United Netherlands has been abbreviated to the Netherlands, and is used interchangeably with the word Holland, even though Holland was only one of the provinces. The word Dutch used as a noun or adjective refers to Holland and/or the Netherlands. New Netherland is singular; it may or may not be preceded by the article.

stock in the Company and supplied a number of warships and yachts to reinforce the Company's fleet. In many ways the Company was a political and military arm of the government. The charter issued by the States General gave the Company a monopoly for a limited time to trade in specified foreign waters, including the full sweep of North and South American coasts and the western coast of Africa. The authority delegated by the States General to the Company seems incredible in contrast to the legal restraints imposed upon modern American corporations. It was authorized to make alliances with native rulers, which included negotiating treaties and agreements with the chiefs of the American Indian tribes. It had the right to establish its own colonies, set up courts to administer justice, appoint governors and other officers to supervise its colonies, build forts, and hire soldiers and sailors to protect its vessels and properties.

Another, and a prime objective delegated to the Company, was to weaken Spain's power by capturing Spanish ships and seizing the gold and silver the vessels were transporting to Spain from the New World. If it served the Company's best interests its ships could attack and raid Spanish colonies.

The Company was divided into five separate units called "Cameren," which a modern corporation might designate as divisional offices, but is literally translatable in English as "Chambers." Unlike the branch offices of modern business organizations each Chamber had its own directorate, and the Chambers often operated independently of each other. There was an overall nineteen-member executive committee representing all the Chambers, known as the Assembly of XIX, where decisions affecting the whole Company were made. The States General had a representative on the Assembly of XIX enabling the government to participate in the Company's deliberations, but policy decisions did not require his approval.[11]

With its fleet of more than 100 well-built, armed ships

and yachts, its wealthy and politically prominent directors and investors, and its 8,000 to 9,000 employes including soldiers and seamen, the Company was primarily motivated by commercial incentives. The directors considered it more important to make profits for its investors than to spread Dutch civilization and culture to Africa or the North and South American continents. The directors had no doubt that the Company's success or failure would ultimately be measured in dollars and cents—or in Dutch terms, guilders and stuivers. The directors believed that colonization should be undertaken only if required to enhance the Company's commerce and contribute to the overall profits.

The Amsterdam Chamber with its twenty directors administered the affairs of the New Netherland through a committee called the "Commissioners for New Netherland." It is reasonably certain that when the initial plans were made for exploiting the New Netherland neither the directors of the Amsterdam Chamber nor the Assembly of XIX knew that the Santhoeck existed. None of them had yet visited the Delaware River valley and they had no reason to recognize the potential importance of the Santhoeck.

To characterize the West India Company solely in terms of its activities in the New Netherland is a very narrow view, because the investors were concerned with the Company's far flung business interests: the gold, ivory, and slave trade of West Africa; the sugar of Brazil and Surinam; the salt of Venezuela; and the cochineal, tobacco, amber, precious stones, drugs, and other products of Saba, St. Martin, St. Eustatius, and Curaçao in the West Indies. The New Netherland was only a small part of the Company's commercial enterprises, and the Company could have survived if the New Netherland never existed.[12] Since the New Netherland looms high in the context of American colonial history, a false impression has been made that the West India Company's dominant commercial activities were along the American east coast. The fact is that South America and Africa each provided much greater profits to the Company than the New Netherland.

Sharp differences of opinion developed among the directors of the Amsterdam Chamber about the most efficacious method for the exploitation of the New Netherland—and that meant the most economical way to get the maximum financial return for minimal expenditures in contrast to the opportunities available in other lands. There was general agreement that emphasis should be given to the fur trade because of the profitable market for furs in Holland and in certain other European countries. For many years Russia had been the premier source of high quality furs, but the supply had thinned because of the decrease in the animal population, and the demand for furs in Russia itself. The profit margin on furs was also an important inducement to the directors, but there was no unanimity about the best way to acquire the furs.

One faction of the Amsterdam Chamber held the view that the Company should establish permanent trading posts strategically located for the convenience of the Indians. Small craft suitable for navigating the inland streams could then be dispatched from these posts to trade farther inland with the Indians. Knowledge of American geography, especially the lands west of the Delaware and Hudson Rivers, was still incomplete, making planning very difficult. Nevertheless, the directors were persuaded that periodically larger vessels sent from Holland could transport goods used in the Indian trade and provisions to supply the Company's agents, and return home with the furs that awaited their arrival. Maintaining ships and compensating captains and crews, as well as the agents employed to handle the Indian trade, had to be evaluated in relation to the net returns from the ultimate sale of the furs.

The question of shipping provisions to the agents and other employes at the trading posts was fully discussed, and some of the directors felt that this was expensive and impractical. It would make the Company's employes in the New Netherland dependent for their livelihood on food and supplies shipped at a distance of 3,000 miles. An alternative plan of having the agents raise their own food and maintain their own communities didn't make good sense either. A trader could not be a farmer, herdsman, and a craftsman at the same time he was expected to develop the full potential of the fur business. There were only two methods to obtain furs—go to the Indians in their towns and camps, or attract the Indians to come to the trading posts. Dutch traders eventually used both methods.

A consensus was reached that small agricultural colonies consisting of non-traders should be established to support the fur-trading personnel. From the little that was then known about New Netherland geography, the directors agreed that fur-trading should be concentrated at trading posts along the Delaware, the Hudson, and the Connecticut or Fresh River, the three major waterways in New Netherland. These posts were intended as combination storehouses and living quarters for the Company's employes, who consisted of traders to negotiate with the Indians; clerks to control the inventories of trade goods and reconcile the accounts with the main office in Amsterdam; and a garrison to protect the post against possible Indian attacks.

The directors also intended that self-supporting farmers would live in houses in the areas around the trading posts and would raise food to provision themselves and the employes at the posts. This was less costly than making transatlantic shipments of foodstuffs which was "ten times the expense" of growing it on the site.[13] In an emergency the farmers and families could find protection in the fortified posts.

This system would also free valuable cargo space to transport the trade merchandise needed to barter with the Indians. The directors recognized what many authors writing about the fur trade do not fully understand. Pelts obtained from the Indians were purchased with merchandise shipped from Holland in sailing vessels during costly voyages of seven or eight weeks duration, and often twice that length of time in bad weather. Ships were also subject to interruption by reason of war, piracy, and shipwreck. The insurance premium alone on ship and cargo was costly, entirely apart from the wages and expense of meals, drink, and medical care for officers and crew.

It goes without saying that the monetary value of the furs was many times the value of cheap trade merchandise if the two commodities were placed side by side. This apparent disparity does not take into account the cargo space required and the shipping costs of transporting large quantities of bulky trade merchandise. The shipments had to be accumulated at ports of departure, carefully packed, especially the breakable goods, and loaded aboard the vessel. Some of the goods had to be specially fabricated to meet the changing demands of the Indian customers, and as the natives became more sophisticated and learned more about the available variety of European merchandise, such as guns, ammunition, fabrics, copper and iron kettles, etc., they became less interested in cheap glass beads and baubles.

If the trade merchandise failed to reach the New Netherland due to bad weather, shipwrecks, or attacks by enemy vessels, the traders awaiting the arrival of the ships could not consummate their negotiations. Since the Indians were impatient to conduct business once they had a supply of pelts to trade, there was always the possibility that they would be diverted to the French, the English, and others, to barter their skins. If everything went according to plan, a Dutch ship would safely make its scheduled arrival and unload its cargo of trade merchandise, as well as tools, weapons, and durable goods for use by the Company's employes. It would then return to Holland with its hold loaded with bundles of animal pelts to be sold at a good profit for use in making robes, cloaks, muffs, coats, and trimming for fine clothing at a substantial profit to the Company. Beaver pelts, highly prized because they could be felted, were used to make

Traders bartering with the Lenape for furs, baskets of corn, and other edibles in exchange for blankets, iron axe heads, scissors, glass beads, pots, gun, and other goods. Two women wearing duffel cloth shawls paint their faces using mirror for first time. Two braves at left enjoy new sensation of drinking rum. Indian pet dogs wonder what is going on. (Courtesy Dr. H. C. Kraft, Seton Hall University Museum, South Orange, N. J.)

the broad-brimmed conical hats worn in the Netherlands, and they brought premium prices in the Dutch market.

If the Dutch vessels were relieved of bringing edibles to the Company's employes they could transport larger cargoes of axes, hatchets, adzes, knives, looking-glasses, gilded chains, finger-rings, combs, earrings, and the fragile white clay smoking pipes prized by the Indians but worth less than a penny in Holland. Another Dutch commodity in demand among all the eastern Woodland tribes was "duffel cloth" (named for Duffel, a suburb of Antwerp where it was made), a coarsely woven cloth dyed blue, red, or brown, shipped in bolts and sold by lengths. The Lenape used the cloth as a shawl worn around their shoulders, or tied around their loins like a girdle with flaps in the front and back, and at night as a blanket. The Lenape had no woven fabrics before the Europeans arrived and were eager to obtain cloth as a substitute for their fur garments.

The early Dutch traders were forbidden to introduce muskets and gunpowder to the Indians in exchange for furs, and the neighboring colonies also passed laws and regulations intended to prevent firearms reaching their Indian customers. It did not take the Indians long to recognize that European guns were more effective hunting weapons than stone arrowheads and spears, and they demanded guns for their beaver pelts. Despite the fact that the risk existed that these weapons could be used against the Europeans, the greed of the traders made the laws unenforceable. One nation blamed another for permitting the illicit trade in firearms, but all must share the guilt.

Dutch traders also had to have a supply of wampum beads, known as sewan or sewant, when bartering with the natives. Indians often demanded so many yards of duffel, for example, plus a certain quantity of sewant in exchange for a given number of pelts. The traders acquired the beads from coastal tribes in New England and at Manhattan and Long Island who made them from seashells; the Nanticokes of the Eastern Shore of Maryland were widely reputed for their skill in fabricating shell beads. As the Dutch population increased, Dutch currency became scarce and sewant was frequently used as a medium of exchange among the settlers in lieu of money.

The directors of the Amsterdam Chamber expected that the farmers who agreed to go to America to grow food for the Company's fur traders would also be able to raise a surplus of wheat, rye, and barley that could be shipped to Holland and sold there. This seemed to be a bonus that an agricultural colony afforded even though the plan never materialized. The directors also thought there was a possibility that ambitious individuals might gather wild grapes that could be converted to grapejuice or fermented to make exportable wines, brandywine, vinegar, or dried as raisins. Oil might be pressed from the many kinds of edible nuts that reportedly grew in the New Netherland; copper, iron, lead, gold, silver, sulphur—or even diamonds and rubies might be found, or a pearl fishery established.[14] Lacking detailed information about the natural resources in the New Netherland, no one in Amsterdam knew what products the undeveloped country might yield in addition to furs, whose availability was already known, but the directors had high hopes, many of which proved overly optimistic.

Some of the investors disapproved the plan of founding agricultural colonies supportive of the trading posts, but there seems to have been general agreement on one issue. There were fears in Amsterdam that a rival European nation might try to seize the territory in America chartered to the West India Company. If the land were only sparsely settled by a relatively few fur traders it could readily be taken over by the English, for example, who claimed the New Netherland by right of the prior discoveries of John Cabot. Colonies of farmers as adjuncts to the trading posts would be good insurance to protect the Company's commerce from such competition. Fears about English intrusion were well founded; the Virginia Company had already settled Jamestown, which had become a Crown colony, and the Puritans in New England were expanding into Connecticut. The

New Netherland lay in a vulnerable position between the threat of the two growing English settlements.

In theory the Amsterdam directors who espoused the program discussed above had found the answer, but in practice they encountered many problems. There was no enthusiastic response to the call for Dutch families to go to America to seek their fortunes as farmers. Exciting and romantic exploits on the high seas and voyages to distant lands had storybook appeal to adventurers, but moving to the American wilderness to settle permanently as dirt farmers and herdsmen was something else. Dutch families were contented at home and too comfortable to leave. They enjoyed religious freedom to a higher degree than people in most other countries, and they were living at the peak of an era of economic prosperity—often referred to as Holland's Golden Age. Why leave their homeland and risk the uncertainties of settling in an undeveloped country, from which they might never return, in order to enrich the coffers of the West India Company?

The Amsterdam Chamber was fortunate that a group of Walloons, French-speaking Protestants, agreed to chance it in America. In the spring of 1624 the directors gave free passage to thirty families "mostly Walloons" to leave for the New Netherland to engage in agriculture.[15] These Walloons went as independent entrepreneurs; they were not paid employes of the Company, although they were sponsored by the Company and beholden to the Amsterdam directors.[16] Ownership of specified tracts of land was transferred free of charge to each family on their arrival, the size depending on the number of members in the family. The Walloons contracted to reside in the New Netherland for at least six years. At the end of that time they could remain if they chose or dispose of their property by gift or sale and return home. The Company decided what products they should sow and cultivate and consented to become the exclusive customer for their crops. Thus, the Walloons were guaranteed a market for their products to be used as provisions by the

Company's employes. During the period the Walloons were building homes and preparing their fields for cultivation the Company provided them with food, clothing, and other supplies at reasonable prices. The Walloons agreed to discharge their debts after they harvested their crops.[17]

The Walloon families were assigned to three or four different locations at or near newly-built trading posts. The location of principal concern to us was a place called Hooghe Eylant ("High Island") in the Delaware River where three or four Walloon farm families settled in the summer of 1624. A trading post "provided with palisades and battlements" was also built on the island for use by the Company's employes. Through careful study of contemporary maps and other source material, the writer identified Hooghe Eylant as present Burlington Island in the Delaware River within the state of New Jersey, north of Philadelphia.[18] Regrettably very little is known about this and the other Walloon settlements because letters, reports, and other papers in the files of the West India Company dated earlier than 1700 were bundled up and sold as waste in Holland in 1821.[19] This has been a serious handicap to the historian, but the early period is not a complete void because notarial records, private correspondence, and journals that have been preserved provide information to fill some of the gaps.

For instance, additional Walloons and some "hired" farmers employed by the Company were sent from Holland in 1625, and they brought livestock with them. The exact number of settlers is unknown, nor do the records indicate how many were placed in Burlington Island; what is known is that the expedition included 103 head of livestock (stallions, mares, bulls, and cows), as well as hogs and sheep, transported in two vessels.[20]

A commander, or chief residential trader, accompanied the second expedition, Willem Verhulst, also referred to as the "provisional director." The original intent of the Amsterdam Chamber was to make Burlington Island the seat of the agricultural colony on the Delaware River, and also the Company's commercial headquarters in the New Netherland. This was before Manhattan Island was purchased from the Indians.

The Walloons sent to plant at Fort Orange (present Albany, New York) sowed grain which was ready for harvesting in the fall of 1625, but the records are silent with regard to the progress of farming on Burlington Island. No doubt the industrious Walloons immediately began to cultivate the fertile land on the island, and Verhulst, who was then in charge of all the settlements in the New Netherland, was instructed to "strengthen the population of the southern colony [on the Delaware] most."[21] In the years 1624 and 1625 the Company's agents shipped 9,295 beaver pelts and 1,136 other pelts to Holland—a promising beginning.[22] The records do not state how many of these furs came from the Delaware nor how many were obtained from the Indians on the Hudson.

A visitor to Burlington Island today might gain the impression that its size scarcely justified its selection as the New Netherland headquarters of the great West India Company. However, the directors did not intend to confine the occupation to the island, but anticipated the population would expand in due course to the mainland. As the following passage indicates, the directors expected to settle the island as well as both sides of the river; the italics are supplied:

> . . . the said island is in itself a level field with a fertile soil and *on both sides has as much suitable arable and pasture land as well as all kinds of timber*, so that a large number of families could support themselves there better than on the North River.[23]

Today the city of Burlington, New Jersey is situated on the eastern side of the river immediately opposite the island, and Bristol, Pennsylvania lies on the western side.[24]

One might ask: What does Burlington Island have to do with the history of New Castle, Delaware? The answer is that New Castle evolved as the culmination of a series of interrelated

events. Each must be seen in proper perspective to understand
what subsequently occurred. If the directors had selected the
Santhoeck as the "capital" of their colony on the Delaware,
which is what later happened, the town's history would have
been different. If the directors then had a full grasp of the
geography of the region, and the territories occupied by the
different Indian tribes, it is not likely they would have chosen
Burlington Island when the Santhoeck would have better served
their goals. It didn't take long for the Company's American
executives to recognize that a mistake had been made, because
neither the Walloon colony nor the trading post on Burlington
Island survived more than two years. Peter Minuit, who succeeded Verhulst, decided in 1626 to concentrate the scattered
Walloon settlements on Manhattan Island (present New York
City) where the Company erected another fort. The town that
sprung up around the fort was called New Amsterdam. Located
at the mouth of the Hudson River it was commercially attractive
because of its access to the Atlantic Ocean and its navigable
harbor. There were also other considerations; Indian troubles at
Fort Orange resulted in the deaths of several Dutch soldiers and
Minuit feared that Indian attacks might wipe out the Walloon
population at Fort Orange and on Burlington Island. A concentration of the settlers at one location meant greater security, and
there were also economic benefits since a small number of
skilled craftsmen could serve the needs of a single colony more
efficiently than duplicating their functions at several locations.

The plan of having scattered agricultural colonies to support a
series of fur trading posts didn't work out as envisioned, and the
directors continued to hold differing views. An articulate faction
of the directorate of the Amsterdam Chamber continued to
oppose long-term investments in any kind of colony in favor of
concentrating on the fur trade at the lowest possible cost, strictly
for short-term profits.

With Burlington Island vacated the Company needed a base
for the fur trade with the Indians on the Delaware River, and

Fort Nassau was erected in 1626 at what is now Gloucester, New Jersey between the mouths of Newton and Big Timber Creeks. The name commemorated the family of the assassinated Dutch hero, William the Silent, Prince of Orange, who was from Nassau. The post was essentially a fortified market place which normally was used only at certain times of the year. In the winter when the animal pelts became thick, luxurious, and more valuable, the Indians roamed the woods trapping and hunting. Instead of incurring the expense of maintaining a garrison at the fort, Minuit found it was more practical and less expensive to send sloops from New Amsterdam with trade goods to meet the Indians at designated times. The traders usually bartered in the spring for the Indians' winter haul and then sailed back to New Amsterdam, their vessels loaded with bundles of pelts.

Fort Nassau also had potential military value if the English attempted to make a foothold in the Delaware Valley, and occasionally soldiers were left to garrison the fort—especially when rumors reached Minuit of other nationalities attempting to compete in the fur trade. Fort Nassau during the early stages of its existence was never permanently occupied, nor was it permanently vacated.

The pelts transported from Fort Nassau were temporarily stored at New Amsterdam along with skins obtained from the Indian tribes along the Hudson and Connecticut Rivers and elsewhere. The furs were then consolidated in periodic shipments to Holland. New Amsterdam became a sort of branch office of the Company with a small staff of bookkeepers, cashiers, and clerks who handled inventories, accounting details, and related communications with the main office in Amsterdam. Initially the number of Company employes was relatively small, but they had to be fed and housed, and like modern corporations the West India Company often transferred key personnel from one location to another. Even those directors who opposed the cost of colonization learned there was no way to avoid the expense of maintaining employes and their families at New

Amsterdam. Although some farming was carried on, New Amsterdam could not feed itself, and the cost of shipping provisions, food, tools, and clothing continued to be a drain on the Company's finances. Making a profit in the New Netherland large enough to satisfy the shareholders was no easy task.

Fort Nassau proved to be on the wrong side of the Delaware River for developing the maximum business in the Indian fur trade, and it was too far up the river to have real military value. It could not prevent enemy vessels from entering Delaware Bay and sailing up the river past the Santhoeck, the mouth of the Christina, and the Schuylkill. Although the local Lenape brought their furs to the fort to trade, the insatiable demand for pelts soon resulted in a scarcity of beavers and otters in the lower Delaware valley. The Dutch traders learned that the beaver population was much larger in the valley of the Susquehanna River and in the mountain tributaries west of the Susquehanna. This area was a hundred miles from the banks of the Delaware River, and some of the best beaver pelts came from even farther west.

The Lenape did not hunt or trap in the Susquehanna Valley which was occupied by a tribe called the Minquas. Another tribe called the Black Minquas (because they wore gorgets of black stone around their necks) lived beyond the Alleghenies. These Minquas people, whose language and culture were different from those of the Lenape, were hostile to the Lenape. Minquas war parties raided Lenape villages burning wigwams and cornfields and killing Lenape males. Many of the Indian families living in Delaware fled across the river to seek haven in New Jersey's pine woods. Lenape people living in New Jersey were also forced to vacate some of their villages due to Minquas attacks. Displaced, unsettled, and living in an area with a diminishing animal population, the Lenape were unable to supply adequate pelts to the Dutch traders.[25]

Learning that the Dutch paid well for pelts, especially beaver skins, the Minquas came to Fort Nassau to barter. They traveled long distances by canoe and overland trails, or portages, connecting the headwaters of the tributaries to the Chesapeake with the tributaries to the Delaware. One of these trails led from the head of the Bohemia River in Maryland to the head of Appoquinimink Creek in Delaware; another brought them from the head of the Elk River to the head of the Christina; still another led them to the southside of the Schuylkill River. All of these routes terminated at places on the west bank of the Delaware, and the Indians had to complete the journey by crossing the river with their heavy bundles of pelts. Then they retraced their steps carrying Dutch trade goods back to their homes on the Susquehanna River.

If the Dutch had relocated Fort Nassau to the west bank of the Delaware it would have been a more convenient location for the Minquas. At this time the West India Company had no competition for the fur trade on the Delaware, and the Company was not inclined to invest in a new trading post. Within a few short years circumstances changed, and the Company regretted not having moved Fort Nassau to a site on the opposite side of the river; but initially Nassau stood as the only European trading post in the sprawling, undisturbed woodlands of the Delaware Valley.

In 1631, five years after Fort Nassau was built, the Dutch made a settlement at present Lewes, known then as Swanendael—the first within the bounds of the present state of Delaware. The West India Company was not its sponsor. It was a private project financed by Samuel Godyn, president of the Amsterdam Chamber, Samuel Blommaert, and several other officials of the Company designated as "patroons." Under the influence of Godyn and other well-to-do directors who strongly favored colonization, the Assembly of XIX approved granting patroonships to members willing to establish commercial colonies at their own expense. The patroons were obliged to select and register land within certain limits approved by the Company and then extinguish the Indian title by purchase. The wages of settlers sent from Holland, the cost of their passage, and the expenses of erecting forts and other buildings were paid for by the patroons. If the venture succeeded, the patroons, not the Company, stood to enjoy the profits.

Godyn received reports that whales had been sighted in Delaware Bay, and whale fishing was uppermost in his plans. Whale oil was in demand in Holland as a fuel for lamps and as a lubricant for machinery in an age when the refining of petroleum was unknown. Godyn dispatched an agent who selected a suitable site along the Delaware Bay and paid the Indians in trade goods for a small tract along the bayshore. Twenty-eight men were sent from Holland as the nucleus of the colony; women and children would come later. The objective was clearly set forth, "to carry on the whale fishery in that region, as to plant a colony for the cultivation of all sorts of grain for which the country is well adapted and tobacco."[26]

The fur trade had very little to do with the settlement; Godyn and the other patroons were prohibited from bartering with the Indians for furs—an activity the Company reserved for itself unless the patroons were given special permission. Godyn believed that whale oil, tobacco, and grains shipped from his colony would make the project a success without the need to export furs.

The settlers built a palisaded fort on a navigable tributary to the bay which became known to the Dutch as the Hoerenkil ("Harlot's River"), later called Lewes Creek, now part of the Lewes Rehoboth Canal.[27] The creek was wide enough to provide a suitable roadstead for sailing vessels and the soil on its banks was fertile. The men immediately began to cultivate the land and plant crops. The advantage of the location was that the bay was readily accessible from the fort by boat, and when whales came into the bay the men could paddle out and harpoon them. When the whales left the bay and went out to sea the men could spend time in the fields. Everything seemed to fit together nicely, but the plans did not materialize. Due to a tragic misunderstanding with one of the Lenape bands called the Ciconicins, or Sickoneysincks, who lived nearby, the Indians turned against the Dutchmen, massacred all of them, and burned down their fort. That was the end of Swanendael, the first and last attempt of the patroons to found a colony on the Delaware.[28]

Would the outcome have been different if Godyn's agent had selected the Santhoeck as the site for the colony? The soil there was also fertile, and a Dutch mariner noted in January of 1633 that he saw a whale at the mouth of the Delaware River and two larger ones farther upstream. A fourth whale was observed in the river north of the Christina.[29] Since there was no Indian town at the Santhoeck, perhaps Godyn's colony might have survived there without antagonizing the natives. If so, it would have changed the course of history.

The fact remains that, despite its impermanence, the first European settlement within the bounds of the state of Delaware was made at the site of Lewes. It was truly the ''cradle of a state'' just as the Walloon settlement on Burlington Island was the first in New Jersey, although neither lasted very long. Meanwhile the Santhoeck lying on the Delaware at a strategic point between the destroyed Swanendael and the misplaced Fort Nassau languished from inattention.

2. THE COMING OF THE SWEDES

ALTHOUGH THE DIRECTORS of the Amsterdam Chamber of the West India Company were apprehensive of foreign intrusion in the New Netherland they did not anticipate a surprise move by a nation with which Holland was then on friendly terms—Sweden. In fact, there were unusually close ties between the two countries, which the leading authority on the Swedish settlements in America characterized as follows:

From Holland, Sweden received many of its best and most useful citizens, capitalists, merchants, and warriors. Dutch soldiers served in Swedish armies and Dutch captains and skippers commanded Swedish ships; Swedish students went to Holland to study commerce, and Swedish scholars gained inspiration from Dutch teachers; Dutch money helped Sweden to support its armies and found its commercial companies and Dutch brains developed the industries of the country, and from Holland came the first impulse for transatlantic trade.[1]

He might have added that the Dutch language was spoken, as well as Swedish, in many cities in Sweden. Attempts were made in the city of Gothenburg to make Dutch the official language of the city administration. It is not surprising that many of the official Swedish documents relating to New Sweden were written in Dutch, and that some soldiers in Swedish service in America, as well as "Swedish" colonists, were born in Holland.

A succession of treaties was made between the two countries to cement their friendship, and the States General apparently had no warning that friendly Sweden would suddenly become a formidable rival in the New World. To make matters worse the rivalry occurred in specific territory, within the Delaware Valley, to which the Dutch claimed ownership.

What had happened was that the Company recalled Peter Minuit from his post at New Amsterdam as director-general of the New Netherland. This decision had a significant effect on Delaware Valley history, although it was unanticipated by the directors. Minuit and several of his associates were ordered to return to Holland in the summer of 1632 for interrogation. Controversies developed in the Amsterdam Chamber about the granting of patroonships, which some of the directors opposed. Minuit was a proponent of the patroon system and this alienated him from the anti-patroon faction in the directorate. His adversaries claimed he incurred unnecessary expenses for the Company, and other charges were made against his administration, some prompted by personal enmity.

The records giving full detail about these accusations are missing, but from the scant information now available it would appear that Minuit was an honest, conscientious Company employe during the six years he held office in New Amsterdam; otherwise he would have been replaced. He was a member of the original Verhulst administration and apparently had formerly lived on the Delaware River, possibly on Burlington Island. In January 1625, more than a year before Manhattan Island was purchased from the Indians, Verhulst was instructed to have "Pierre Minuyt and others whom he shall deem fit investigate what minerals and crystals there may be both on the North River and South River . . ." and send samples of each mineral that looked promising to Holland, as well as "dyes, drugs, gums, herbs, plants, trees, and flowers."[2]

As Verhulst's successor, Minuit administered the Company's business from his office on Manhattan Island. He issued patents there on behalf of the Company for the patroon settlement at Swanendael; he was in office when the Indians massacred the settlers at Swanendael, news that must have grieved him because he, Samuel Godyn, and Samuel Blommaert were friends. During his administration, 47,196 beaver pelts, 5,388 otter skins, and an unrecorded quantity of bear, fox, raccoon, muskrat, mink, and other animal pelts had been shipped to Holland for the Company.[3]

The farms, or boweries, as they were known, which Minuit laid out on Manhattan Island produced the earliest tobacco crops grown by the Dutch in the New Netherland. Other crops were grown and livestock raised, although they were insufficient to provision the Company's employes. Food, tools, clothing, and other necessary supplies continued to be shipped from Holland to maintain the fur trading establishment.[4] Since it was never the Company's intention to support a full-scale government in the New Netherland, Minuit innovated a quasi-military system of law and order which adequately served its purpose. At the time of his recall the total population of the New Netherland was slightly in excess of 300 men, women, and children, not an auspicious growth to culminate a six year period of Dutch occupation.

The small population cannot be blamed on Minuit, an advocate of colonization. It was the result of the vacillation of the directors on the issue of supporting agricultural colonies as opposed to extracting the maximum profits from the fur trade without the expenses of colonization. The failure of the Amsterdam Chamber to subsidize farmers to reinforce the Walloons sent to the New Netherland also weakened the colonization effort.[5]

The aggressive colonization of Pennsylvania, which came more than two decades later, provides a sharp contrast to the feeble efforts of the West India Company to settle the New Netherland. In the three years following William Penn's arrival in 1682 the population of Pennsylvania grew to 7,200 persons and continued to increase.[6] Penn was intent on attracting new settlers to his province, and he did not have to debate the issue with a contentious board of directors. The twenty directors of the Amsterdam Chamber failed to agree on a unilateral policy, and the population of the New Netherland remained static.

Did Minuit resign or was he discharged? The answer is not known, but after the hearing ended in Amsterdam, Minuit was no longer in the Company's employ. Resentful over his treatment, Minuit left Holland and became associated with a new Swedish company headquartered in Stockholm, which has been told in detail by Johnson.[7] The Swedes found that Minuit was an unusual executive who probably knew more about the New Netherland than any other living person. He subsequently played a dominant role in organizing a New Sweden Company; he gave the colony the name New Sweden before it was actually founded. He was a dominant figure in outfitting two vessels, the *Kalmar Nyckel* (*Key of Kalmar*) and the *Fogel Grip* (*Bird Griffin*), and engaging their crews. The directors of the new company had no reservation about placing him in command of the first Swedish expedition to America.

The objective of the New Sweden Company, operating in cooperation with the government that provided the two vessels, ammunition, and cash, was to compete with the Dutch in the fur trade, raise tobacco and other grains for export, and expand Swedish civilization. Converting the Indians "in the true religion and worship" was also one of the Company's aims. The underlying motive was commercial, but the difference between

Holland and Sweden was that the New Sweden Company intended a transplantation of Swedish society to the New World.

Minuit made detailed plans before the two vessels sailed from Sweden. He probably knew where he intended to make a settlement—on a stream the Dutch called the Minquas Kill ("the River of the Minquas") because it was one of the waterways leading to the country where the Minquas lived. The stream is specifically named in the instructions he took with him when he sailed from Sweden.[8] Minuit knew that a trading post on the Minquas Kill would be a convenient location to negotiate with the Susquehanna tribe and would divert the trade away from Fort Nassau. His vessels carried quantities of duffels, axes, hatchets, mirrors, gilded chains, finger rings, combs, and other trade merchandise he knew would appeal to the Indians. The spiritual needs of the crews and passengers were not overlooked; Minuit was instructed to have prayers read and a psalm sung every morning and evening.

The two Swedish vessels arrived in Delaware Bay in the spring of 1638, and Minuit carefully avoided the shoals by guiding the skippers up the river following the channel that ran close to the Santhoeck. The *Kalmar Nyckel*, the larger of the two craft, was a man-o-war requiring deep water, and Minuit couldn't take the chance of having her stranded on a sand bar in the river. If Fort Nassau had been located at the Santhoeck the two ships would unquestionably have been challenged. Had this occurred, an aggressive leader with Minuit's boldness would probably have resisted any effort to thwart his plans. If Dutch cannon had been fired during such a confrontation, it is possible the Swedish vessels may have been damaged before reaching the Minquas Kill. If so the expedition could have been a costly failure and the "incident" could have disrupted friendly relations between Sweden and Holland.

Minuit knew there was no Dutch fort at the Santhoeck, and after sailing past it he directed the skippers of the two vessels into the mouth of the Minquas Kill, well out of sight of the garrison at Fort Nassau farther up the Delaware. About two miles up the Minquas Kill (known today as the Christina River) he brought the two vessels to anchor at a rock outcropping which served as a natural wharf; in a nearby cave there was a spring of cool, fresh water.[9] Minuit considered "the Rocks" an ideal location for a fort because it was less vulnerable to Dutch attack than one built on the banks of the main river. Minuit had explored this area fourteen years before in search of precious metals, and he knew it was used as a landing place by the Lenape, who had two names for it, Hopokahacking meaning "place of tobacco pipes," and Pagahacking, "land where it is flat."[10]

Before planting the Swedish flag and setting up the Swedish coat of arms Minuit went some distance up the Minquas Kill to make certain there was no European occupation along the stream. This was an essential step in legalizing the occupation under the Swedish interpretation of international law, although no one knew better than Minuit that the Dutch had been sailing up and down the Delaware River for almost twenty-five years and had made prior settlements at Swanendael, on Burlington Island, and at Fort Nassau. An affidavit later made by four members of the *Kalmar Nyckel*'s crew stated that they "neither found nor observed any sign or vestige of Christian people," a document intended to refute any Dutch claims of possession and continuous occupation.[11]

The next step was to obtain a title deed from the Indians, "the rightful owners," which, according to Swedish law, would further secure possession of lands on the western side of the Delaware River. This was consummated in a conference with five chiefs who were more than willing to share their rights to the land with Minuit for the desirable European goods he offered to them.[12] One of the chiefs, a respected Lenape sachem named Mattahorn later said he had a "house" (wigwam) at Hopokahacking when the two Swedish ships arrived.[13] Another Lenape chief, whose name is important in the history of New

Castle, "Mitot Scheming" (Metatsimint) will turn up again in the next chapter.

At this early date the Lenape living in the Delaware River valley did not understand what it meant to own and sell land according to European concepts. There were no private land owners in aboriginal Lenape society because land, like air and water, was considered a natural resource necessary for survival. If Indian families did not have free access to the land known to them as "Mother Earth" they could not plant corn and other edibles, and they would be excluded from their hunting and fishing grounds and could not survive. In their contact with Europeans during the next several decades the Lenape learned what it meant to sell land in fee simple.

In 1638, the Lenape were under the misapprehension that they were granting Minuit and the Swedes usufruct rights; namely the privilege of sharing the land with them. When the five chiefs affixed their marks to the deeds prepared by Minuit they did not know they were transferring permanent ownership to the Swedes. They never intended to sacrifice their own right to continue to use the same land for hunting, fishing, planting, and gathering. Whereas Minuit considered the trade goods he gave the Indians as compensation for the land, the chiefs accepted the goods as gifts generously offered for the right to share the use of the land.

Under the Lenape concept they could also sign a parchment deed and accept presents from other persons, Dutch, for example, to use the identical land. Since private land ownership was alien to Lenape culture there was no reason why a European "buyer" who elected not to settle or use a particular tract of land should not at a later date again offer presents for the right of occupancy and use. Even in those instances where Europeans made settlements on land they thought they had bought outright with trade goods, the Indians had no hesitancy at a later date to request additional presents for the continued use of the land by the settlers.

Minuit obviously did not understand these nuances in Lenape culture, and he no doubt believed he was paying for outright ownership irrespective of whether or not the Swedes occupied all the land bounded in the deeds. There is no reason to accuse him of intending to deceive the natives. In European society land ownership was part of the culture and the conveyance of land to a new owner by a title deed was legal and customary. In negotiating with the Indians, Minuit, and other Swedes and Dutch, simply followed the practice of their native lands. By the time the Indians learned that when they deeded lands to European buyers they had expatriated themselves it was too late to do anything about it. This does not excuse some unprincipled Europeans from deliberately cheating the Indians, but this was not Minuit's intent. His objective was to establish amicable relations with the Lenape chiefs leading to a lasting friendship.

The two deeds Minuit executed with the Lenape chiefs are now among many missing Swedish-American papers; perhaps some day they may be found in one of the repositories in Sweden. From other documents that refer to Minuit's purchases, the writer believes that he acquired the land from the Minquas Kill south to Bombay Hook (corruption of the Dutch Boomptjes Hoeck which means "little tree point"), a distance of approximately forty miles, and the area north of the Minquas Kill as far as the Schuylkill River, a distance of perhaps twenty-seven miles.[14] No western bounds were named in the deeds because of the lack of knowledge of the geography west of the Delaware River. Discussion in a later chapter will bring this purchase into sharp focus when Stuyvesant disputed Swedish ownership of the Santhoeck, although he had no prior Indian deed for this territory.

One way of looking at the early history of New Castle is that the large tract Minuit purchased from the Lenape in 1638 included the Santhoeck although it was not specifically mentioned by name. An opposing view would be that the Swedes were latecomers and trespassers, having neither discovered nor explored the territory, and that the Santhoeck belonged to the

Dutch because they were the first nation to discover, explore, and settle the Delaware Valley as previously discussed. There is no question that they were well established at Fort Nassau when Minuit sailed up the river passing the ruins of an earlier Dutch colony at Swanendael.

Minuit was not concerned about these technicalities. As a practical business executive, stockholder, and promoter of the New Sweden Company he lost no time building a stronghold at "the Rocks," which he named Fort Christina in honor of Sweden's child queen. He intended it as a place of residence for the twenty-four men he decided to leave there as the nucleus of a colony; as a post to trade with the Indians; and as a fortress to repel hostile natives or unfriendly Europeans who might try to interfere with the settlement.

Fort Christina was well situated as a trading post, accessible to both Lenape and Minquas, and, as previously pointed out, it was a more convenient location for the Minquas than Fort Nassau. With the advantage of hindsight one can now see that as an offensive military facility its value was limited because it could not command the Delaware River. Dutch ships in the river were well beyond the range of the cannon Minuit placed in the three bastions. From the viewpoint of defense it was vulnerable to attack by enemy vessels, and the soldiers left to occupy two log houses built within the palisades would have had difficulty defending themselves from a surprise Indian attack over the fastland on the northeastern side of the fort. Fortunately, the Lenape were then friendly and welcomed the newcomers.

When the Dutch commandant at Fort Nassau learned that the Swedes were constructing a fort on the Minquas Kill he protested to Minuit, and Minuit replied that "his Queen had as much right there as the [West India] Company." His message was transmitted to Director-General Willem Kieft, the West India Company's ranking official recently arrived at Manhattan Island from Holland. Kieft lost no time in sending a messenger to Minuit with a threatening letter objecting to the trespass on lands that both he and Minuit knew had been in Dutch possession for many years.[15] By the time Minuit received Kieft's letter the fort was nearing completion.

Minuit was not disturbed by Kieft's complaint, because Kieft was a newcomer to a position Minuit had held for six years. He knew the limits of the office and that Kieft had no authority to make a decision that might disrupt the then friendly relations between Holland and Sweden. Minuit took what he believed was a reasonably safe chance that any retaliation from the small garrison at Fort Nassau would be in words, not bullets, and he paid no attention to Kieft's letter. After 1655, when Swedish-Dutch relations rapidly deteriorated, Minuit's defiance would certainly have provoked hostilities, but in 1638 the risk was worth taking, and Minuit knew it.

Shortly after Minuit's arrival in the Minquas Kill he dispatched the *Grip* to Virginia to trade her cargo for tobacco, and the *Grip* arrived in Jamestown in the middle of April. This visit has led to an erroneous assumption that the Swedish vessels stopped in Jamestown *before* coming to the Delaware, but the dates of the voyage of the *Grip* disprove this notion. The governor of Virginia would not cooperate, and the *Grip* returned to Fort Christina without any tobacco. About May 20 the *Grip* weighed anchor again and set sail for Caribbean waters hoping to capture a Spanish prize carrying gold and silver.

In June, the *Grip* had not yet returned to Fort Christina from the Caribbean, and since Minuit had been away from Sweden for more than seven months he decided it was time to return home. The *Kalmar Nyckel* still carried wine in her cargo, and Minuit sailed to St. Christopher to trade the liquor for tobacco. While in St. Christopher, Minuit and the captain of the *Kalmar Nyckel*, Jan Hendricksen van de Waeter, accepted the invitation of a skipper from Rotterdam to visit his ship the *Flying Deer* lying at anchor in the harbor with many other vessels. During their friendly visit, a hurricane suddenly swept through the harbor where twenty of the vessels at anchor, including the *Kalmar*

Nyckel and the *Flying Deer*, were driven out to sea. The *Kalmar Nyckel* returned undamaged after the storm subsided, but the *Flying Deer* never returned, and was never seen again. Thus ended the life of the founder of New Sweden, and the captain of the *Kalmar Nyckel*. After a careful but futile search the crew of the *Kalmar Nyckel* took the vessel safely home.

After Minuit's departure from Fort Christina for St. Christopher, the *Grip* again returned to Fort Christina, and although she had obtained some tobacco in the Caribbean she had not taken any Spanish vessels. Very little is known about her adventures in the West Indies. Due to contrary winds the *Grip* was unable to leave Fort Christina until late April of 1639, and traveling alone, safely returned to Sweden.

The twenty-three men left behind at Fort Christina, and their commander Måns Kling, were expected to take care of their own needs, maintain control of the fort, trade with the Indians, and keep peace with the Dutch at Fort Nassau where Governor Kieft had now stationed a permanent garrison to keep an eye on the trespassers. These unsung heroes at Fort Christina were left to face a coming winter in an unfamiliar land separated by thousands of miles from their native country and their loved ones. They must have frequently scanned the horizon from the yacht, or "ship's boat" Minuit left with them, but there was no sign of ships from Sweden bringing reinforcements. Two long years passed before a second expedition arrived on April 17, 1640.

Peter Hollender Ridder, of Dutch or low German origin, was in charge of the second expedition, and he served as the governor of New Sweden from 1640 to 1643. He found Fort Christina in disrepair following two years of wear and tear and exposure to the weather. He managed to mend the breaks in the walls and repair the ramparts, but he had neither the material nor sufficient skilled workmen to do a thorough job. The settlers who came with him from Sweden erected three new dwellings, a storehouse, and a stable, probably all of logs, within the palisades of the fort. Settlers who came later built cabins outside the fort and planted vegetable and tobacco patches.

Ridder, who had been in Swedish service for some years as an officer in the Admiralty, was not impressed with the location of Fort Christina, which he recognized had questionable military value. In a letter, he proposed that the Swedish government build a new stronghold on or near the Delaware River "so that the Crown's fort would be the key to New Sweden."[16] Is it possible that Ridder may have had the Santhoeck in mind as a prospective site of a new fort? He must have recognized its advantages as the site of a citadel to defend the Delaware River, and he must have learned enough about the geography of the Delaware Valley to conclude that permanent possession would be vested in the nation that controlled the ship traffic in the river that constituted the transportation corridor.

While awaiting the approval of his recommendation to build a new fort, which never came, Ridder did the next best thing by extending the bounds of New Sweden. He purchased land from the Lenape on the west bank of the river from the Schuylkill to "the falls" opposite present Trenton; from Duck Creek south to Cape Henlopen; and on the New Jersey side of the river from Raccoon Creek south to Cape May.[17] These acquisitions gave the Swedes additional Indian deeds to support their claim to ownership of the territory now constituting the state of Delaware, as well as parts of Pennsylvania and southern New Jersey.

Subsequent expeditions bringing men, women, and children from Sweden reinforced the colony, but the population growth of New Sweden was by no means spectacular. This was not due to the New Sweden Company's failure to encourage settlement, but to the reluctance of Swedes, like the Dutch, to leave their homeland and settle in America. A large percentage of the Swedish colonists were really Finns, some of whom were forcibly sent to America. Finland had been a country with its own government, but in the Middle Ages was absorbed by Sweden. Many Finns then settled in the northern and central parts of

Sweden where the forested land was to their liking. Their method of clearing the forests by burning the trees was at first approved by the Swedish government, but was later found objectionable. The Finns continued the practice illegally, and they also disregarded the Swedish laws regulating hunting. Punitive ordinances were enacted against them, and efforts made to drive them back to Finland or over the ocean to America.

Even though Finland and Sweden were politically united, the people differed in culture and language. Some colonists spoke Swedish and others Finnish, but most of the Finns had Swedish names, making it impossible to separate Swedes from Finns on the basis of their recorded names. In some instances certain individuals are referred to as Finns, e.g., "Lars Anderson the Finn," "Peter Stalcop's wife, a Finn," etc., but many things attributable to Swedes were nevertheless accomplishments of Finns.

Despite the relatively small number of Swedes and Finns who arrived in New Sweden, the Dutch West India Company continued to protest that they were trespassing on Dutch territory, but the Swedish officials paid little attention to these protests. During this early period the Dutch made no attempt to negotiate deeds with the Indians to reinforce their claims of ownership. The instructions issued to Willem Verhulst in 1625 cautioned him that if he found any Indians living on High (Burlington) Island he should not drive them away by threats or force, but negotiate deeds for their lands "since such contracts upon other occasions may be useful to the Company."[18] No deeds have yet been found indicating that he purchased land from the natives, but it goes without saying that the West India Company could have obtained Indian deeds for all of the Delaware Valley, if it chose to do so, long before Minuit arrived with the first Swedish expedition. The earliest Dutch-Indian deed on record in Delaware is one previously mentioned, covering land Godyn's agent bought for the ill-fated Swanendael colony. This conveyance was for a narrow strip of land only thirty-two miles long and about two miles wide.[19]

The Company's officials in New Netherland apparently felt it was unnecessary to negotiate deeds with the Indians in the Delaware Valley. For example, there is no evidence that the Dutch West India Company ever had an Indian deed for the land where Fort Nassau was built, although the Company obtained Indian deeds for lands on the Hudson, the Connecticut River, Staten Island, Manhattan, and at Albany.[20] Perhaps the Company's American representatives believed that land ownership along the Delaware was not a prerequisite to conducting the Indian trade. Conversely, the Swedes were concerned with colonizing the Delaware—that's why Minuit and Ridder made certain that title deeds were executed as proof of Swedish land ownership.

The ambivalent policies of the West India Company are difficult to understand; the Amsterdam Chamber, as the reader has seen, did its utmost to promote the fur trade, but failed to make adequate investments in colonization, which under proper direction, could have been the key to commercial success. Some years later the States General took the position that the Company's objective was to colonize, but this is not supported by the evidence.[21] The records are also clear that the Dutch government through the States General took no initiative in colonizing the New Netherland.

After the Walloon farmers had been transferred to Manhattan Island (some of them returned to Holland disenchanted with the New Netherland), the Assembly of XIX ruled that agricultural colonies to support the fur traders were unpromising and dissuaded the Amsterdam Chamber from making further investments to achieve that end. Nevertheless, the Company did not want to give up the fur trade, and some way had to be found to provision the fur trading establishments. As an alternative the directors encouraged settlers not subsidized by the Company to go directly to the New Netherland as independent artisans and farmers. The directors now believed that a large Dutch residential population would strengthen the Company's ability to meet English threats in America. By so doing the directors negated their own commercial monopoly because those who went on their own had no loyalty or obligation, directly or indirectly, to the Company, and they found ways to involve themselves in the fur trade. Smuggling and private trade defrauded the Company's agents who were supposed to retain exclusive control of the fur trade. The Company asserted that persons living in the New Netherland not in the Company's employ obtained more furs from the Indians in the winter of 1637–38 than the Company did.[22]

Although the West India Company claimed that the Connecticut Valley was part of the New Netherland, the New Haven English also offered aggressive competition in the fur trade. The Dutch protested, but their complaints were ignored. The New Englanders far outnumbered the Dutch because of the emphasis that had been placed on colonization, and the persecuted Puritans had better reasons for coming to America than the Dutch. The French were also diluting the West India Company's business by diverting Indians from the Dutch trading post at Fort Orange to French posts on the St. Lawrence.

On April 30, 1638 (at about the same time the Swedes were building Fort Christina) the Assembly of XIX received a questionnaire from the States General asking for information about the status of the Company's affairs. The Assembly of XIX declared it had suffered a cumulative financial loss in the fur trade in the New Netherland, a damaging admission in view of the time, effort, and money spent to support the business. The Assembly of XIX then went on to say that if the Company were able to raise sufficient grain in the New Netherland and sell it in Holland the loss could be turned into a profit.[23] Grain, in terms of shipping costs, a paramount factor in importation and exportation, had a high value-to-volume ratio in the hold of a vessel compared, for example, to common timber, which had a low value ratio in relation to weight and bulk.

The paradox is that this is what the proponents of colonization had proposed in the first place as an expedient to augment
the fur trade. Facing a critical situation the Amsterdam Chamber
took action that completely reversed all previous decisions made
by the directors. A new policy was adopted in May of 1639
whereby all inhabitants of the New Netherland, irrespective of
whether or not they were Company employes, were given tacit
permission to trade with the Indians or engage in any other kind
of business with other inhabitants of the colony.[24] Under this
free trade policy all pelts, grains, and other products were
supposed to be transported to Holland in the Company's ships at
freight rates set by the directors, and a "recognition" (impost
tax) had to be paid to the Company on both exports and
imports.

The directors advocating free trade were convinced that the
duties the Company would receive from free traders, added to
the freight receipts, and supplemented by income from the
Company's own trade, would wipe out the deficits without
incurring the expense of colonization. The new policy encouraged some Dutch freemen living on Manhattan Island to go to
the Delaware in an attempt to start trading with the Indians. It
also stimulated immigration from Holland by private merchants,
artisans, and fortune hunters having their own selfish interests.
Free enterprise offered opportunities that had not previously
existed, and as a consequence the population of New Netherland
after 1639 began to grow with an influx of adventurous Dutch,
French, Walloon, German, English, and others. Ironically, the
impetus for the growth of the New Netherland (which reached
10,000 men, women, and children during the next two decades)
did not come from the West India Company's initiative nor
from the States General, but from individuals interested in
advancing their own personal economic interests.

The free trade policy was not intended to benefit interlopers
like the Swedes who were thought of by the Dutch West India
Company as violators of international law. Nevertheless, the

Swedes were directly affected because the added competition tended to drive up the price of furs, which necessitated more aggressive activity to maintain a share of the market. Governor Kieft complained to the Commissioners of the Amsterdam Chamber that the Swedes undersold the Dutch by giving the Indians more trade goods for a specified quantity of pelts than the Dutch. This practice was not new—it began with Minuit who undersold Dutch traders in his initial contacts with the Minquas. When his two vessels left Fort Christina they carried away 2,200 beaver, bear, and otter pelts, and Swedish merchants in Stockholm sold 1,505 of these pelts in Amsterdam![25] Sweden was never as good a market for furs as Holland, Poland, or Germany, but Swedish merchants had no difficulty finding customers in other markets for all the furs imported from New Sweden.

The Swedes developed an excellent rapport with the Minquas, who considered them special friends. Minquas trading parties came to Fort Christina when they had furs for sale, and Swedish traders made their way on foot to the Susquehanna River, and beyond, once or twice a year carrying merchandise to barter for beaver and otter pelts.[26] As long as the Swedes had sufficient trade merchandise the Minquas were good friends and customers, but when ships bringing trade goods did not arrive, the Indians affections began to wane. The natives were opportunists and patronized those Europeans who best served their needs. The Europeans also viewed the Indians in terms of their own interests, and the natives complained that friendship "lasts only as long as we have beavers."[27] Mutual friendship seems to have depended upon an uninterrupted flow of goods.

Sweden was an excellent market for tobacco; by 1629, for example, tobacco smoking was common among students at Uppsala University. On a voyage in 1640, the *Kalmar Nyckel* returned from America with 11,878 pounds of tobacco, the largest importation of tobacco to Sweden up to that time. The tobacco was readily sold in Gothenburg and Stockholm.[28] English merchants in Maryland and Virginia supplied the Swedes with tobacco, and also cattle, flour, seed corn, sewant, and other commodities. Tobacco was also raised in moderate quantities in New Sweden.

The Swedes were on friendly terms with the English in Maryland and Virginia, but the English living in the Connecticut colony were viewed as unwelcome competitors. Furs were important to the success of the English settlement in New Haven, because they could be used to purchase bills of exchange in London. The problem was that the coastal beaver population had been practically depleted through the activities of both English and Dutch traders. Connecticut merchants turned to the Delaware River region as a new source for pelts, and two prominent members of the New Haven colony, George Lamberton and Captain Nathaniel Turner, were among the active promoters in organizing the Delaware Company of New Haven. Both men were familiar with the Delaware valley, which they saw not only as a place to obtain furs, but as territory where New Haven could expand its population and influence.

In the spring of 1641, Lamberton and Turner came to the Delaware in a small sloop, well provided with trade goods, to buy land from the Indians and also to exchange for beaver pelts. They sailed up and down the Delaware River and into its tributaries seeking suitable locations for a colony and also bartering for furs with the natives. The Englishmen purchased land from the Indians along present Salem Creek in New Jersey leaving fourteen men there as the beginning of a colony. Ridder protested but the Englishmen paid no attention; the next year they returned with a cargo of trade goods and additional colonists to reinforce those settled on Salem Creek, and to establish a second colony.

Lamberton and Turner renewed friendship with the Lenape chiefs Usquata and Wehwsett (also spelled Wehhewsett) who had sold them the land in New Jersey the previous year. Then they sailed up the Delaware River and purchased a second tract along the Schuylkill, within the bounds of present Philadelphia, from Mattahorn and several other chiefs, where they made a small settlement.

Finally they purchased a third plot from the chief Wehwsett on the west bank of the Delaware south of Fort Christina "extending from a stream called Tomguncke to another stream called Papuq . . ." The latter word is only fragmentary in the document reporting the transaction, which makes it impossible to identify the stream.[29] Tomguncke is one of the forms of Tamakonck—the Indian name for the Santhoeck, and also for a tributary immediately south of New Castle to which previous reference has been made in the first chapter as "a lost creek."

What merchandise Lamberton and Turner paid Wehwsett and what right a New Jersey chief had to sell land on the opposite side of the river that had already been purchased by Minuit and Ridder are questions that remain unanswered. What is significant is that the two English adventurers from New Haven recognized the potential value of the site of present New Castle that had failed to impress either their Swedish or Dutch contemporaries. Not willing to risk Swedish reprisals, the New Haven promoters never made a settlement at the Santhoeck, although English colonists were placed on the Schuylkill where they also built a blockhouse. The Dutch from Fort Nassau burnt down this blockhouse and adjacent dwellings, took the colonists as prisoners, and carried them back to New Haven.[30] The English settlers on Salem Creek fell under the jurisdiction of the government of New Sweden, and New Haven's expansion program proved to be a failure.

In 1643, Lieutenant-Colonel Johan Printz was sent from Sweden to replace Ridder as governor. The Swedish government had become more deeply involved in the success of the colony, and New Sweden became the joint concern of the monarchy and the New Sweden Company, which now was also referred to as the South Company. Printz's salary was paid by the Swedish government. He wrote progress letters to government officials, particularly the Lord High Chancellor, and he submitted detailed reports to the South Company, which he persisted in addressing as "the Noble West India Company in Old Sweden." Much has been written about this gargantuan governor who supposedly weighed 400 pounds and "had an eye as cold as an icicle, a nose that seemed to have been pounded into distorted prominence, and a jaw that jutted like the prow of a ship."[31] Nothing new can be added about his personality that has not already been written, but new interpretations can be made of events during his administration that had a direct bearing on the early history of New Castle.

During Printz's administration, Swedish and Finnish farmers cleared and cultivated land along the Christina River and north of Fort Christina in an area of a thinly dispersed population at places now known as Marcus Hook, Chester, and Essington. Like his predecessor Ridder, Printz recognized the military limitations of Fort Christina. Ridder's recommendation that the Swedes construct a fort on the Delaware proper must have been discussed in Stockholm. This can be inferred from the instruction given Printz before he left Sweden that he should erect a fort at a suitable place on the river "that through such a fortification the South River might be closed or commanded by this fortress . . ."[32] Two sites were suggested as possible locations: Cape Henlopen or Jacques Island, but nothing was said about the Santhoeck. Swedish officials had not yet recognized its importance.

After inspecting the territory from Cape Henlopen to the Sankikans (near present Trenton), Printz decided to build not one but two forts on the Delaware. The first completed in 1643 was on the east bank of the river near present Salem, New Jersey diagonally southeast of the Santhoeck. He named it Fort Elfsborg, perpetuating the name of a large imposing fortress near Gothenburg, Sweden. Printz conceived it as a military barrier, which could prevent all vessels, English or otherwise, sailing up the river without permission of the Swedish commander in charge of the garrison. The fort could also keep the little English community on the Salem River under the "jurisdiction, devotion and dominion of the Swedish Crown," as covered in Printz's instruction. He gave the English colonists the choice of evacuating or swearing allegiance to the Swedish Crown, and they chose the latter option.

Printz intended the second fort he built to be his residence and the new "capital" of New Sweden instead of Fort Christina. It was located near the water's edge on the high point of Tinicum Island, not far from the present Philadelphia International Airport. This triangular island, which seemed to be part of the mainland, was insular because of a narrow creek on one side. The fort Printz erected commanded the riverside with four copper cannon, and on the land side he built a storehouse-redoubt, which could be used for defense in the event of an Indian attack by land. He named the fortress New Gothenburg, but the imposing two-story log gubernatorial manse he erected, with brick fireplaces, brick chimney, and glass windows, was called Printzhoff. Here the public records of New Sweden were kept, including salary rolls, Indian deeds, and copies of official correspondence. Treaties were negotiated with the Indians at Printzhoff, private conferences were held with merchants and leaders from the other colonies, and it also served as the seat of the court.

Printz also put Fort Christina in good repair, assigning his son-in-law, Johan Papegoja (married to his daughter Armegot), to command the garrison. He also erected smaller posts on the Schuylkill and its tributaries primarily to protect the trade route used by the Minquas. Despite the numerous problems he faced in New Sweden, Printz was able to report to his superiors on June 11, 1644 that he was shipping 2,142 beaver pelts to the homeland and 20,467 pounds of tobacco of which 15,476 pounds were purchased in Virginia and 4,991 pounds were raised in New Sweden.[33] If adequate trade goods were sent to him from Sweden he said he could continue to enjoy the beaver trade with the Minquas, and, if he were supported by new colonists, and if the weather was favorable, he could send larger shipments of tobacco to the homeland. He did not then know of the disappointments the future held in store for him.

As subsequent events revealed, Printz would have been better advised to have selected the Santhoeck as the site of Fort Gothenburg, the ''capital'' of New Sweden, instead of Tinicum Island. This would not have solved all of his problems, but would have blocked Dutch expansion. He, too, was denied historical hindsight, and the Santhoeck continued to remain unoccupied.

Printz and Governor Willem Kieft developed a good rapport, which largely sprang from their mutual desire to exclude the English from the Delaware River valley. At this particular period their principal apprehension was associated with the English of New England, and Kieft was especially sensitive to this threat because he had seen how the English had overrun the Connecticut Valley to the detriment of the Dutch-Indian trade. Kieft was aware that he could not spare troops to defend the Delaware from English expansion; he needed his soldiers to protect New Amsterdam because of the hostilities that had developed with the Indian tribes of upper New Jersey and the lower Hudson. Due to his rash policies many Dutch colonists were massacred and women and children taken prisoners in the so-called Governor Kieft War. Kieft did not have sufficient soldiers to provide an adequate garrison at Fort Nassau. His best recourse was to lean on Printz, and Printz's manpower, limited though it was, recognizing that the forts Printz had built provided the only defense against English intruders and served the best interests of both Dutch and Swedes.

Fort Elfsborg, according to a Dutch report, ''closes the entrance of the river,'' and incoming vessels were compelled to lower their colors and drop anchor for boarding and inspection. If the English vessel was from Virginia bringing supplies to sell

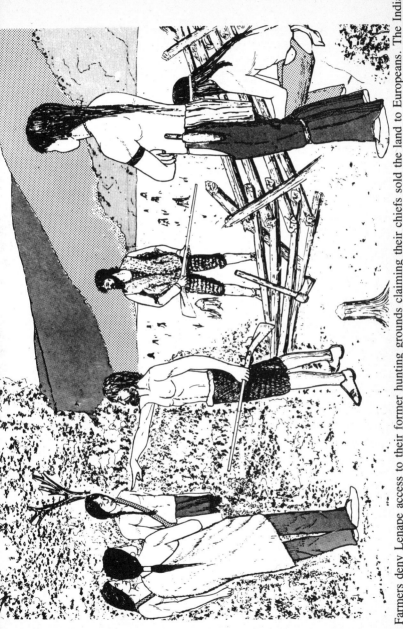

Farmers deny Lenape access to their former hunting grounds claiming their chiefs sold the land to Europeans. The Indian reply was that they gave the whites the rights to use the land, but didn't intend them to fence it in and exclude the Indians from hunting and fishing. (Courtesy Dr. H. C. Kraft, Seton Hall University Museum)

to the Swedes, or if it belonged to an English merchant from New England engaged in commerce with the Swedes, it was allowed to pass. English vessels attempting to settle colonists, or to engage in the fur trade, were turned back, and some English vessels from New England never reached the mouth of Delaware Bay, because they were detained at Manhattan Island by Kieft and forced to return.

Printz is often portrayed as an uncompromising tyrant constantly at loggerheads with the Dutch, and there can be no question that he was despotic, but from the time of his arrival until Stuyvesant's appointment four years later, he and Kieft were on friendly terms. Kieft, who received news from the numerous Dutch skippers who disembarked at Manhattan Island, kept Printz posted about events taking place in Holland, Sweden, and elsewhere. There were also times when the Dutch supplied the Swedes with food, such as occurred in 1644 when Printz sent a sloop to New Amsterdam where seven oxen, a cow, and seventy-five bushels of seed rye were purchased from the Dutch.[34]

Printz reported that when he arrived in America, and met Governor Kieft for the first time, the Dutchman warned him he was trespassing on Dutch territory, just as he had protested to Minuit five years before. Printz, who had seen the Indian deeds in Stockholm, replied that the Swedes had purchased the land from the rightful Indian proprietors and he had no intention of vacating real estate his Queen had legally acquired. Kieft knew that both he and Printz were beholden to their superiors in Holland and Sweden, and to keep the peace he stopped protesting. He did not have the soldiers to spare even if he wanted to take military action, and he didn't want to do so because it might lead to a war between the two countries. So he resorted to coexistence and allowed Printz more or less to have his own way.

Although Printz objected to Dutch competition in the fur trade, he tolerated the Dutch because Kieft confined Dutch occupancy in the Delaware Valley to Fort Nassau, which was not within the bounds of New Sweden. If Kieft had attempted to settle colonists on the western side of the Delaware, Printz would have considered that an affront to his Queen, calling for retaliation. Thus, for a few years amicable relations and an uneasy peace existed between the West India Company's officials and the Swedes on the Delaware, but there were dark clouds ahead.

3. STUYVESANT BUILDS FORT CASIMIR

A TURNING POINT in the amicable relations between Governor Printz and Governor Kieft occurred when Kieft provisionally transferred Andries Hudde from Manhattan Island to Fort Nassau as the commis, or acting commander. Hudde, a well-educated employe of the West India Company held the position of surveyor at New Amsterdam. At a time when property was being laid out and new homes were being built, a surveyor, who also knew how to make maps, served a useful purpose. With his awareness of topography, Hudde quickly sized up the situation after he arrived at Fort Nassau on November 1, 1645. If the Company expected to block Swedish competition and retain a maximum share of the fur trade, the Dutch had to have ready access to the Minquas trade route along the Schuylkill River on the opposite side of the Delaware River from Fort Nassau.

A number of Swedish and Finnish colonists laid out farms near the fortified posts Printz built in the Schuylkill territory. This enabled the Swedes to dominate the Minquas trade as long as they had goods to barter. Dutch barks and yachts sent across the river from Fort Nassau were at a disadvantage because Printz could prevent their anchoring except where he specified, and to Hudde this interference was intolerable. The answer to the dilemma, as he saw it, was to build a permanent Dutch trading post on the Schuylkill and induce Dutch freeholders living in New Amsterdam to immigrate to the west side of the Delaware River and build homes and lay out farms. In his opinion this was the most effective way of protecting the beaver trade and securing the territory for the Dutch West India Company.

Governor Kieft agreed with Hudde and concurred with the surveyor's recommendations. He immediately took steps to urge Dutch freemen in New Amsterdam to move to the environs of what is now Greater Philadelphia. Land was offered free of charge provided the prospective owner agreed to cultivate it within a year. Kieft also authorized Hudde to buy the land from the Indians on behalf of the Company with suitable trade goods.[1] Acquiring Indian deeds was a change in Dutch policy on the Delaware.

Kieft's decision to promote a settlement of non-Company employes was also a significant change in the long-standing policy of confining Dutch activities to the Company's settlement at Fort Nassau. Kieft expected that some of the colonists who took advantage of the offer would engage in the fur trade as well as land cultivation. This was in accord with the decision made by the directors of the Amsterdam Chamber in May of 1639 to allow private persons to trade with the Indians, paying a duty to the Company on the furs they obtained, as explained in the previous chapter.

Kieft's plan met with Governor Printz's outspoken objections. It made no difference to him whether the intruders were private settlers or employes of the West India Company. A Dutch incursion on New Sweden's territory, and the erection of a trading post by the West India Company, were more serious offenses than the periodic trading by Dutchmen who came into the Schuylkill in sailing crafts and were soon gone again.

Four residents of New Amsterdam promptly took advantage of Kieft's generous offer, Abraham Planck, Symon Root, Jan Andriesen, and Peter Harmensen; they were granted 100 morgens of land, about 200 acres, for four boweries of fifty acres each. Others were later given permission to build, including Hans Jacobsen, Thomas Broen, and Cornelis Mauritsen. (These names are variously spelled in the Dutch records and some of the men later settled at New Castle.)

Neither Kieft nor Hudde were deterred by Printz's protests, and when construction began on the first houses Hudde replied to Printz's protests by writing, "The places which we occupy we occupy in rightful ownership; we have also occupied them perhaps before the South River was heard of in Sweden." The facts, as the reader is well aware, bear out his statement. He signed the letter "your honor's affectionate friend."[2] Hudde and his wife were Printz's dinner guests at Printzhoff following their arrival at Fort Nassau, which is suggestive that Printz wanted to continue friendly relations. No doubt the new political situation brought an end to the Huddes socializing with the Swedish governor, his wife, and their four unmarried daughters, Catharina, Christina, Elsa, and Gunilla. The governor's son, Gustav Printz, served under his father in New Sweden as a military officer, and reference has already been made to his sister Armegot's marriage to Johan Papegoja.

A new Director-General employed by the West India Company arrived at Manhattan Island on May 11, 1647 to replace Willem Kieft—the legendary Peter Stuyvesant. He had served the Company in Europe and Brazil, and was promoted as director of the Dutch possession in the Caribbean with his headquarters in Curaçao. His right foot was mangled by a Portuguese cannonball during a siege on the island of St. Martin in 1644, and the leg was amputated. Three years later, after convalescing in Holland, he arrived with his wife at Manhattan limping on a

silver-banded peg leg. The new post was his country's reward
for faithful and meritorious service as a soldier and administra-
tor; his appointment was made by the States General on July 28,
1646 in order to maintain "in all things there good order for the
service of the United Netherlands, and the general West India
Company."[3]

Stuyvesant was placed not only in charge of the government,
the commerce, and the administration of civil and criminal law
in the New Netherland, but he was also responsible for govern-
ing the "Islands Curacao, Buenaire [Bonaire], Aruba, and their
dependencies." These Dutch possessions in the West Indies
were also under the supervision of the directors of the Amsterdam Chamber. Administering the Company's affairs in the New
Netherland and in the Caribbean from his office in Fort Amsterdam was an important and difficult assignment. The Delaware
River was probably furthermost from Stuyvesant's thoughts when
he arrived at Manhattan, but he later became responsible for
making the first Dutch settlement at the Santhoeck. Peter
Stuyvesant might be called New Castle's founding father, but it
took three years and a political crisis before he first saw the
Delaware River.

Stuyvesant and his Swedish counterpart, Governor Johan Printz,
were alike in many ways. Both were minister's sons, raised
under strict Christian disciplines, who grew up as God-fearing
men. Both were intelligent, well-educated, bold, and hot tem-
pered, with strong prejudices and passions. As former army
officers both were accustomed to having their orders obeyed
without question. Of the two, Stuyvesant may possibly have had
more personal integrity, because after nine years as governor
Printz returned to Sweden a wealthy man, having engaged in the
fur trade for his own profit. Although he denied any malfea-
sance there is no record that he cleared himself of the colonists'
accusation that he sold beaver pelts to the English for gold that
went into his own pocket, and that he shipped pelts to Holland

to be sold for his personal account without the knowledge of the Swedish government.

The Delaware lawyer-historian, one-time president of the Historical Society of Delaware, Christopher Ward, believed that Printz lacked the good judgement, adaptability, and farsightedness that characterized Stuyvesant's single-minded devotion to the welfare of the Dutch colony and the West India Company. Ward felt that Printz could not have governed the New Netherland as well as Stuyvesant governed it, but this is the opinion of only one historian.[4] It could be argued that Stuyvesant could not have governed New Sweden as well as Printz did in view of the minimal support he received from Sweden. In 1653, Printz wrote that he had not received a letter or message from the Fatherland in six and one-half years! The Swedish colony was left to wither on the vine due to wars and other problems taking precedence in Sweden.

Stuyvesant was well aware that the Swedes occupied lands claimed by the West India Company, and that one of his predecessors, Peter Minuit, defected to Sweden, built Fort Christina, and laid the foundation for a Swedish colony on the Company's lands. Stuyvesant no doubt believed that Minuit had betrayed the West India Company. On the other hand, Printz had no question in his mind about the Swedish right to occupy the land even though Stuyvesant considered them trespassers. Printz must have recognized that a confrontation with Stuyvesant was inescapable, but his problem was that the Swedish forces under his command were pathetically weak in contrast to the number of Dutch soldiers and vessels at New Amsterdam.

Printz wrote in 1647 (the year Stuyvesant arrived in New Netherland) that the population of New Sweden was only "183 souls" by which he meant men, women, and children. The army he brought with him from Sweden consisted of Lieutenant Sven Skute, a head guard, a gunner, a corporal, a trumpeter, a provost-marshall, and twenty-four soldiers. He placed Lieutenant Sven Skute, his second in command, in charge of his key defensive position at Fort Elfsborg, even though he could spare only thirteen soldiers and "eight 12 lb. iron and brass guns and one mortar" to arm the fortress. Additional soldiers later reinforced Printz's Lilliputian army, but the total number of adult males able to bear arms, including soldiers, freemen, and employes and servants of the Swedish company, never exceeded 90 or 100.[5]

In letters to his superiors in Sweden, Printz twice requested that at least 100 soldiers be sent to strengthen his command, but no action was ever taken.[6] His military forces were always inadequate to man the major forts intended to control the Delaware River—Elfsborg, Christina, and New Gothenburg—and to garrison the smaller fortified trading posts in the Schuylkill watershed. How could he discharge his duties by maintaining Swedish sovereignty, as his instructions required, in lands obtained "by virtue of deeds entered into with the wild inhabitants of the country as its rightful owners?" This, of course, referred to the Indian deeds negotiated by Minuit and Ridder then on file in the chancery in Stockholm. The territory comprising New Sweden in 1643 was defined in the instruction issued to Printz under the royal seal: from Cape Henlopen on the west side of the Delaware River north to Sankikans, and on the east side from Narraticon Creek (present Raccoon Creek) south to Cape May.[7] Later land purchases from the Indians increased the size of this territory.

Printz was in a particularly sensitive situation because Sweden and the Netherlands were still at peace and neither wanted a rupture in their friendly relations. His instruction cautioned Printz to "hold good friendship" with the Dutch officials in America, but if they displayed open hostility he was authorized to repel "force by force."[8] He was also directed to undersell the Dutch in the Indian fur trade as Minuit and Ridder had done, in order to divert the pelts to the Swedes.

How could one "hold good friendship" with a rival occupying lands that he claimed belonged to him under international law, erecting forts on both sides of a river he claimed he owned, and then adding further insult by underselling him in the fur trade he had originally established? Printz never questioned the inconsistency of his instruction, but proceeded as ordered to make himself master of New Sweden with as little offense as possible to the Dutch. Their common interest, opposition to the English getting a foothold in the Delaware Valley, was in Printz's favor, but it did not change Stuyvesant's mind that the Swedes were trespassers on lands "that have belonged to us since many years." Meanwhile in a report to his superiors in Sweden, Printz wrote:

> It is of utmost necessity for us to see to how we can get rid of the Dutch from the river, for they oppose us on every side: (1) They destroy our trade everywhere (2) They strengthen the Savages with guns, shot and powder, doing with these things a public trade against all Christian laws (3) They stir up the Savages to attack us, which (but for our prudence) would already have happened (4) They begin to buy land from the Savages within our boundaries, which we had purchased already eight years ago, and are so impudent that they here erect the seal of the West India Company, calling it their coat of arms, and New Sweden they call New Netherland, and are not ashamed to build their houses there . . . And those who are doing this mischief are merely a lot of Dutch freemen, provided with their Governor's passport, and trading on their own account, paying duties therefor but the [West India] Company itself does not trade at all, and has little profit from it.[9]

In support of the building program begun by Kieft, Stuyvesant sent a carpenter from Manhattan to Hudde with orders to put Fort Nassau in good repair and to construct new houses there. The intent seems to have been to make Nassau a stronger base of supplies and a home for the families of officers, soldiers, and

other Company employes. At the same time Stuyvesant continued to encourage individual Dutch settlers to build houses in the
Schuylkill watershed. Confronted with this construction activity
on land he was sworn to protect for his Queen made Printz
furious. The friendly relations he had with the Kieft administration gave way to heated rivalry because of Stuyvesant's determi-
nation to occupy land that he claimed belonged to the Company.

During the latter part of Kieft's administration the directors of
the Amsterdam Chamber criticized him for being too lenient
with the Swedes, and this gave Stuyvesant further justification
for becoming more aggressive. At the same time he had the
good sense to know the directors did not want him to take any
action that might open a breach with Sweden. It was a delicate
situation for a man with Stuyvesant's temperament to handle.

While Stuyvesant was suppressing his urge to provoke trouble,
Hudde's letters from the Delaware recommended that the director approve the construction of a fortified trading post on the
Schuylkill as reinforcement for the houses then being erected by
the settlers. The numerous letters exchanged between the two
men, of which only a few survive, were carried back and forth
by vessel from Fort Nassau to New Amsterdam or by Indian
runners traveling overland. The Indian messenger was not paid
in advance, but the letter advised the recipient what trade goods
had been promised him when delivery was made. This was
supposed to assure safe and prompt delivery of the message,
although in some instances the runner was waylaid or the message lost.

Although Stuyvesant was apprehensive of the risk of maintaining a Company installation among many unfriendly Swedes
and Finns, he approved Hudde's recommendation. It is uncertain
whether or not Hudde knew that the Schuylkill lands were
included in the territory Minuit and Ridder had purchased from
the Indians for the Swedes, but if so it didn't deter him. On
April 24, 1648 he conferred with old Mattahorn and another
Lenape chief, and they "gave" him land on the east bank of the

Schuylkill in the present district known as Passyunk ("in the valley"). There he erected a trading post surrounded by palisades which he named Fort Beversreede.[10]

Stuyvesant had now become fully conscious of the importance the Swedes attached to Indian deeds as evidence of ownership, and to make the gift official he resorted to the Swedish criteria. He sent two learned members of his council, Vice Director Lubbertus van Dincklaghe, a doctor of law, (also spelled Lubbert van Dincklage) and Dr. Johannes de la Montagne, a University of Leyden graduate and an esteemed physician, to pay the Indians in trade goods and draw up a deed transferring title to the Dutch.[11] Since Minuit bought lands south of the Schuylkill in 1638, and Ridder acquired Indian title north of the Schuylkill in 1640, a Dutch deed executed for the same land in 1648 would not nullify the earlier Swedish purchases. When the deed was being executed the Dutch emissaries reminded the Indians that a West India Company employe, a former commis at Fort Nassau named Arent Corssen, purchased this identical land for the Company in 1633, five years prior to the arrival of the first Swedish expedition. They said that Corssen neglected to pay for the land in full, and the new 1648 deed now served to renew and confirm the sale made fifteen years before, and trade goods were given to the Indians to compensate them for what was long owed them. The writer has failed to find a transcript of the alleged 1633 deed and nothing is known about the boundaries of the lands that Corssen is supposed to have bought. A transcript of the 1648 deed has been preserved but it refers only to "the Schuylkill and adjoining lands" with a note that it corresponded with the missing 1633 deed.

Dutch-Swedish relations progressively deteriorated as a series of incidents occurred when the Swedes resisted Dutch intrusion of New Sweden. Printz's officers, soldiers, and some of the freemen participated in acts of violence against the Dutch freeholders. One of the Swedes tore down the West India Company's coat of arms that Hudde erected on the land the Dutch purchased from the Lenape, an act of vandalism then deemed a national affront. Others pulled apart the Dutch houses under construction, burnt down fences and newly planted fruit trees, seized Dutch boats, and confiscated powder and guns from one of the Dutch traders. The principal activists who harassed the Dutch were Lieutenant Gustav Printz, Lieutenant Johan Papegoja, Commissary Hendrick Huygen, Sergeant Gregory Van Dyck, Lieutenant Måns Kling, and a bookkeeper named Carl Jansson. One of the soldiers, Peter Yochim (Yochimson), who lived at Aronameck on the west bank of the Schuylkill, tore down some of the palisades at Fort Beversreede in the dark of the night. When the Dutch repaired the palisades the Swedes tore them off again, "hacking with great violence the woodwork to pieces."[12] When the Dutch again replaced the palisades the Swedes retaliated by erecting a blockhouse between the fort and the river which prevented the Dutch from having access to their trading post.

With his limited manpower at Fort Nassau, Hudde could put up little defense against a "friendly" enemy thoroughly familiar with the terrain and determined to repulse intruders. Hudde realized the odds were with the Swedes and that Printz had the upper hand. Not only could the Swedish commando raids destroy houses or trading posts at will, but Printz's fortified posts on the Schuylkill commanded the Minquas trade route. Fort Christina where Papegoja was in command controlled a second major trading path used by the Minquas. Fort Elfsborg could keep Fort Nassau or Fort Beversreede from being supplied or reinforced if Printz decided to take drastic action, and he had also built a small log blockhouse at Upland, present Chester.

The situation was beyond Hudde's competency to handle, and taking the offensive that might result in bloodshed was not within his authority. He personally went to Manhattan to confer with Stuyvesant, who found himself on the horns of a dilemma because Dutch honor was at stake, but he did not want to be responsible for provoking a war. After studying his maps and charts he decided on a big bluff which he believed would overpower the Swedes without provoking military retaliation. Fully aware that Printz was not being supported from Sweden with the supplies and manpower he needed to defend New Sweden against a major attack, his objective was to confront the Swedes with such a formidable display of strength that Printz would realize the futility of further resistance.

After secret preparation Stuyvesant led an army of 120 men, the largest military force ever seen on the Delaware River, overland from Manhattan Island to Fort Nassau, with every man armed to the teeth. The idea was to give the impression that the Dutch were about to launch a major assault on New Sweden. By the time Stuyvesant's forces reached Fort Nassau on June 25, 1651, Indians who had seen the long column of soldiers on the march, the sun reflecting from their swords and helmets, carried the news to Printz at New Gothenburg on Tinicum Island. Printz scarcely had time to summon Lieutenants Papegoja, Kling, and Gustav Printz for a strategy meeting when he received further alarming news. Eleven Dutch vessels that had sailed down the Atlantic coast into Delaware Bay were already in the river on their way to rendezvous with Stuyvesant's troops at Fort Nassau.[13]

This first flotilla of "tall ships" in the Delaware must have been spectacular, one riding in the wake of another, sails bellied in the wind with the flags of the Prince of Orange and the West India Company streaming from their masts. The vessels encountered no resistance as they followed a single-file course up the river from Cape Henlopen. Not a single cannon was fired from Fort Elfsborg. Lieutenant Sven Skute had been sent back to Sweden the previous year by Printz to make a report on the colony. The garrison he left at Elfsborg consisted of five or six frightened Swedes who apparently did not dare to fire on what appeared to be an unconquerable fleet sent by one of the world's great maritime powers.

When the vessels reached Fort Nassau they sailed down the river and back up again, on Stuyvesant's orders, drummers beating a military cadence that reverberated from one shore to another, and cannons blasting into the empty air. All of the Dutch ships had some kind of armaments, but only four were really well armed, but Printz didn't know that until later. It made little difference because the Dutch soldiers and sailors outnumbered the *total population* of New Sweden by at least three to one. Printz was helpless to repel this pincer movement applied by land and water, and he offered no resistance from Fort Christina or Fort Gothenburg.[14] Stuyvesant's bluff proved to be a notable success.

Stuyvesant conducted this invasion of New Sweden without the knowledge or permission of the directors of the Amsterdam Chamber. Even though he knew he was taking a risk, he did not advise the directors in advance of what he intended to do and what he hoped to accomplish. The only reasonable explanation that can be given for his conduct is that he was afraid the directors would not approve his plan, and he was probably right. Their political conservatism would not have allowed them to accept the responsibility for any action that might antagonize Sweden, whose military might was respected throughout Europe.

At some stage of the invasion Stuyvesant saw the Santhoeck for the first time. Perhaps he went down the river on one of the vessels during "the cannonading and drumming," which would have given him the opportunity to view the territory that Hudde had described in his letters and reports. The Santhoeck was still unoccupied either by Dutch or Swedes, and when Stuyvesant saw the site it appealed to him as an excellent location for a fort as well as for a Dutch town where trade and commerce could be developed. Stuyvesant recognized that a fort at the Santhoeck would give the Dutch military and political advantages and a deep harbor that Fort Nassau lacked. Furthermore it was on the west side of the river where the Minquas trade was conducted. A concentration of weaponry at the Santhoeck could, if the situation required, prevent supplies reaching the Swedes at Fort Christina, Upland, Fort New

Gothenburg, and the Swedish posts on the Schuylkill and its tributaries. A fort at the Santhoeck would also render Fort Elfsborg on the opposite side of the river powerless because the Dutch could cut Swedish lines of communication between Elfsborg and Fort New Gothenburg and isolate the garrison at Fort Christina. The fort could also protect a Dutch town at the Santhoeck from any Swedish mischief.

Stuyvesant's decision to construct a fort at the Santhoeck was the mark of military brilliance, but he wrestled with a political problem. How could he justify building on land that the Swedes had purchased from the Indians? Printz never allowed him to forget that the Swedes possessed deeds signed by the Indians as proof of ownership. Stuyvesant could fall back on the argument that the valley in which the Santhoeck was located was discovered, explored, and first settled by the Dutch. But his two learned legal advisors, van Dincklage and de la Montagne, may have pointed out that the question about what constituted ownership of new lands was debatable. Some authorities on international law held that legal and binding claim to new land could be acquired three ways: (1) by discovery (2) by permanent occupation (3) by conquest. Queen Elizabeth had laid down the principle that the Spaniards, regardless of prior discovery or anything else, had no right "to any places other than those they were actually in possession of." Her ruling meant that discovery alone was not sufficient for valid title unless the land was actually settled and continually occupied. This would tend to lend weight to Printz's argument that since the Dutch had never occupied the Santhoeck, they did not own it, but the Swedes possessed it by another criterion, which the Dutch could not claim; namely, they purchased the lands from the rightful Indian owners.

Stuyvesant apparently was convinced that he needed a document signed by the Indians to validate Dutch ownership. That would enable him to use his own deed as a weapon in the duel with the Swedes over land tenure at the Santhoeck. In retrospect it is apparent that trying to justify his actions by accumulating parchment deeds signed by the Indians' marks was absurd because the Swedes possessed deeds dated earlier for the same territory. Stuyvesant had no way of knowing that some years later William Penn would use the prior Dutch settlement at Swanendael (irrespective of Indian deeds) as the winning argument against Lord Baltimore to prove the Dutch had settled and cultivated the land there prior to the date of the Crown's patent for Maryland. That's why Delaware today is a state in its own right and not part of Maryland. Stuyvesant's most persuasive argument was to invoke prior discoveries, exploration, and settlement by the Dutch, and by negotiating with the Indians for title deeds at this late date he weakened his position.

The West India Company officially took the position that it had erected forts in the New Netherland:

> not only for the purpose of closing and appropriating the aforesaid rivers, but likewise the lands around them and within their borders (being then about sixty leagues along the coast), and on the other side of the rivers so far as title by occupation tends to possession, to declare as their own and to preserve them against all foreign or domestic nations who would endeavor to usurp the same contrary to the Company's will and pleasure.[15]

Stuyvesant abandoned this principle when he insisted on having Indian deeds for the Santhoeck.

Andries Hudde arranged for Stuyvesant to meet at Fort Nassau with three prominent Lenape chiefs, the patriarch Mattahorn, Sinquas, and Pemenacka whose name is sometimes spelled Pemenetta. The Indians were undoubtedly impressed by the great white chief whose right leg was like the smooth branch of an oak tree encircled with silver, and who wore at his waist a sparkling scabbard containing a long sword with an ivory handle. They were also awed at how Stuyvesant commanded the Dutch forces at the fort, and directed the movement of a fleet of

Count Ernst-Casimir (1573-1632), Earl of Nassau-Dietz, stadholder of Friesland, namesake of Fort Casimir, from an oil painting by Wybrand de Geest, c. 1632. Top of right boot is sagged to reveal frills above the knee, as Dutch military heroes were often portrayed. (Courtesy of Fries Museum, Leeuwarden, The Netherlands)

The Adversaries

Governor Johan Printz (1592-1663)

Copy of an oil-on-canvas portrait in the parsonage at Bottnaryd, a village near Jönköping, Sweden where Printz was born and where his father served as the pastor for more than seventy years. The original painting by an unidentified 17th century artist is badly faded; see photograph taken by Amandus Johnson in *Instruction*, p. 3.

The copy, also in oil, was presented by King Gustaf V of Sweden to the Swedish Colonial Society in 1909, and is now owned by the Historical Society of Pennsylvania whose permission to reprint it is acknowledged. The original was possibly painted some time after Printz's return from America to Sweden in 1654 after which he was made governor of the district of Jönköping. The copyist has superimposed the Printz coat-of-arms in the right corner.

Governor Peter Stuyvesant (1610-1672)

Dated c. 1660, this portrait has long been attributed to an "unidentified artist," and since it is one of the earliest and most important paintings in American art history many attempts have been made to identify the artist. Evidence gathered by the author indicates the artist was Henri Couturier, a Dutch merchant-official who lived for a time in New Amstel, and is believed by the author to have been Delaware's first portrait painter.

The painting was a gift to the New York Historical Society in 1909 by Robert Van Rensselaer Stuyvesant, the four times great-grandson of the subject. The painting executed in oil on a wood panel measures 21½ x 17½ inches. There is no author's signature or mark on the front or back. See Appendix 3 below for further information that Couturier was the painter. (Courtesy New York Historical Society, New York City)

Nicholas William Stuyvesant (1648-1698)

Unsigned painting of Peter Stuyvesant's fifteen-year-old son on a pony is attributed to an unidentified artist, but the author's historical evidence in Appendix 3 indicates that Henri Couturier of New Castle was the painter. The boy's head is too large for the gnomelike body, but it allowed the artist to emphasize the son's striking resemblance to his father. The right hand, indistinct in this photograph, holds a whip, with the back of the hand turned and the wrist bent against the hip.

A gift to the New York Historical Society in 1905 by Robert Van Rensselaer Stuyvesant. Executed in oil on a wood panel measuring 35 x 25⅝ inches. (Courtesy New York Historical Society, New York City) vessels whose cannon belched smoke and thunder. But the Lenape chiefs were no fools. William Penn wrote that they could not be outwitted in any treaty "about a thing they understood,"[16] and the three chiefs fully understood Stuyvesant's artifice as the minutes of the conference clearly reveal to one reading between the lines.

Through his interpreter Alexander ("Sander") Boyer, Stuyvesant asked the chiefs if they were proprietors of land on the west side of the river where the Swedes were then living. Mattahorn speaking for the three sachems answered in the affirmative, and his answer leaves little doubt that the Indian concept of "use" rights had given way to the European institution of individual land ownership. Stuyvesant then asked how much land the Swedes had purchased from them, and Mattahorn dodged the question by asking, "Why was not the Sachem of the Swedes present that they might ask himself and hear him?" Stuyvesant replied that he had invited Printz to attend the conference, but he apparently was unwilling to come. This was a bald-faced lie—Stuyvesant didn't want any Swedes present to listen to his dialogue with the Indians.

Stuyvesant pressed Mattahorn further, and the chief's reply was that all the European nations coming to the *Lenape Wihittuck* were welcome, and the Lenape sold their lands to the first who asked them. Mattahorn was reverting to the ancient concept of sharing the land in contrast to European private ownership, and he added that the Dutch were "the earliest comers and discoverers of the river, who also, first of all settled thereon among them."[17] Mattahorn elaborated by saying the Indians had always maintained good friendship and commerce with the Dutch and they had often exchanged presents as a gesture of mutual friendship. Mattahorn did not say the Dutch had paid the Indians for use rights to the land south of the Minquas Kill as far as Bombay Hook, which included Tamakonck, nor are there any deeds in existence which indicate the Dutch "bought" this land from the natives. Mattahorn was careful *not* to say that the

Swedes paid for rights to this land as evidenced by deeds possessed by the Swedes. He wanted to please Stuyvesant but he did not want to say anything that might be interpreted as antagonistic to Governor Printz.

Stuyvesant then tried a different approach; he asked the Indians what lands belonging to the Lenape were still considered unsold. Once again he insisted upon imposing Dutch concepts of land tenure on the Indians and Mattahorn's answer was what Stuyvesant wanted to hear. Mattahorn said that Minuit "bought" only the land where Fort Christina was built, a small tract bounded by six trees, and that all other lands then occupied by the Swedes still belonged to the Indians. Mattahorn had learned a great deal about European real estate ownership, in contrast to Lenape aboriginal concepts, since his negotiation with Minuit thirteen years earlier, and now he wanted to apply the European system of outright sale. It is difficult to reconcile his ambivalence with an affidavit made by four members of Minuit's crew on December 29, 1638, when they returned to Europe, in which they all swore that five Indian chiefs, including Mattahorn, had, in exchange for gifts "ceded, transported, and transferred all the land, as many days' journeys on all places and parts of the river as they requested; upwards and on both sides."[18]

Stuyvesant was not familiar with this deposition or he would not have asked the next question: if the land at Tamakonck had not been sold to the Swedes would the chiefs now sell this territory to him? In characteristic Lenape fashion when confronted with a controversial question, the three chiefs withdrew from the meeting to deliberate and arrive at a consensus. When the conference reconvened, Pemenacka, characterized in the minutes as "the present and ceding proprietor," spoke as follows through the Indian interpreter:

> The Swede builds and plants, indeed, on our lands without buying them or asking us. Wherefore should we refuse you, Great Sachem, the land? We will rather present than

sell the Great Sachem the land, so that, should the Swedes again pull down the Dutch houses and drive away the people, you may not think ill of us, and we may not draw down your displeasure.

The minutes go on to say that, Stuyvesant having consented, the chiefs presented the land to him as a gift; namely, from the west point of the Minquas Kill where Fort Christina stood unto "Boompgens Hook" (presently Bombay Hook). The chiefs sealed the bargain by shaking hands with Stuyvesant and the witnesses.[19] There is no record that Stuyvesant presented gifts to the three chiefs although it was the usual custom for both Dutch and Swedes to give presents to the Indians when negotiating treaties or holding conferences. Pemenacka requested that if his gun needed repair that the Dutch would accomodate him without charge. Indians had not yet learned how to repair broken firearms, and were dependent upon European gunsmiths just as they relied on European traders for lead and gunpowder. Pemenacka also requested that if he came to the Dutch in need of food they would give him some corn. Stuyvesant agreed to comply with both reasonable requests.

Having gained possession of the land where the town of New Castle is now situated Stuyvesant lost no time in laying the foundations for a fort on the Santhoeck. Printz, who was kept informed of the Dutch activities, learned that Pemenacka had given the land to Stuyvesant with the approval of Mattahorn and Sinques, both friendly with the Swedes. Printz lost no time in summoning the chiefs to a meeting at Fort New Gothenburg to try to jog their memories. Of course, Mattahorn who was party to the negotiations with Minuit knew exactly what had transpired during the transaction in 1638 when the Lenape did not fully understand the consequences of outright land sale. Another sachem who was present in the 1638 transaction, Metatsimint, had since died, but in 1638 he was considered chief of the hunting territory south of the Minquas Kill on which Tamakonck was located.

Printz wanted to know why Pemenacka claimed ownership of Tamakonck, as the chief maintained in his discussions with Stuyvesant, when it was part of the territory Metatsimint ceded to Minuit on March 29, 1638? Pemenacka replied that prior to Minuit's arrival Metatsimint had sold the land to him, and since Metatsimint was no longer the owner in 1638, he had no right to sell it to Minuit. Mattahorn and Sinques corroborated Pemenacka's statement, which meant that (according to Dutch and Swedish laws) Pemenacka's gift of the land to Stuyvesant was legal and binding since Minuit had not purchased the land from the rightful owner!

Printz then produced three surprise witnesses—Metatsimint's widow Notike, her son Kiapes, and another relative named Quenieck. They testified that Metatsimint did not sell any land to Pemenacka—conveyances of land from one Indian to another were alien to Lenape culture. What happened was that by common understanding Metatsimint claimed the right to hunt on certain lands by the consent of the tribe, and according to acceptable Lenape practice, he gave Pemenacka the right to hunt on the same land, but that did not make Pemenacka the proprietor. Metatsimint retained prior right to the full use of the land and he was the bona fide owner when the land was sold to Minuit and consequently the land at the Santhoeck (Tamakonck) belonged to the Swedes as Printz claimed. It is quite clear that both Printz and Stuyvesant were manipulating the strings of the Indian puppets and the questions of use rights versus outright land sale became confused and inconsistent.

The document recording Printz's meeting with the Indians dated July 13, 1651 was preserved in the Royal Archives in Stockholm, but it was not available in the English language until 1954 when Professor Dunlap published a translation. Therein it is stated that after listening to the witnesses Pemenacka himself admitted that he was convinced of the truth and that "her [Metatsimint's wife] husband never gave him that land, but merely allowed him to hunt thereon . . ." After listening to this admission Metatsimint's wife said that she desired that "Pemenacka should revoke his compact with Stuyvesant."[20]

Since there was general agreement that Pemanacka had no authority to give land to Stuyvesant that he did not own, the Swedes were, and continued to be, the real owners. In the presence of Pemenacka, Mattahorn, and Sinques, Printz renewed the original contract with Notike, Kiapes, and Quenieck in which they reconfirmed Swedish ownership. No compensation is mentioned in the document, but it goes without saying that as an astute negotiator Printz must have given suitable trade merchandise to Metatsimint's heirs.[21]

Fortified with this new information Printz protested in writing to Stuyvesant, but Stuyvesant paid no attention and continued with the construction of the fort. Nevertheless, Printz's protests seemed to have raised questions in Stuyvesant's mind about the propriety of Pemenacka's gift of the land to him. He still lacked a legal contract conveying the Santhoeck to him for a stated consideration, and since all the land as far south as Bombay Hook was included in the gift he needed evidence that there had been no coercion.

On July 19 (probably by the Dutch calendar) Stuyvesant held a second conference with the Indians. Those in attendance were Pemenacka, Sinques, Mattahorn, and Mattahorn's son Ackahorn. The conference was held "on the land Camecouck [Tamakonck] itself," according to the document recording the transaction. The fort under construction must have been nearing completion and the conference was probably held in one of the buildings within the palisades. Stuyvesant may have believed that conducting the negotiation on the property then in dispute would make it appear more official. He invited four or five Minquas chiefs and thirteen prominent Dutchmen, who had accompanied the invasion forces, to witness the proceedings. Among the Dutch witnesses were Cornelis van Tienhoven, the Secretary of the New Netherland, second in rank to Stuyvesant, Martin Crieger, a New Amsterdam burgomaster, Dr. Abraham Staats, a physician and elder in the Dutch Reformed Church, Egbert van Borsum, master of the yacht *Prins Willem*, one of the vessels in the flotilla, Captain Jacob Jansen Huys, skipper of another Dutch vessel, and a young clergyman Domine Wilhelmus Grasmeer. If any questions were later raised in Holland or Sweden about the legality of the transaction Stuyvesant could point to the signatures of these respected Dutchmen.

This time the chiefs were paid for the land with "twelve coats of duffels, twelve axes, 12 adzes, 24 knives, 12 bars of lead, and four guns with some powder." The bounds of the land were explicitly given—from the Minquas Kill south to Bombay Hook— and the Indians conveyed "the aforesaid lands, trees, fruits, kills and rivers, solely and absolutely (the hunting and fishing excepted) to the disposal and pleasure of the aforesaid Sachem or Director, Peter Stuyvesant."[22]

Mattahorn, Ackahorn, and Sinques signed the parchment with their marks, but Pemenacka did not sign. His renunciation of ownership in the earlier conference with Printz may have made him wary of signing, and Stuyvesant may have preferred that Pemenacka's signature be omitted for the same reason. This deed of sale would have little validity in a modern court of law, because it was the result of Stuyvesant's conniving with the Indians. The Swedish government possessed earlier deeds in Stockholm indicating the Indians had conveyed title for the identical property to the Swedes. Stuyvesant could be accused of conspiring with the Lenape chiefs to defraud the Swedes of property they legally owned. Of course, Stuyvesant could argue that the Dutch possessed the rights of prior discovery, which invalidated the Swedish deeds.

These technicalities did not deter Stuyvesant from erecting the new fort with the assistance of soldiers, sailors, artisans, laborers, and one surveyor—Andries Hudde. Possibly 200 men participated in the work, and the fort was built with all deliberate speed because Stuyvesant wanted to get back to New Amsterdam as soon as possible. By August 1 the fort was ready for

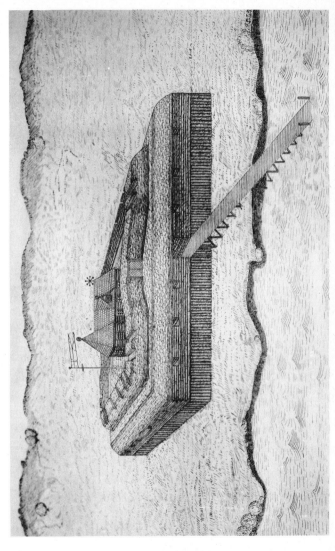

Sketch made in 1905 purporting to be Fort Casimir, built in 1651. No contemporary drawings of Fort Casimir are known to exist, and this is actually the artist's attempt to refine Lindeström's drawing of Fort Trinity after the Swedes rebuilt and renovated it in 1654-55. (Courtesy Historical Society of Delaware)

occupation; the armament, supplies, and trade goods at Fort Nassau were brought down the river to the new fort, and Fort Nassau was completely dismantled. No drawing was made of the new fort—at least none has survived as of its completion in 1651. Speculations have been made about its size, the number of cannons installed on the parapet, but this is all guesswork. It seems probable that a storehouse and barracks were built within the palisades, and several small dwellings erected outside the walls to house the families who formerly lived at Fort Nassau, but this, too, is speculative. Although the appearance is uncertain, the location of the fort is discussed in Appendix 1.

Neither are there records as to the number of soldiers and settlers left at the Santhoeck when Stuyvesant departed, but it is certain his intention was to encourage families from New Amsterdam to populate a town at the fort. No church was built, but as a religious man one assumes that Stuyvesant insisted that Dutch Reformed Church services be conducted by Domine Grasmeer, chaplain of the expedition. If so, this was New Castle's first Christian service, dating back to the summer of 1651.

When Stuyvesant returned to New Amsterdam he left two armed vessels temporarily on the Delaware to give added strength to the new fort and protect the families from possible Swedish reprisal. A contemporary Dutch report states that before his departure Stuyvesant had "divers verbal conferences with Johan Printz, the Swedish Governor, and they mutually promised not to commit any hostile or vexatious acts against one another, but to maintain together all neighborly friendship and correspondence as good friends and allies are bound to do."[23] Printz's correspondence negates this statement, which may have been Dutch propaganda intended to show that Stuyvesant bore no animosity toward the Swedes and that what he had done was not an act of war. In a letter written to Chancellor Oxenstierna in Sweden, Printz said he dispatched a message to Stuyvesant protesting his actions while the new fort was under construction, and he had protested verbally in a conference with Stuyvesant.

He added that if two men-of-war were sent to him from Sweden, the Dutch, as well as the English, would "right away abandon their violent enterprises."[24]

Before his departure Stuyvesant gave Sergeant Gerrit Bicker the military command of the fort and placed Andries Hudde in charge of civilian affairs. He also gave the fort a name—Fort Casimir. Stuyvesant was obliged to write to the directors in Amsterdam giving an account of the expedition and the construction of the new fort. The directors were astonished to receive the news, "which has taken us by surprise, as your Honor had not previously made any mention of this intention; God grant that what your Honor has done, may turn out for the best . . ." They continued to be apprehensive of what action the Swedish government would take when Printz's report of the attack was received. They went on to say that they did not know "whether the demolition of Fort Nassau was a very prudent act, and we are in the dark as to the reasons the [new] fort has been given this name."[25]

If Stuyvesant replied to the directors giving his reason for naming Fort Casimir, which he probably did, his letter is among many that are missing. It seems likely that Stuyvesant named the fort after Count Ernst of Casimir, Earl of Nassau, distinguished stadholder and hero of Friesland, Stuyvesant's home province. Count Ernst was a military hero during Stuyvesant's boyhood, and when Stuyvesant entered the services of the West India Company in 1635 the count had been dead for three years. His memory was preserved in the name Nassau used for forts in New Netherland and on a New Jersey stream "Graf [Count] Ernst's rivier" shown on a map dating from the early 1630s.[26] It was quite fitting for Stuyvesant to select the name Casimir, frequently referred to in Dutch records as Casimier, Casemier, or Casemiris, in honor of Count Ernst.[27]

No matter how the directors felt about it in their comfortable offices in Amsterdam, Stuyvesant's bluff worked. He made the Dutch West India Company master of New Sweden without shedding the blood of a single Swede, Finn, or Dutchman. He conquered New Sweden by his bravado and succeeded in making the Delaware and Hudson Rivers the axis of the New Netherland.

4. THE SWEDES CAPTURE FORT CASIMIR

PETER STUYVESANT DID NOT seize any forts or supplies belonging to the Swedes in his invasion of New Sweden, but before returning to New Amsterdam he left the Dutch West India Company in full control of the Delaware River valley. Governor Printz wrote that Stuyvesant cut down a standard at the Santhoeck bearing the coat of arms of Queen Christina; he invited the Swedish freemen to break their oaths with Sweden and swear allegiance to the Dutch; he did his utmost to convince the Minquas that they should trade with the Dutch at the new fort and have as little as possible to do with the Swedes; he gave orders that all ships sailing up the Delaware should be detained at Fort Casimir for inspection; and that tolls and custom duties should be demanded of all foreign vessels.[1] Thus, the West India Company not only regulated the river commerce, but it possessed land on the west shore from the Christina River south to Bombay Hook by virtue of Stuyvesant's land purchase from the Indians.

By the summer of 1653 Printz wrote there were twenty-six

Dutch families settled at Fort Casimir, the first reference to the number of Dutch householders.[2] By this time the Dutch had abandoned other locations on the Delaware, including Fort Beversreede, and had consolidated the settlers at the Santhoeck. The records do not give the size of the garrison nor the number of soldiers' families in contrast to traders, craftsmen, and others living in private houses near the fort in the area then known as the Strand. These inhabitants of what would later become the town of New Castle were not immigrants newly arrived from Holland; some had formerly lived at or near Fort Nassau and others came from New Amsterdam.

Printz had neither the manpower nor the military resources to attack Fort Casimir, nor would such action have received the support of the majority of Swedish colonists nor the soldiers who had grown resentful of the autocratic methods of their governor. Commandant Bicker and Commis Hudde did not interfere with the Swedish settlers on the river, and the Dutch and Swedish families were on friendly terms. The two Dutch warships had been withdrawn to New Amsterdam and there was peace in New Sweden, although many of the Swedes had little love for Governor Printz.

Following Printz's arrival in 1644 to take charge of the colony, vessels from Sweden brought supplies, a few new settlers, and letters from the government and the New Sweden Company. After 1648 no vessels arrived from the homeland, and he received no reinforcements, no supplies, no goods for the Indian trade, and no letters. He was left to his own devices to rule a fast-fading colony. He did his best to make the colony self-supporting agriculturally, but there were droughts and periods of too much rain when he had to rely upon shrewd bargaining with English and Dutch merchants to obtain food for the soldiers and company employes.

As the chief executive and legislative officer, as well as prosecuting attorney and judge of the court of law, Printz was a despotic ruler of a small body of people, many illiterate. His decisions were final and if he was unjust or abusive the people had little recourse. So far as the Swedes were concerned Printz was their commanding officer regardless of the Dutch at Fort Casimir who had their own leaders. Printz insisted upon enforcing the New Sweden Company's policy of confining the Indian trade to the company's agents. The Swedish freemen strongly opposed this restriction because they could not deal with the natives for beaver pelts, which could be used in lieu of scarce currency to obtain goods from English and Dutch merchants. The Swedes complained that the Dutch West India Company permitted their freemen to engage in the Indian trade and that Printz traded with Indians, Dutch, and English without hindrance, for his own personal gain. Why didn't they have equal rights?

Printz's despotism caused some Swedes and Finns to desert the colony and flee to Maryland where the people were governed by a less autocratic governor and an assembly consisting of a council and a lower house with elected representatives. Furthermore, at this particular period almost anyone in Maryland could engage in the Indian trade; raising tobacco in Maryland was also a profitable activity where soil and weather were conducive to bumper crops. As a result of Printz's harsh rule, twenty-two settlers signed a petition accusing him of being brutal, avaricious, and unjust. An enraged Printz arrested, tried, and executed the ringleader on a charge of treachery, and berated the other signers.[3] Printz nipped the mutiny in the bud, but the seeds of discontent were still there.

Some of the Swedes died of illness, and a few were killed by Indians, and by 1653 New Sweden's population had declined to "200 souls." The soldiers and company employes were having difficulty sustaining themselves. The Minquas proper and the Black Minquas "from whom the beavers come" were warring against each other, which kept them from trapping and hunting.[4] Even if the furs were available Printz's trade goods were insufficient to sustain commerce with the Indians, and this tended to alienate the Lenape who expected gifts periodically to cement the bonds of friendship.

The Dutch in New Amsterdam were also having problems. Holland had gone to war with England; money was short and times were hard in the New Netherland. Stuyvesant had been quarreling with the New Englanders over the northern bounds of the New Netherland, and the war in Europe made him apprehensive of an attack from New England. He hired workmen to repair and strengthen Fort New Amsterdam and enlisted private citizens to serve as soldiers at a monthly salary paid by the Company.[5] Faced with a potentially critical situation at New Amsterdam, Stuyvesant was unable to enlarge the settlement at Fort Casimir as he intended, and the population at the Santhoeck remained static. Even if he had the manpower to reinforce Fort Casimir, he was inhibited by letters from the directors of the Amsterdam Chamber cautioning him not to antagonize the Swedes and give them cause for complaint. "It is not very desirable," the directors wrote, "to add to the number of the Company's enemies at this critical period."[6]

The directors were well aware that Swedish generals led victorious armies over half of Europe and that Sweden's highly organized military system was the best in Europe. Sweden had fought against Russia, Poland, and Germany, and in the spring of 1643 struck a decisive blow at Denmark. It is not difficult to understand why Holland's engagement in a war with England was not the time to antagonize a first class nation like Sweden, the leading power in northern Europe.

In May of 1654, Stuyvesant was so concerned about the safety of New Amsterdam that he discussed with his council the advisability of abandoning Fort Casimir and bringing the freemen as well as the members of the garrison to reinforce the defenses at Manhattan. If that had happened the town of New Castle may never have come into existence. One of the members of the council suggested transferring only the soldiers, leaving the freemen in control of Fort Casimir's armaments.

Since the freemen and their families were "few in numbers," if left without military protection the council feared they might be in danger of being massacred by Indians.[7] While Stuyvesant was trying to resolve the issue a message arrived from Fort Casimir requesting reinforcements for the garrison. The message stated if reinforcements were not forthcoming for protection against the Indians, the civilians threatened to leave the river altogether, which would again make the fort vulnerable to Swedish occupancy. The message dissuaded Stuyvesant and the council from moving the soldiers at Fort Casimir to Manhattan, but leaving a weak garrison on the Delaware proved to be the worst mistake they could have made.

While Stuyvesant was preoccupied with strengthening his command at New Amsterdam, Governor Printz had grown unhappy about the situation on the Delaware and he wrote his superiors in Sweden for "gracious delivery from this place." He was able to get his letters through on Dutch vessels and his mail eventually reached Stockholm, sometimes months later. Inasmuch as no ships sailed from Sweden to America his letters went unanswered. Queen Christina's original instruction stated that he should occupy the position of governor of New Sweden for three years at which time he was free to return "after the necessary arrangement has been made for his successor . . ."[8] At the end of three years while he was still in direct contact with the homeland he respectfully requested permission to return home. The Queen's answer came a year later. She told him to remain at his post for a few years longer because no worthy successor could then be found.

Printz was an obedient soldier, but three years turned into nine, and his subsequent requests for relief were still not answered; perhaps they never reached the Queen. Who can blame him, at the age of sixty-one, still tied to a frustrating command in New Sweden, for deciding to take matters into his own hands? He was tired of his job in an undeveloped land separated by thousands of miles of ocean from his beloved country. Since no one in Stockholm would issue orders relieving him, he furloughed himself.

About the beginning of October 1653 he packed up his personal belongings and went to New Amsterdam with his wife and four daughters (Armegot remained in New Sweden). From New Amsterdam he set sail for Europe on a Dutch vessel accompanied by about twenty-five soldiers and settlers who decided to return with him. These men were referred to as the best in the colony.[9] One of them was "the wise and faithful" Hendrick Huygen, a native of Wesel on the lower Rhine in Germany who originally arrived as a member of Minuit's expedition in 1638 and became chief commissary of the colony under Printz. Printz left New Sweden in charge of his son-in-law Johan Papegoja, promising him that he would return within ten or twelve months, or at least arrange for a ship to be sent from Sweden to bring relief to the colony.

If Queen Christina had devoted more attention to the American colony the story would have been different, but she had little interest in New Sweden. After taking up the sceptre at the age of eighteen she seemed principally interested in advancing learning and the arts in Sweden and making her royal court in Stockholm famous for its balls, masques, and pageants. She kept spending the royal revenues with such recklessness that she nearly bankrupted the kingdom. Queen Christina's disinterest in the American colony was not the sole reason New Sweden did not receive support; Sweden was involved in wars; the leader of the New Sweden Company died; and there were other reasons not relevant to the present account.

In 1652, at the time Printz was weighing his decision to return to Sweden, the Queen suddenly displayed an unexpected, but momentary interest in the colony. She decided that an expedition with 300 new colonists and a large cargo of supplies should be sent to New Sweden. If Printz had known about this he probably would have remained at Printzhoff, at least until the expedition arrived. At the Queen's direction a branch of the government known as the Commercial College, with salaried officers, was given the management of the former New Sweden Company. The special function of the Commercial College was to supervise, increase, and extend foreign trade. Johan Rising, the secretary of the Commercial College, was an economist who had traveled in a number of European countries and was considered an outstanding authority on commerce, trade, and agriculture. The government commissioned Rising as the head of the expedition, and he agreed to serve in New Sweden as Printz's chief commissary and councillor, a sort of lieutenant-governor.[10] He was knighted by Queen Christina before leaving Sweden.

It was originally intended to send two vessels in the expedition, the *Örn* (*Eagle*) and the *Gyllene Haj* (*Golden Shark*), but for several reasons the *Haj* was not ready at sailing time, and the *Örn* left Gothenburg alone. Since this expedition is of special interest in the history of early New Castle, certain of the details are worth noting. The captain of the *Örn*, a vessel belonging to the Crown, was a Dutchman named Jan Janson Bockhorn, but during the voyage he took his orders from Rising. As preparations were being made, which required several months, it was not then known in Sweden that Printz was on his way back home. It had already been decided that he would be ordered to remain in America since the expedition would bring the additional colonists he had repeatedly asked for as well as an experienced economist to share in the administrative work.

Lieutenant Sven Skute, who had not yet returned to New Sweden after making Printz's report on the affairs in the colony, was ordered to return with Rising on the *Örn*, and was promoted to a captaincy. Peter Mårtensson Lindeström, a tall, robust, handsome engineer aged twenty-one, who had specialized in mathematics and the science of fortifications at Uppsala University, was given free passage with an officer's rank. After the vessel arrived in New Sweden, Rising gave him the official title of "Engineer and Clerk of the Court," a unique multi-purpose assignment.

Skute was assigned to hire soldiers and laborers to go to New Sweden as employes and to prevail on others to go on their own as settlers. He had no difficulty in recruiting all the people that were needed which may seem unusual in view of the unrest and hardship in the American colony. Lindeström, who was present at the time, said that those who had been deported on earlier expeditions were believed to be living rich and comfortable in New Sweden, and had no desire to return home—at least this was the impression many Swedish farmers had. He added that some volunteered because of a passion to travel and see the world; others to seek prosperity through trade and commerce; and still others were looking for new homes for their wives and children in a land of opportunity.[11] This especially applied to the Finns and many were included in the applicants who came mostly from Värmland and Västergot where most of the potential colonists lived.

The credentials of those seeking passage were carefully examined to exclude criminals and lawbreakers, which was in sharp contrast to earlier expeditions where malefactors, poachers, forest-burners, and deserters from the army were forcibly exiled to New Sweden. On this expedition 100 families were left behind because there was no room for them on the vessel, although many of them had already disposed of their homes and property. When the *Örn* sailed on February 2, 1654, breaking through the ice in the harbor, she was overcrowded with about 350 persons, including crew members. Her cargo consisted of a large assortment of trade goods to be used in commerce with the Indians: muskets, clothing, implements, and tools, several hogsheads of wine, and barrels of beer. Bread and butter were also included to help feed the passengers, but the *Örn* carried only a limited quantity of foodstuffs sufficient to sustain passengers and crew during the passage. Her cargo space was used to accomodate the people, and the intent was that the *Haj* would follow bringing food to help support the colonists after they landed in New Sweden. During the voyage the company provided food for the soldiers and the colonists, whereas the Admiralty paid for the food for the sailors. There was only one galley on the vessel, which must have been a busy place!

Before the *Örn* hoisted anchor news reached Rising that Governor Printz had arrived in Holland enroute to Sweden and had become ill. After leaving America, Printz was at sea more than ten weeks due to adverse weather; the vessel made a landing in France, and from there he went to Amsterdam. His illness and the severe winter weather in the English Channel delayed the completion of his journey from Holland to Sweden. Rising was not fully informed about what had happened to Printz, and when the time came for the *Örn* to leave Gothenburg, Printz had not yet arrived in Sweden and Rising had no opportunity to discuss the situation in New Sweden with his predecessor. Rising realized before sailing that it would be necessary for him to take the executive position when he arrived and his instructions provided for that eventuality. He also knew that Stuyvesant had invaded New Sweden and built a new Dutch fort at a "place called Sandhauk," because Printz had given Oxenstierna that information in a letter written August 1, 1651.[12] What was not known to the Queen, the Commercial College, nor to Rising was whether Stuyvesant had subsequently seized Fort Christina, Fort Elfsborg, or Fort New Gothenburg. Consequently, the instructions to Rising stated that in the event that these forts had been captured and Printz had departed the country, "he shall demand their return in the name of Her Royal Majesty and seek to get them into his possession in all possible manners, otherwise settle and fortify some other place in the river."

If the Dutch could not be persuaded to vacate Fort Casimir, Rising was cautioned to avoid hostility, because he was told it was better to tolerate the Dutch there than have the English in control of the fort. Rather than have a confrontation with the Dutch, Rising was directed to proceed with the erection of a

Swedish fort on the Delaware south of Fort Casimir which would control the river and make the Dutch fort powerless.[13]

If the situation on the Delaware appeared precarious Rising was supposed to consult with his officers and decide whether it would not be better to return to Sweden with the colonists.[14] His lack of information on what awaited him when he arrived in the Delaware River must have given Rising considerable concern but a more realistic worry was the voyage itself and the problems that beset the *Örn* on the high seas. The vessel followed a circuitous route from Gothenburg, Sweden to Calais, Dover, the Canary Islands, and the Caribbean. Lindeström wrote in a journal he kept of the voyage that she was fired on in the English Channel by British warships who mistook her for a Dutch vessel; the Spaniards shot at her off the Canaries; and she narrowly escaped being waylaid by three Turkish privateers. Bad weather dogged the voyage, and an epidemic broke out among the closely packed passengers. Corpses sewn in sheets were cast overboard each morning, with weights on their legs and arms to take them to the bottom before sharks ate their bodies. Some passengers delirious with burning fevers jumped overboard. One hundred deaths occurred during the voyage.

When the *Örn* reached St. Christopher in the Caribbean, 230 passengers were ill, but they were rested and refreshed with food and fresh water before departing. Driven off course by a hurricane that ripped the sails off the masts, Captain Bockhorn entered the Chesapeake under the assumption he was at the mouth of the Delaware Bay. Lindeström noted in his journal, "The person who cannot pray to God, let him be sent on such a long and dangerous voyage and he shall surely learn to pray."[15]

At long last, after repairs were made in Virginia, the *Örn* arrived opposite Fort Elfsborg on May 20, after a voyage of more than three months. Captain Sven Skute, looking from the deck, must have been impatient to visit the site of his former command, but what he saw when he and Rising went ashore must have come as a shock. Lindeström noted:

There we cast anchor and landed finding the fort, with the houses and ramparts totally in ruins. This fort had been abandoned on account of the mosquitos, because there was such an immense number of them that they almost ate up the people there, and they could not be driven away, though they tried to do this in all kinds of ways. They sucked the blood from the people so that they became very weak and sick from it. In the daytime they had to fight continually with the mosquitos so that they could not see with their eyes, and in the night they could neither rest nor sleep. From the continued stinging and sucking of the mosquitos the people were so swollen, that they appeared as if they had been effected [sic.] with some horrible disease. Therefore they called this Fort Myggenborgh [Mosquito Fort].[16]

Whether or not Lindeström exaggerated the reason for this incident name is not known, but this appears to be the earliest account, frequently repeated, that New Jersey mosquitos caused the fort to be vacated. One wonders if mosquitos were not also bothersome in the marshlands at Fort Nassau, Fort Christina, and Fort Casimir, and yet these forts were not vacated for that reason.

When Commandant Gerrit Bicker saw the *Örn* anchored in the river he sent Adriaen van Tienhoven, clerk of a rudimentary Dutch court at Fort Casimir, and four freemen, Egbert Gerritse, Cornelis Teunisse, Cornelis Mauritz, and Peter Harmans in a small boat to learn the identity of the vessel and whence she came. Rising permitted them to board and treated them in a friendly way. He learned from them that the garrison at Fort Casimir consisted of only nine soldiers and the fort was in such disrepair that it could easily be taken. The five men remained on the *Örn* overnight and then returned to the fort early the next morning, Sunday May 21, with information for Bicker that an armed Swedish vessel was bringing new colonists and the leader of the expedition intended to demand the surrender of Fort Casimir.

Van Tienhoven later testified that when he reported to Bicker the latter informed the freemen and the Company's employes all of whom requested that he give orders to defend the fort, and Bicker replied, "What should I do? There is no powder."[17] Bicker apparently did not issue orders to the soldiers or freemen to prepare to defend the fort.

In the meanwhile, with the wind in his favor, Rising ordered Captain Bockhorn to cross the river to the Santhoeck and cast anchor before the fort. The majority of the passengers, and some of the members of the crew, were still seriously ill, but Rising was unwilling to proceed to Fort Christina without trying to gain possession of Fort Casimir "without force and hostility" according to his instruction. About eleven o'clock in the morning, following the conclusion of church services, the *Örn* arrived at the fort and gave a salute by firing two of her cannon. There was no answer from the fort. Rising then dispatched Captain Sven Skute and Lieutenant Elias Gyllengren ashore with three squads of musketeers, about twenty or thirty men.

When the soldiers landed Commandant Bicker came to meet them, welcoming them as friends, and he and Skute went into the fort together for a discussion that lasted about two hours. Rising, still aboard the *Örn*, became impatient and fired another salute on the cannon, which was not answered. Lindeström later wrote that the fort was armed with twelve iron cannon and one brass gun, but Bicker had no powder and only sixty three-pound cannon balls. Apparently during Bicker and Skute's conference the latter made a strong case for Swedish ownership rights to the land and the fort, and undoubtedly promised freedom to Bicker and his men if they would peacefully surrender.

There are several accounts of what then ensued, told by men who were there at the time, such as Lindeström who gave the Swedish view, and several members of the Dutch garrison who later gave their depositions in New Amsterdam about the conduct of Rising, Skute, and the Swedish forces. Their names, as well as their ages and places of residence, are on record. The spellings below are given in their depositions:[18]

Corporal Jan Adamse of Worms, aged 28
Hans Aelbertss of Brunswick, aged 24
Matthew Boucheine of Calis, aged 28
[who became court messenger under Jacquet; see chapter 6]
Godefried Cloeck of Aldernag, aged 30
Peter Ebel of Meckelenburch, Burgher Sergeant, aged 40
Elias Emmens of Swol, aged 37
Jan Hendrickse of Struckhausen, aged 25
Hendrick Siliacques of Groeningen, aged 44
Symon van Straten of Nimwegen, aged 31

These men seem to have been the nine previously referred to as soldiers at Fort Casimir, although Peter Ebel was a freeman not in Bicker's command. With the five freemen who boarded the *Örn*, they were among New Castle's earliest known occupants.

Following his discussion in the fort with Captain Skute, Bicker requested a little time for consultation before deciding to surrender the fort, and he again sent Adriaen van Tienhoven and two others to board the *Örn* to request three day's delay. Rising replied that he would rather have an immediate answer, but would await a report from Skute before taking further action. Bicker then sent van Tienhoven and Peter Ebel to confer again with Rising and learn under whose authority he demanded the surrender of the fort.

Van Tienhoven accordingly asked Rising to show him his commission that justified his taking possession, and Rising replied, according to van Tienhoven's and Ebel's depositions, that he did so on Queen Christina's authority. He also told them that her Majesty had addressed the West India Company, whose directors had given for answer, that they had not authorized the encroachment on the Swedish limits, much less the building of

Fort Casimir in the South River, and they had further told the Swedish ambassadors: "If our people are in your way there, drive them off." Then to add emphasis to his statement, "the Governor [Rising] slapped Adriaen van Tienhoven on the breast with his hand and said: Go your way and tell your Governor that."

Rising was correct that the West India Company had not authorized Stuyvesant to build Fort Casimir, but the available records do not support his statement that the Company officials told the Swedish ambassadors to oust their employes from Fort Casimir. If this had occurred, the instructions given him when he left Sweden would doubtless have made reference to such an important concession. Rising may have embellished the story to justify his assault on the fort.

Commandant Bicker later submitted a report to Stuyvesant explaining what took place and why he had no alternative except to surrender. He said he welcomed Skute when the Swedish landing party came ashore, but at the point of a sword Skute immediately demanded surrender of the fort and the river. Bicker claimed the side arms were taken from his men and their "muskets torn from their soldiers." He said Skute seized the cannon in the bastions and that Rising refused to give him an hour's delay before the Swedes would begin firing from the *Örn*. He added that the Dutch soldiers were driven out of the fort and all the property in the fort confiscated by the Swedes, and he was scarcely able to convince Rising not to disseize his wife and children.[19]

Rising minimized any violence in his account of the incident. He said the Hollanders were promised freedom of their persons, property, occupation, and religion; that scarcely any watch was kept in the fort and that the Swedish soldiers went into the fort and occupied it without hostility. He admitted the Swedish soldiers took charge of the guns, but they did not seize any personal property. Rising wrote that he told Commandant Bicker that every discretion would be shown him and his people, and if they elected to remain at the Santhoeck they would enjoy all the liberties bestowed on Swedish subjects; if not, they could depart unhindered with their belongings whenever they desired.[20]

The Prince of Orange's flag flying over the fort was lowered by Bicker's son on his father's instructions, and the Swedes ran up the gold-blue Swedish flag brought ashore from the *Örn*. Rising gave the fort a new name, Fort Trefaldighet ("Fort Trinity") because it was taken on Trinity Sunday, so called by Swedish Lutherans from the feast held annually in honor of the Trinity. Rising had a second reason for giving the fort a new name—he stated in his journal that he wanted to eliminate Dutch place-names on the Delaware as far as possible.

Vice-Director Papegoja, hearing the cannon fire at Fort Christina, sailed down the Santhoeck to investigate, and one can imagine his astonishment to see the Swedish colors flying over the fort and a Swedish vessel anchored in the river. He boarded the *Örn* and welcomed Rising, but was dismayed to see the condition of the passengers who "were now very ill on the ship and the smell so strong it was impossible to endure it any longer. . ."[21]

Papegoja agreed with Rising that the passengers and crew should be landed at Fort Christina, and on May 22 after a voyage of 109 days they came ashore, many so ill they had to be carried and others so weak they could not walk unassisted. Some remained at Christina to recuperate and others were distributed among the families of Swedish and Finnish freemen to be cared for until they were strong enough to build their own cabins. Lieutenant Gyllengren and a squad of soldiers remained at the Santhoeck in command of Fort Trinity. Rising must have felt that the capture of Fort Casimir was a notable and successful conclusion to a distressing and tragic voyage. The Dutch menace to New Sweden had been eradicated; Fort Casimir was in Swedish hands; the Delaware Valley from Bombay Hook to Fort Christina and northward was again in Swedish possession, and not a drop of blood had been shed on either side.

* * *

In his first report to the Commercial College written at Fort Christina July 13, 1654, Rising said that when he landed at Fort Christina with ''a lot of weak and sick people,'' he found an ''empty country partly disturbed by despondency, partly by mutiny and desertion.''[22] He, of course, learned of the opposition to Printz, and that, following Printz's departure, fifteen men (some with their families) deserted the colony and settled in Maryland without Papegoja's permission. This was considered a serious offense because those in the company's employ had contracted to remain for a stated length of time and many owed the company money for food and supplies; in the case of soldiers it was more serious because desertion was punishable by death. Rising wrote that when he arrived there were only seventy people in the colony. With the soldiers, servants, and freemen who debarked with him at Fort Christina the total population of New Sweden escalated to about 370 people.[23]

The second day after he arrived at Fort Christina, after taking a day to rest, Rising set up a provisional government consisting of himself, Captain Sven Skute, and Vice-Director Johan Papegoja, again resuming his rank as a lieutenant. Papegoja was probably glad to be relieved of the full responsibility that devolved on him after Printz's departure; in fact, he was eager to go back home, and when the *Örn* sailed back to Sweden he returned with her.

Rising summoned Commandant Bicker, Commis Hudde, and the Dutch colonists and soldiers from Fort Trinity to come to Fort Christina where they were required to take an oath and sign a document pledging they would henceforth be faithful subjects of Queen Christina, and as honest neighbors and fellow citizens would submit to Swedish protection. Bicker and Hudde set the example by first taking the oath in the open air with Swedish banners waving overhead, but some of their followers had reservations about deserting the Stuyvesant government even though they were promised more privileges by the Swedes. Six

Dutch soldiers requested permission to go to New Amsterdam where they would take their leave and return to become freemen, provided the Swedish colony prospered. They did not take the oath. The remaining three soldiers owned land under cultivation at Fort Trinity and decided to take the oath and remain.

Two of the colonists, Adriaen van Tienhoven and Cornelius de Baer (de Boer) were rejected and denied permission to take the oath. Both had reputations of being unfriendly to the Swedes and making insulting remarks about their Queen. They were sent back to New Amsterdam.

A question was raised about the integrity of three others willing to take the oath—Sander Boyer, and two Englishmen, Simon Lane and Thomas Brun (Brown). Papegoja knew that Boyer and Brown made trouble on the Schuylkill during the Printz administration, and none of the three were well disposed to the Swedes. The question as to whether they should be accepted as Swedish subjects was deferred for further consideration.[24] They returned to their homes at the Santhoeck to await a final decision.

A number of Swedish and Finnish freemen living upriver came to Fort Christina to witness the proceedings, and also to meet Rising and his staff and to greet Captain Skute on his return to the colony. They were all well pleased when Rising made an important announcement: it had been decided in Sweden that the New Sweden Company would no longer retain the exclusive right to conduct the fur trade with the Indians. Henceforth, private colonists were granted permission to trade freely with the natives or with other Europeans. Allowing the colonists to barter with the Indian tribes or engage in commercial negotiations with English and Dutch merchants was a significant change in Swedish colonial policy. The colonists would be charged a modest 2% export duty on all furs and other products shipped to Sweden, but were exempt from paying any import duties at Swedish ports. Another privilege granted the settlers was the right to buy land from the company or from Indian owners, if the land had not already been deeded to the company, and to hold it as personal property.[25]

On May 28, a week after the *Örn*'s passengers landed at Fort Christina, Rising sent Peter Yokum, one of the Swedish freemen, to Manhattan with an Indian guide to inform Governor Stuyvesant of his arrival in America and to assure him of his intent to be a friendly neighbor. In his letter he said that Fort Casimir with its garrison and the colonists living in the village had voluntarily taken an oath of allegiance and fidelity to the Queen of Sweden. Rising had the best of intentions when he wrote the letter, but he should have known how the hot-tempered Dutch governor would react.

Stuyvesant never answered Rising's letter, but before the summer was over Rising heard rumors that Stuyvesant was secretly planning an attack to recapture the former Dutch fort.

Rising apparently was still concerned about the loyalty of the inhabitants at Fort Casimir. Although the majority had already sworn allegiance to the Swedish government, Rising wanted the oath fully understood and, if necessary, reaffirmed. He, Skute, Papegoja, and others went to Fort Trinity, and there on June 3 they read the oath for a second time, and once more the Dutch agreed to it. The Swedes also consented to accept Sander Boyer, Simon Lane, and Thomas Brown as citizens of New Sweden and the oath was also administered to them.

Rising noted in his journal that twenty-two colonists at Fort Trinity had been added to the rolls of New Sweden. He was speaking only of the males because the oath was not taken by females. In none of the contemporary records is there an exact figure of the total population at the Santhoeck at this time. The reader will recall that a year before Printz reported that twenty-six Dutch families were settled at Fort Casimir. His reference was to families, not houses or colonists, but Lindeström observed that there were twenty-one houses "built by the Hollanders." If the twenty-one or twenty-two dwellings were all occupied, the total population of those living beyond the palisades of the fort must have been in excess of sixty or seventy men, women, and children. Whether some of the houses were occupied by soldiers who had families, or whether all of the soldiers lived within the confines of the fort, is not known.

No surveyor's drawings exist which pinpoint the locations of these houses nor are the houses described in contemporary accounts. The records at this time do not refer to streets, a public square, or a Green. What is certain is that the total population was well in excess of the population of any other single community in the Delaware Valley. The Swedish and Finnish settlers were scattered on farms along the streams north of Fort Christina, with small clusters here and there. At a very early date New Castle seemed to be taking on the character of what would later become a cosmopolitan town.

The same day Rising and his associates administered the oath to the Dutch at Fort Trinity, June 3, 1654, Rising also convened a court where a few cases were heard. Although this was the first Swedish court in New Castle very little is known about it except for a brief mention in Rising's journal. Who was involved in the initial litigation, how the cases were tried, and the decision rendered by the court (probably consisting of Rising, Skute, and Papegoja) are not documented. There was no courthouse at this early date and the trials were probably held in an upper room in the fort, and the litigants must have been residents of the Santhoeck. Since Rising was fluent in Dutch, as well as Swedish, there would have been no language problems.

(In 1881, 227 years later, the county seat was moved from New Castle to Wilmington, terminating a judicial continuum dating back to Rising's Swedish court of 1654. Actually there was an earlier Dutch court of which Adriaen van Tienhoven was the clerk, but nothing is known about it.)

One of Rising's first concerns was to improve the defenses of New Sweden, and he ordered high priority given to Fort Trinity which he recognized "is as a key to the river." He instructed Captain Skute, who was in charge of all the ammunition, guns, and cannon in the colony, to repair and strengthen the fort with Lindeström's assistance. Lindeström wrote that the fort "had fallen into almost decay," which may be an exaggeration since Lindeström had a tendency to over-dramatize, and the structure was only three years old. He went on further to say in his journal, referring to himself in the third person, that "the said fortress was built up anew, practically from the foundation, much stronger fortified and improved with bastions by the above-mentioned Mr. Peter Lindheström."[26] Captain Skute directed the work of reconstruction, and he doubtless had something to say about the new features that were added, although Lindeström may have been responsible for the design since he had been educated in the field of military fortifications. No description or drawing of the original Fort Casimir is known to exist, and it is impossible to determine precisely what enlargements or renovations were made.

Evidently all of the Dutch cannons were not functional because four cannon, which could fire fourteen pound balls, were transferred from the *Örn* to the fort. They were not set on the parapet, but behind an entrenchment and bulwark built on the river side of the fort "the better to sweep the river straight across." Balls, powder, and lead were also taken from the vessel to the fort, and since the *Örn* carried thirty-four to forty cannon, she still had sufficient armament to protect her on her return voyage to Sweden. According to an agreement made with the Hollanders, every man living at the Santhoeck spent fourteen days working along with the Swedes and Finns during the reconstruction.

Whereas the original Fort Casimir was a Dutch production, Fort Trinity, due to Lindeström's designs, incorporated some of the latest concepts in Swedish military science, consonant with the building material then available. Lindeström made a drawing of the reconstructed fort, which accompanied the finished manuscript of his journal entitled *Geographia Americae*, completed in Stockholm in 1691 some years after his return to Sweden, but it was not then published. Thomas Campanius

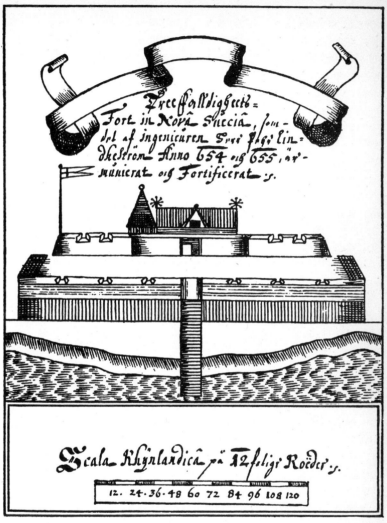

Peter Lindeström's contemporary drawing of Fort Trinity which accompanied his manuscript, *Geographia Americae*. Caption reads, "Trinity's Fort in New Sweden which partly by the engineer Mr. Pehr Lindheström in the years 1654 and 1655 is armed and fortified." (trans. by Dr. Richard H. Hulan.) The bottom line states the measurements are in the Rhinelandish scale of 12-foot rods, which means the front measured approx. 210 feet. (Courtesy of Hagley Museum and Library)

Holm, grandson of Johannes Campanius, had access to the drawing and recopied it as an illustration in a book he published in Stockholm in 1702. Holm's version of Lindeström's drawing was published for the first time in America in 1834 to accompany an English translation of his book.[27] Not until 1911 was a faithful reproduction of Lindeström's drawing published in Johnson's *Swedish Settlements*. The illustration in the present text is a photographic copy of Lindeström's original drawing borrowed from *Swedish Settlements*.

The reader will note that a ramp or elongated pier ran from the front gate of the rampart to the Delaware River, thus permitting passengers, livestock, and supplies to be disembarked without being lightered to shore in small landing craft. This was probably a feature of the original fort built by Stuyvesant because ready access to the river was one of the reasons he selected the site.

Lindeström's drawing clearly shows the high bank of the tapered promontory responsible for the name, "long sandy point." There is little doubt that Skute's men had to rebuild this wooden ramp exposed to storms and high tides.

The central building shown on the drawing in the rear of the rampart appears to have been constructed of hewn logs laid horizontally with a planked roof, a non-Dutch type of housing, probably erected by Skute's men familiar with log dwellings. The two gadgets on the roof seem to be weather vanes intended to give sailing craft some indication of wind velocity. The pennant shows the direction the wind is blowing. The log house seems to have been constructed behind the bastions of the fort proper, probably having its own protective palisades, which Lindeström could not show on his drawing that depicts the fort as seen from the Delaware River. The conical tower, which seems to be part of the log building may have been built on or behind the rear wall, not necessarily attached to the log dwelling. It may have been a watchtower accessible by steps not shown in the drawing. Admittedly, the drawing leaves much to be desired in trying to visualize the reconstructed fort—but it is the best we have.

When Rising took Fort Casimir the Dutch West India Company had twenty morgens of land (a little more than forty acres) under cultivation near the fort at the Santhoeck. The records do not state the nature of the crop, but this was the time of year when corn was coming in tassel and vegetables were ripening. Skute did not disturb the Dutch crops, but ordered a nearby tract owned by the Swedish company to be plowed and seeded with winter grain for the company's benefit. A visitor to New Castle today might have difficulty imagining farm fields between Harmony and Chestnut Streets, which was arable land behind the fort in 1654.

Some of the newly arrived Swedish and Finnish families who accompanied Rising moved to the Santhoeck, and Swedish freemen and servants cleared additional tracts for farming using horses and oxen that Rising made available to them.[28] Initially some of the cattle owned by the company were rented to the colonists at moderate prices for limited periods, but as contact was reestablished with English merchants from Virginia and Maryland, Rising was able to purchase mares, horses, and oxen from them, as well as some edibles. Rising noted in his journal on May 29 that supplies were exhausted and he and the other leaders of the colony were afraid the people would perish from hunger or run away. A sloop owned by the company was sent to New England in an effort to obtain food.

The *Haj* had not arrived with the food that was intended to sustain the colonists while they were building cabins and planting crops, and it was feared she may have been driven off her course by storms and wrecked. To help support the colonists during the winter Rising bought corn from the Lenape at Passyunk, and on October 14 he transported forty bushels to Fort Trinity for the maintenance of the Swedish garrison. He also sent Vice Commissary Jacob Swensson, who was held in high regard by the Lenape, to Appoquinimink (present Odessa) to trade cloth, powder, and lead for deer meat.

Rising ordered the repair of Fort Christina, which had also deteriorated, and he commissioned Lindeström to lay out plans for a town immediately behind the north side of the fort. In this first Swedish attempt to build a town at "the Rocks" the young engineer designed it as a rectangle with square blocks and streets running parallel to each other. Rising gave it the name Christinahamn ("Christina Harbor") in honor of the Queen.

Christinahamn is often referred to as the forerunner of the city of Wilmington but this statement should be qualified. This area is now part of the city of Wilmington, but when Wilmington was founded in 1731 (then called Willingtown after Thomas Willing, one of the developers) it was laid out some distance up the Christina River between present French and West Streets. The elevation and fastland had more commercial and residential advantages than the low-lying site of Christinahamn. The latter area did not become part of Wilmington for many years.

Rising brought a new and enlightened administration to New Sweden that revived the colony. He did his utmost to make living conditions better for the people in the colony and to be just in all legal proceedings. He moved the "capital" of New Sweden back to Fort Christina from Tinicum Island. He improved relations with the Minquas, and he tried to maintain friendship with the local Lenape who had become troublesome under the Printz administration. He was deeply interested in extending the bounds of New Sweden and in making the colony a successful venture for the Commercial College. He hired Andries Hudde, the Dutch surveyor who had signed the oath of allegiance to the Swedes, to make a map of the territory from Delaware Bay to present Trenton. He encouraged Lindeström to make maps of the Delaware River system and identify the tributaries and other physical features by their Indian names. Lindeström's maps have survived, and while not precise, are extremely valuable to the historian, the geographer, and the ethnologist.[29]

Rising had many problems to solve, some of which he inherited from Printz, dealing with unrest in the colony, and others attributable to food shortages and adverse weather conditions. The severe winter of 1654-55 followed a terrible storm on October 22 when a blustering northwestern wind and unusually high tides did considerable damage at Fort Trinity, washing away a wall under the parapet that Captain Skute and his men had worked on all summer.

Although they had twice signed oaths of allegiance, the Dutch freemen at Fort Trinity were discontented and a report reached Rising that they were threatening mutiny, claiming he had forced them to sign the oath. On December 7 Rising held another court at Fort Trinity, and he took advantage of the occasion to reassemble the Dutch colonists and reread to them the oath they had taken. They all stated they remembered taking the oath, and they had not been forced to take it. A third document was then prepared, which they all signed. One of the cases tried in court involved the Dutch burgher, Peter Ebel, found guilty of having spoken scurrilous words about the Swedes. Ebel was later pardoned.

Rising also faced serious external annoyances. The New Englanders under the influence of Governor Theophilus Eaton of New Haven, a large investor in the unsuccessful English colony on the Salem River in New Jersey, continued to claim ownership of lands in the Delaware River valley. At the same time the Maryland provincial government maintained that all of the Delaware Valley under the 40th degree of latitude (approximately at present Philadelphia) belonged to Lord Baltimore on the basis of the patent issued to him by Charles I. Commissioners from Maryland visited Rising to argue about their rights, and Governor Eaton wrote letters of protest, all of which Rising refuted by resorting to the old, but persuasive, argument that Sweden possessed legal title to the lands by right of deeds granted by the

Indian owners. Nevertheless, with English pressures from the north and southwest, and a potential Dutch enemy on the east at Manhattan, New Sweden was in a precarious position. Emboldened by the hope of support from the homeland, Rising's second report to the Commercial College dated June 15, 1655 outlined some of his needs, but he did so with considerable optimism.[30]

Our present concern is not with Rising's broad activities as the new "Director of New Sweden" but with those events that directly relate to New Castle. In the second report he said that the Hollanders dwelling at Fort Trinity who had thrice taken the oath of allegiance decided to vacate their homes and departed for Manhattan two or three weeks before, namely in late May or early June of 1655. What prompted them to change their minds after pledging their loyalty to the Swedes is unknown, but Rising was not unhappy. He said in his report that they "were out of their element here in the river. The land is now practically clear of the Hollanders."[31]

What had formerly been a little Dutch hamlet at the Santhoeck was then starting to be occupied by Swedish families owing their allegiance to King Charles X, who grasped the reigns of the government after his cousin the twenty-nine year old Queen Christina abdicated, accepted the Catholic faith, and went to Rome to live. Her deceased father, Gustavus Adolphus, the warrior king who fought bloody religious wars in the name of Protestantism, would have been, to put it mildly, disappointed in his only daughter.

Very little is known about the Swedish and Finnish occupants of the Santhoek during Rising's administration. The withdrawal of the Dutch made their houses available, and although the names of the residents at this time are not known, it was a growing community. Two ministers arrived with Rising on the *Örn*, Matthias Nertunius and Peter Laurentii Hiört, who were sent to extend the ministry of Pastor Lars Carlsson Lock the only minister in New Sweden from 1648 to 1654. Rising assigned the Reverend Hiört to Fort Trinity although there still was no church there. Rising described him as "both materially and spiritually a poor priest," but the presence of the minister suggests that the Swedish families on the Santhoeck and the garrison at the fort must have constituted a parish of reasonable size. Pastor Hiört no doubt moved into one of the better houses vacated by the Dutch, and since there was no church, he may have conducted Lutheran services in the fort.

Important and welcome news was received by the Dutch at New Amsterdam on July 16, 1654—peace had been agreed upon between Holland and England, and Rising learned about it shortly after. He should have known that relief from the fears of an attack from New England would allow Stuyvesant to take action against the Swedish interlopers who had insulted the West India Company and the government of the United Nether-lands by seizing the fort he had built on the Delaware River.

5. STUYVESANT SEIZES FORT TRINITY

Dɪᴅ JOHAN RISING exceed the authority delegated to him by the Swedish government when he boldly took Fort Casimir at present New Castle? Was he guilty of a hostile act against the Dutch that he had been cautioned to avoid? Was he foolish or naive and oblivious to the likely retaliation by the West India Company? Many historians incline to place the blame on him for imprudence that had dire consequences in Dutch-Swedish relations and proved to be the direct cause of the downfall of New Sweden.

Rising was guided by three documents, an Instruction issued December 15, 1653, a Memorial dated December 18, and an Authorization also dated December 18.[1] These instruments originated with the Crown, the Commercial College, or a combination of both of them, and are subject to different interpretations. Although the documents told him to avoid provoking any hostility, nevertheless, Section 5 of the December 15 Instruction ordered him "with all possible care, to get rid of the Hollanders who have erected a fort on the land and settled there." One wonders how his superiors thought this could be done without antagonizing the Dutch. The reader will recall that the Instruction given Governor Printz was to "repel force with force," undersell the Dutch in the Indian trade, but to hold good friendship with them. The Swedish authorities wanted both Printz and Rising to assert the country's sovereign rights, and at the same time avoid offending the Dutch. Printz learned that this was an impossible task, and the similar inconsistency of Rising's instructions led to his ultimate failure.

One cannot read Rising's journal without concluding that he was convinced that his seizure of Fort Casimir was consistent with the written orders given him before he left Sweden.[2] Rising maintained that he did not launch an assault on Fort Casimir, but that Commandant Bicker gave up the fort with no resistance when Rising convinced him that the fort was built on territory rightfully owned by the Swedes. Rising's position was that Stuyvesant built Fort Casimir on land the Lenape Indians deeded to the Swedes as evidenced by the deeds preserved in Stockholm. Moreover, Rising maintained that Stuyvesant had no authority either from the Dutch government or the West India Company to build Fort Casimir, and that he had exceeded the limits of his office. The previous chapter makes it clear that when he erected the fort in 1651 Stuyvesant did so without authorization from his superiors. He was also guilty of an infraction of international law, Rising claimed, when he tore down a standard at the Santhoeck bearing the insignia of the Swedish queen, proof of ownership. Rising insisted that as a rule of law, which he defined as "quicquid inaedificatur fundo, fundo cedit," anything built on another's land becomes parcel of the land and the property of the owner of the land. This concept, if not the Latin phrase, still survives in contemporary law. Bicker and other members of the Dutch garrison, as well as residents at the Santhoeck, tacitly admitted Swedish ownership when they took an oath of loyalty to the Swedish Crown, not once, but at three different times. In Rising's opinion he was repossessing lands that belonged to Sweden, which had been illegally seized by Stuyvesant. It was unfortunate for the Dutch, in his view, but they built a fort on property that didn't belong to them!

Rising also insisted that, if he had landed his tired and ailing passengers at Fort Christina without first securing Fort Casimir for Sweden, that he would have disobeyed his orders to take control of the territory if it was within his means to do so. He maintained that Fort Casimir was so weakly defended by nine Dutch soldiers having inadequate armament, the English could have readily taken it, thus closing the river and blocking access to Fort Christina and the Swedish settlements upstream. In his judgement he could not allow New Sweden to be bottled up from overseas commerce either by the Dutch or English without violating his instructions.

Rising was no fool; he was fully aware that he was responsible for creating a sensitive situation, which is the reason he promptly wrote to Stuyvesant at New Amsterdam to advise him that Fort Casimir had voluntarily surrendered to him. This may seem to have been an indiscreet and unnecessary gesture, but Rising believed that offering his friendship and expressing the desire to reconcile differences between them in a peaceful way could result in compromise.

Stuyvesant's response was to ignore the letter and inform the directors of the Amsterdam Chamber of the Swedish governor's audacity and his insult to the West India Company and the Dutch government. Rising also sent details of the surrender of Fort Casimir on the *Örn* when she returned to Sweden in July, reminding his superiors that military assistance was promised him to withstand a possible attack, if it should materialize. Rising was optimistic about Swedish relations with the Dutch government. Having made a number of visits to Holland to study the Dutch commercial system he knew that friendly relations existed between business and political leaders in the two countries, at least at the time of his visits. He nurtured the vain hope that the differences between the two countries originating in their American colonies could be resolved through diplomatic channels in Europe.

Rising did not know that his capture of Fort Casimir ignited a fire among the directors of the West India Company that arbitration between the West India Company and the Swedish Commercial College could not extinguish.

On November 16, 1654 the directors wrote Stuyvesant charging him to avenge Rising's infamous behavior "not only by restoring matters to their former condition, but also by driving the Swedes at the same time from the river as they did us, in such a manner however that those of them who should desire to come under our jurisdiction may be allowed to do so . . ." If the Swedes refused to be governed by the Dutch he was ordered to move them elsewhere so the Delaware River would be populated exclusively by Dutch subjects. The directors specified that speedy action should be taken before reinforcements were sent to Rising, and they reminded Stuyvesant that since Holland was then at peace with England he didn't have to worry about New Englanders attacking New Amsterdam while he was invading New Sweden. The directors also ordered him to punish Commandant Gerrit Bicker who was accused of conducting himself faithlessly and treacherously by surrendering Fort Casimir to the Swedes.

After further discussion in Holland the directors softened their position somewhat in a letter to Stuyvesant on May 26, 1655. They wrote:

> We still retain and persist in these orders and directions, only we have after precarious deliberation, resolved, that, when your Honors shall have carried the expedition to a successful end, the land upon which Fort Christina stands, with a certain amount of garden-land for the cultivation of tobacco shall be left to the people, as they seem to have bought it with the knowledge and consent of the Company [!] under the condition that the aforesaid Swedes shall consider themselves subjects of this State and the Company.[3]

Despite his efforts to keep his invasion plans a secret, Stuyvesant could not prevent Rising from learning through two spies he sent to New Amsterdam that the Company was planning to avenge his capture of Fort Casimir with warships and an army of 700 or 800 men.[4] Having received this unwelcome news Rising made a costly miscalculation. He expected Stuyvesant to select Fort Casimir as his only target, but not to disturb other Swedish installations. This can be inferred from his report of June 14, 1655 in which he said he believed Stuyvesant "will come here and capture Fort Casimir which we now call Trinity." He had no inkling that Stuyvesant was instructed to take Fort Christina, which had never been in Dutch possession, and to enforce Dutch claim to the whole Delaware River valley. He did not know that the Company directors, exerting a powerful influence on Dutch international affairs, decided the time had come to rid themselves of the Swedish threat on the Delaware. Charles X of Sweden went to war against Poland in 1655, and he was involved in a continuous series of battles and sieges with Poland and her allies until 1660. There was little chance that he would march against Holland because of an issue involving a handful of Swedish and Finnish colonists in far-off America.

A large warship owned by the City of Amsterdam named the *Wagh* (meaning *Scales* or *Balance*) with Frederick de Coningh (Coninck) as captain, carrying 200 men, was chartered by the burgomasters and Amsterdam council on April 26, 1655 to sail to New Netherland to assist Stuyvesant.[5] Captain Coninck was instructed to obey the orders of Stuyvesant and his council when he arrived in the New Netherland. The *Wagh* alone with its thirty-five cannon could reduce Fort Trinity to rubble, but Stuyvesant wanted the support of a preponderant attacking force. He and his council had the power to impress ships in the New Amsterdam harbor to join the *Wagh* in the command position. Their owners and captains were assured proper compensation, and Foppe Jansen Outhout was appointed Provincial Commissary to make certain the flotilla was well provided with ammunition and victuals, supplied by the Company. Outhout later moved to the Santhoeck where he opened a tavern, and still later became a member of the early court at New Castle.

In preparation for the attack on New Sweden Stuyvesant and his council named August 25, 1655 as a day of fasting, thanksgiving, and supplication, thus encouraging the New Amsterdam community to offer prayers to God to bless the expedition. On the designated day, "ploughing, sowing, mowing, fishing, hunting, and all amusements" were forbidden, such as "playing at tennis, ball playing, drinking, carousing and selling liquor, under the penalty of an arbitrary punishment."[6]

The attacking flotilla was composed of the *Wagh* and the following six vessels: the *Dolphijn* (*Dolphin*) with four guns; the *Liefde* (*Love*), a flyboat with four guns; the *Hoop* (*Hope*), a galiot with four guns; and two armed yachts, the *Hollandse Tuijn* (*Holland Garden*), and the *Prinses Royael* (*Princess Royal*). The Dutch spellings are those given by Johannes Bogaert, an employe of Hans Bontemantel, a director of the Company. Bogaert came to America on the *Wagh* as a secretary-clerk apparently to keep records for his employer, and since he remained aboard the *Wagh* during the attack on Fort Trinity his detailed letter to Bontemantel provides a reliable eyewitness account.[7] Bogaert said there were 317 men on the seven vessels, which varies from figures given by Rising and Lindeström, but one must keep in mind that defenders tend to exaggerate the numbers of enemy attackers.[8] Bogaert gave precise details as to the number of seamen and soldiers in each company and the names of the company commanders, which lend credence to the accuracy of his figures.

Stuyvesant's manpower was more than three times larger than his forces in the bloodless invasion of 1651, and his naval complement was much stronger. In the first pretended invasion he had eleven vessels but only four were armed because he did not intend to subdue the Swedes by force. In the 1655 invasion all seven of his ships were armed, and this time he meant business, having the full support of the Amsterdam directors.

Stuyvesant and one of his councillors who accompanied him, Nicasius de Sille, were in command when the flotilla sailed from New Amsterdam on September 5, according to the Dutch calendar, which the reader will remember was ten days later than the Swedish calendar. The differing dates given in Swedish and Dutch accounts of the attack must be reconciled to adjust for the discrepancy. Two councillors, de La Montagne and Cornelis van Tienhoven, remained in charge of New Amsterdam assisted by Allard Antony, burgomaster of the city, and Martin Crieger, first captain of the "Trainbands," a term applied to a volunteer militia.[9]

On August 27 (the Swedish date which will be used during the remainder of the chapter) the Swedes recorded the appearance of the Dutch flotilla in Delaware Bay. The vessels were piloted by Wessel Gerritsen and Pieter Lourissen, who were thoroughly experienced with the banks and shoals in the river, and the flotilla appeared before the abandoned Fort Elfsborg three days later.

Rising had adequate time to strengthen the remodelled Fort Trinity when he first learned that Stuyvesant planned to seize the fort, and he lost no time. He concentrated his forces there under Captain Sven Skute as the commandant with Lieutenant Elias Gyllengren, Ensign Peter Wendel, and Peter Lindeström as staff officers. He supplied the fort with forty-seven bushels of rye, fourteen gallons of brandy, a quantity of beer and other "necessities."[10] He transferred a large quantity of powder and some of the best soldiers from Fort Christina to Fort Trinity, which increased the garrison at Fort Trinity to about fifty men. This reduced the garrison at Fort Christina to about thirty men. Two officers newly arrived from Sweden were placed in charge at Christina, Hendrick van Elswick, the factor, assisted by Lieutenant Swen Höök. Van Elswick, a merchant, was in command of the *Haj*, bringing the long awaited supplies to Rising, and Höök was an officer on the voyage. Due to carelessness on the part of a first mate who was navigating the *Haj*, the vessel missed Delaware Bay and arrived in an estuary behind Staten Island on September 12, and several days later Stuyvesant commandeered the Swedish vessel and put her officers under arrest. The officers were shortly released, and van Elswick and Höök made their way overland to New Sweden. In retaliation for Rising's seizure of Fort Casimir, Stuyvesant confiscated the vessel and sold the precious cargo with all the foodstuffs intended for the hungry Swedes on the Delaware. Stuyvesant impressed the *Haj* into the service of the West India Company under a new name, the *Diemen*.

Van Elswick and Höök were competent men, and they arrived in New Sweden in time to be of assistance to Rising during the Dutch invasion. Unfortunately, through miscalculating Stuyvesant's objectives, Rising weakened Fort Christina in order to strengthen Fort Trinity. By doing so, the capture of Fort Christina became a certainty if Fort Trinity fell to the Dutch. The situation at Fort Christina was beyond salvation even by two proficient leaders who gave Rising their full support.

In anticipation of the arrival of the Dutch flotilla, Rising and his officers prepared a written resolution for Skute's guidance. He was told that when the Dutch ships appeared opposite Fort Trinity he should send a party in a small boat to board their principal ship to ask if they came as friends. If so, he was advised to arrange for a peaceful discussion of bounds and territories. Rising, who was still disposed to friendship, clung to the notion that he and Stuyvesant could negotiate a solution to their differences. Skute was told that if the Dutch failed to negotiate he should stand firm and not allow the vessels to sail past the fort "upon pain of being fired upon, which in such case they could not reckon [it] an act of hostility."[11]

According to Lindeström's account the Dutch vessels cast anchor at the decaying Fort Elfsborg on the opposite side of the river "where they blockaded, shot, and thundered the whole night." This appears to be an example of Lindeström's hyperbole; it seems unlikely that Stuyvesant would have wasted ammunition firing at the abandoned Swedish fort and alerting the garrison at Fort Trinity to the presence of his vessels. The next day, August 31, according to Lindeström, the Dutch vessels crossed the river diagonally to the present New Castle shore "amidst the beating of drums and the blowing of trumpets and a great bravado." No shots were fired by the defenders as the ships sailed past Fort Trinity, and for reasons that remain unexplained, Skute did not send out a party, as ordered, to board the *Wagh* and discuss an armistice. The Dutch vessels then anchored at a place Lindeström called Strand Wyk on Map "B" (not the present Strand) a short distance above the fort, where the troops landed and began to construct breastworks cutting off the approach to the fort by land from the north. They were so close to the fort that some of the Dutch soldiers occupied a Swedish guardhouse, which had formerly been used as a powder magazine. By holding this position Stuyvesant effectively cut the lines of communication between Fort Trinity and Fort Christina, and he dispersed some of his troops as far north as the Christina River, which crossed the terrain between the two forts.

As the original builder of Fort Trinity, Stuyvesant realized that its strongest defense faced the river, and he deliberately avoided a frontal attack. Lindeström wrote that on the side of the fort where the Dutch built their breastworks and pitched their tents "the walls are lowest and weakest."

Although the Dutch vessels were in command of the river, Skute was able to get the news of the attack to Rising by two Swedes who slipped past the Dutch vessels in a canoe, probably after dark. Rising who was either at Fort Christina or at his recently-built dwelling on nearby Timber Island received the request for reinforcements with some puzzlement. He later wrote bitterly that Skute "suffered the Dutch ships to pass the fort without remonstrance or firing a gun."[12] Lindeström, who was present at Fort Trinity during the siege, practically accused

Skute of traitorous conduct, although Lindeström himself wrote about the cowardice of some of the soldiers under Skute's command. Lindeström also believed that Skute was too willing to surrender because he left the fort and conducted peace negotiations with Stuyvesant at the Dutch camp even though not a single gun had been fired. While Skute was conferring with Stuyvesant, Lindeström states in his journal that he, Lieutenant Gyllengren, and other officers ordered the defenders to strengthen the north side of the fort. Before their work was finished Skute returned, having agreed to surrender terms, followed by a column of Dutch soldiers marching to occupy the fort. Lindeström and the other officers "admonished their people to stand firm and resist the Dutch, but they made themselves rebellious and jumped over the walls to the enemy, which caused us to wound and shoot down some of our people as they fled." One of the would-be deserters, Gabriel Forsman, was shot through the leg by Lieutenant Gyllengren as he climbed over the embankment, and later died from the wound.[13]

The most accurate account of the surrender is probably one written by Stuyvesant reading as follows:

> We passed Fort Casimier about eight or nine o'clock [the morning of August 31] without any display of hostility on either side, and anchored the distance of a salute gun's shot above the said fortress. We landed our men immediately and sent Capt. Lt. [Dirck] Smith [one of the company commanders] with a drummer into the fortress to demand restitution of our property.
>
> The commander [Skute] requested a delay until he had communicated with Governor Rysingh [at Fort Christina]; his request was denied. Meanwhile, with 50 men drawn from our companies we occupied the roads to Christina. The commander Schuts, was warned by a second message that in order to prevent bloodshed and other grief he should not await the attack of our troops which will be

covered by our cannons. In reply, the commander requested permission to speak with us; which was granted.
He met us in the marshland about halfway between the
fortress and our not yet completed battery. He immediately
requested that he be allowed to dispatch an open letter to
the governor [Rising] which would be shown to us. His
request was firmly denied and he left discontented. After
this the troops advanced to the marshland in sight of the
fort. In the meantime our works were raised about a man's
height above the thicket, and the fortress was summoned
for the last time. He humbly requested a delay until morning; this was granted because we could not be ready with
our battery that evening or the following night, in order to
advance closer under its cover. The following morning
[September 1] the commander came out and surrendered to
us under the conditions sent herewith. About midday our
force marched in and today we offered insufficient thanks
at our first church service.[14]

When Skute and Stuyvesant went aboard the *Wagh* to sign the
surrender terms, cannons were fired from the Dutch camp ashore
as well as from the vessels anchored in the Delaware as a
victory signal. Johannes Bogaert on the *Wagh* found an opportunity to copy the surrender terms, which he could transmit to the
Honorable Hans Bontemantel in Amsterdam:

First, The commander, whenever he pleases and shall
have the opportunity, by the arrival of private ships or
ships belonging to the crown, shall be permitted to remove
from Fort Casemier the guns of the crown, large and
small: according to the statement of the commander [Skute],
consisting of four iron guns and five case-shot guns, of
which four are small and one is large,

Second, Twelve men shall march out as the body-guard
of the commander, fully accoutred with the flag of the
[Swedish] crown; the others with their side-arms only. The

guns and muskets which belong to the crown shall be and remain at the disposition of the commandant [Skute], to take or cause them to be taken from the fort whenever the commander shall have an opportunity to do so.

Third, The commander shall have all his private personal effects uninjured, in order to take them with him or have them taken away whenever he pleases, and also the effects of all the officers.

Fourth, The commander shall this day restore Fort Casemier and all the guns, ammunition, materials, and other property belonging to the General Authorized West India Company [materiel the Swedes retained after Rising repossessed the fort].

Done and signed by the contracting parties the 11th September, 1655 [September 1], on board the ship *De Waegh* lying at Fort Casemier.

(Signed) Petrus Stuyvesant, Swen Schuts.[15]

Lindeström wrote that Skute marched his troops out of the fort "with flying banners, burning fuses, loaded guns, beating drums and pipes, and bullet in the mouth and such things." These details signified it was an honorable and voluntary surrender without vanquishment. Rising did not negotiate the terms nor sign the surrender document; Skute was responsible for the capitulation which took place on a Dutch warship. After Skute signed the document, the *Wagh* and the other Dutch vessels celebrated by firing their cannon, which Rising could hear at Fort Christina. Since the guns at Fort Trinity remained silent Rising must have known that the cannon fire meant a Dutch victory.

After the Dutch flag was raised over Fort Trinity, known again as Fort Casimir, and the fort vacated by the Swedish soldiers, Stuyvesant played his trump card. He asked Skute what he intended to do with his soldiers. Skute replied that they would march to Fort Christina, but Stuyvesant refused permission because Skute had not provided for the disposition of the Swedish troops in the peace terms. This was a technicality that Skute overlooked, which Rising later termed a "disadvantageous capitulation, in which he forgot to stipulate a place which he, with his people and effects might retire . . ."[16]

There was still no church within the fort and the services to which Stuyvesant referred in his account of the surrender were conducted by Johannes Megapolensis the chaplain of the expedition. This is the second reference to Dutch reformed services conducted at New Castle; the first was noted in chapter 3. Stuyvesant never missed his daily prayers, and the occasion of a military victory meant that God had provided favorable weather, success, and the weakening of the opponent. In his letter reporting victory, Stuyvesant asked the council in New Amsterdam to offer further prayers so that God would grant his forces additional support and blessing.

When Stuyvesant moved his headquarters from the *Wagh* to the fort he was doubtless very much interested in the modifications made by Lindeström and Skute in the fortress he had originally built. If the renovations were extensive as Lindeström indicated in his journal, Stuyvesant was no doubt impressed with what the Swedes had accomplished. All the Swedish officers, including Gyllengren, Lindeström, and Skute were placed under technical arrest although they were not jailed. They were treated as officers and gentlemen, even dining with Stuyvesant at his own table. Thirty of the Swedish common soldiers were placed aboard the *Liefde* and taken to New Amsterdam; Stuyvesant sent a message that they should be treated well, and doubtless they were soon released. Those who remained took an oath of allegiance to the Dutch; no harm was done to the Swedish and Finnish residents living near the fort. The change in administration had no important immediate effect on their way of life.

During the siege when Rising received Skute's message requesting reinforcements, he sent ten of the best freemen he could muster to assist Skute. They crossed the Christina River in a small boat and then encountered Dutch soldiers in the general area where present New Castle Avenue intersects Heald Street. After a skirmish all but two were taken prisoners and the two who escaped fell back to their boat and retreated across the river to Fort Christina, the Dutch firing after them. The men who were left in the garrison at the fort fired at the Dutch from a cannon on the sconce, but the Dutch retired safely into the woods. Skute should have known that reinforcements could not get through the Dutch lines, and Rising should have realized that even if they got through, ten civilian-soldiers would have little to do with the outcome of the siege.

After losing the eight men Rising began to worry about the safety of Fort Christina. It was beginning to dawn on him that Stuyvesant would not be satisfied by taking Fort Trinity. He decided to send van Elswick under a flag of truce to ascertain Stuyvesant's real intentions and to dissuade him from further hostility "as we could not be persuaded that he seriously purposed to disturb us in the lawful dominions of His Royal Majesty [Charles X] and our principles."[17]

When Elswick put Rising's question to Stuyvesant about his plans he received a brief but direct answer, "To take and hold what belongs to us."[18] Elswick requested Stuyvesant to be content with taking Fort Trinity and not advance on Fort Christina. Like Rising, he, too, didn't realize until it was too late that Stuyvesant's objective was total conquest. When van Elswick returned to Rising with Stuyvesant's answer there was no doubt that the Dutch forces, having seized New Sweden's stronghold without the loss of a single soldier, would soon lay siege to Fort Christina. The paradox was that the only casualty was one Swedish soldier shot by his own officer.

Having weakened Fort Christina by diverting men, powder, and supplies to Fort Trinity, Rising had neither adequate manpower or materiel to put up an effective defense. He ordered the handful of men left in the garrison to work strengthening the ramparts and gabions, but the effort was too little and too late.

Rising must have known that he didn't have a ghost of a chance of resisting Stuyvesant's superior forces. By September 5 Stuyvesant's troops had Fort Christina practically surrounded on the land sides, and Dutch warships blockaded the mouth of the Christina. For the first time since Minuit erected the fort in 1638 it was put to a true military test which exposed its weakness. Stuyvesant sent an Indian courier to Rising with a message "in which he arrogantly demanded the surrender of the whole river, and required me and all the Swedes either to evacuate the country or remain there under Dutch protection, threatening with the consequences in the case of refusal."[19]

Rising then held a general council of war with his officers and it was decided to put up the best possible defense so long as they could. Rising also sent messages to Stuyvesant protesting against his invasion of New Sweden and attempted to dissuade him from assaulting Fort Christina; he still hoped that Stuyvesant would listen to reason. Meantime, Dutch soldiers set fire to the houses in Christinahamn, the village behind the fort laid out by Lindeström, and pillaged Swedish farms north of the Christina. Even Armegot Printz, still living at Printzhoff, was robbed of her valuables and her neighbors' possessions, which they had brought to her for safekeeping. Rising complained about the unnecessary plundering stating that:

> females have partly been dragged out of their houses by force, whole buildings torn down, even hauled away, oxen, cows, pigs and other animals daily slaughtered in large numbers; even the horses were not spared but shot wantonly, the plantations devastated and everything thereabouts treated in such a way, that our victuals have been mostly spoiled, carried away, or lost somehow.[20]

The village at the Santhoeck seems to have escaped this kind of looting; the fort and the resident population were already under Dutch control and nothing would be gained by destroying their properties and livestock.

Rising's little force at Fort Christina was getting short of food; some were tired and worn out; others were ill. Rising prepared to surrender on the most favorable terms he could negotiate. In the meantime, an Indian messenger from Manhattan Island brought alarming news to Stuyvesant. The Dutch governor was guilty of an error of judgment no less serious than Rising's miscalculation of Stuyvesant's intent. Stuyvesant had not fully realized what could happen in New Amsterdam after he sailed away with the best of his fighting men to reduce the Swedes on the Delaware.

The mistreated and embittered Indians, suspicious of Dutch intentions ever since Governor Kieft's War, saw a chance to retaliate. There had been sporadic bloodshed and unrest in the outlying communities of New Amsterdam, but after Stuyvesant's departure Dutch families found themselves fiercely embattled by Indians representing members of many bands the Dutch had earlier antagonized.[21] Guns Stuyvesant had permitted to be traded with the Indians (to be used for hunting) were turned against Dutch boweries, and 100 people were killed within a nine hour period.

"My lord," a passage read in the council's letter to Stuyvesant, "may it please you to consider this letter and reflect whether you and that force would not be needed more here than to subdue that place there. We deem it better to protect one's own house rather than to go conquer one that is far away and lose the old one in the process."[22]

Another message delivered to Stuyvesant urged him that if Fort Christina had not yet fallen into his hands he might make a provisional contract with Rising "concerning the fort and the lands at Cristina, with the most favorable conditions possible for this country and which honor allows; and to return here [New Amsterdam] at the first opportunity with the ships and men in order to preserve what is left."[23] Rising, despite his lack of provisions, powder, and soldiers, may have been less willing to surrender so quickly if he had known that an emergency required Stuyvesant to return to New Amsterdam with all possible speed. Before he knew about the Indian uprising, Rising surrendered Fort Christina and all of New Sweden to Stuyvesant on September 15. Stuyvesant's troops marched into the fort that afternoon, occupied the batteries, lowered the Swedish flag and replaced it with the Dutch flag.

The capitulation terms were not as harsh as might have been expected. Lindeström wrote that "we immediately marched out, over to Timber Island, in full arms, flying banners, beating drums, and pipes, burning fuses, bullet in mouth, etc., where all our soldiers should remain until our departure but we officers in Fort Christina."[24] Evidently the Swedish officers detained at Fort Casimir were set free to come to Fort Christina. The surrender was an honorable one; the Swedish soldiers allowed to carry their sidearms, with musketballs in their mouths, the face-saving symbol indicative of an honorable capitulation.

Rising and several officers, and their servants, had already decided they wanted to return to Sweden, and Stuyvesant agreed to this in the discussion of the surrender terms. Stuyvesant consented to transport Rising and others who wanted to return to Sweden on the *Wagh* to Manhattan where they would be given passage gratis on other vessels bound for Europe. No soldiers, officials, or freemen were to be detained against their will, but were also permitted to depart from New Sweden free and unimpeded. Those who did not want to leave were allowed to remain on the Delaware provided they took an oath of allegiance to the Dutch. Those who remained were permitted to practice their Lutheran faith and have their own pastor.

After the Swedish soldiers marched out of Fort Christina, Stuyvesant, with some of his officers, came to the fort to confer with Rising. Stuyvesant was eager to withdraw his troops and sail back to New Amsterdam without further delay. By this time Rising knew that many Dutch settlers had been slain by the Indians, and he must have realized that Stuyvesant could not spare troops for an occupation army to take advantage of his military coup.

An unexpected offer by Stuyvesant must have come as a surprise. He asked Rising if he did not want to take back Fort Christina again on the condition that Rising would assure him that no ill feeling or trouble should result from what had happened and that the Swedes and Dutch should make an offensive and defensive alliance with one another. This was a complete reversal of his previous demands of unconditional surrender of the whole river. Stuyvesant even admitted that some of the land belonged to the Swedes by right of their earlier Indian purchases, as the directors conceded in their letter to him of May 26, 1655.

Rising said he would confer with his officers about Stuyvesant's offer, which he did. The unanimous vote was not to rescind their surrender and they refused to reoccupy the fort!

In retrospect, Rising's rejection of Stuyvesant's conciliatory offer seems to have been an error of judgment. If he had accepted it, the Swedes would have had an opportunity to regroup at Fort Christina and compromise the differences over possession of the land. Rising's rationale for his decision, which he recorded in some detail in his journal, can be paraphrased as follows:

1. He had no authority to enter into an alliance with the Dutch without the knowledge and permission of his superiors.
2. The Indians who attacked New Amsterdam were friendly toward the Swedes, and a Swedish alliance with their Dutch enemies would antagonize them.
3. He could not guarantee Stuyvesant that Swedish colonists would not retaliate against the Dutch in view of their hostile and unprovoked attack.
4. An alliance with Stuyvesant would prevent the Swedish government from claiming compensation for the injuries and personal damage suffered during the Dutch invasion.

5. Rising and his men could not subsist at Fort Christina because their food supply was exhausted, their cattle slaughtered, and Dutch soldiers had confiscated all the Indian trade goods in the storehouse.[25]

The irony is that at the time of Rising's surrender preparations were being made in Sweden to send the vessel *Mercurius* to New Sweden with the supplies and reinforcements that Rising had requested. By the time the vessel arrived in March of 1656 with Hendrick Huygen as head commissary in charge of the ship, and John Papegoja in command of the people, Rising had departed and all of New Sweden was under Dutch control.

Rising did not allow Stuyvesant to assume the role of a conqueror and confiscate the property belonging to the Swedish company or the Swedish government, and evidently this was not Stuyvesant's intention. Rising prepared a written inventory of all the assets in the territory seized by Stuyvesant so that he could return to Stockholm with an accurate record for the King and the Commercial College. On September 25 the inventory was signed and sealed by Rising and Stuyvesant, the latter signifying that he had received all the fortifications in New Sweden, houses, buildings, estates and farms, all the guns, ammunition, cattle, horses, oxen, swine, and everything of importance that belonged to the Crown of Sweden.[26] Apparently Rising sold some of the New Sweden Company's private holdings on credit to those servants and freemen who decided to remain on the Delaware.

Rising stipulated that Stuyvesant should retain the property temporarily transferred to him only until such time as the King of Sweden demanded its return, and at that time the Swedish government would be indemnified for all the damage done during the invasion. As Lindeström interpreted this agreement, "the Hollanders were placed as inspectors over New Sweden, but not with the right of a possessor or owning master." Rising may have been convinced that he was turning over Swedish possessions to Stuyvesant in trust, but the land and other property was never returned to Sweden, nor did Holland ever pay reparations for the considerable damage done by Stuyvesant's forces.

Most of the Swedish common soldiers who had farms on the Delaware elected to remain as Dutch subjects, and the majority of freemen continued to live unmolested on the lands where they were living. Approximately thirty-seven males, including some soldiers, several freemen, and Lindeström, Hendrick van Elswick, Lieutenant Höök, and the two pastors, Matthias Nertunius and Peter Hiört, returned to Sweden with Rising at Dutch expense. Their wives and children presumably accompanied them, but the number is unknown. Rising himself was a bachelor. It is of interest to note that Hiört, the first "permanent" Dutch Reformed minister at New Castle became "impermanent" and disappears from the pages of Delaware Valley history.

Gregorius van Dyck, Lieutenant Elias Gyllengren, and Captain Sven Skute decided to remain behind as civilians, the latter two taking up residence at the Santhoeck. However, in the surrender terms Stuyvesant agreed that Rising should be permitted to examine the conduct of Skute leading up to his surrender of Fort Trinity. Rising subsequently held an inquest, which, in effect, amounted to court martial proceedings, concerning Captain Skute's behavior during the Dutch invasion. Testimony offered at the hearing by some of the officers and soldiers was damaging to Skute, but he was not sentenced to any punishment.

In his own defense Skute claimed the soldiers at the fort were mutinous and when he ordered them to fight like men they refused. He prepared a formal statement signed by Lieutenant Gyllengren, Pastor Hiört, and some others, exonerating him from any blame, which he sent to Chancellor Eric Oxenstierna in Sweden.[27] It is not known what, if any action was taken in Sweden, but Skute remained in America immune from any decision made by a Swedish tribunal.

Apart from whether the blame should be placed on Skute or

the cowardice of some of his soldiers, there isn't the slightest doubt that Skute, not Rising, was responsible for surrendering New Castle to Stuyvesant. The downfall of New Sweden was triggered by Skute's surrender, which Rising did all he could to prevent. The irony is that Rising bears the onus and died in 1672 in abject poverty, still suffering the disgrace of surrender.

Before Stuyvesant sailed victoriously back to New Amsterdam from Fort Casimir he administered an oath of allegiance to the Swedes and Finns who chose to remain on the Delaware. The oath obligated them to be loyal to the United Netherlands and the officials of the Dutch West India Company. All former Swedish subjects—servants, employes of the Swedish company, freemen, soldiers, and officers—were invited to take the oath. Thereafter all were permitted to remain and make their living as "good and free inhabitants." Nineteen male signers put their signatures or marks on the document; fourteen could not read or write.[28] By no means was this the total male population of New Sweden in 1655, and others may later have agreed to sign, but this is the only document that is now available. Eight of the signers were later recorded as residents of the Santhoeck, but whether they were residing there at the time of the invasion is uncertain. Their names are given here as spelled in the oath; namely, Jan Eckhoff, Constantinus Gronenbergk, Harman Jansen, Jan Justen, Thoomas Bruyn, William Morris, Lucas Petersen, and Moens Andriesen. All the former Swedish subjects living at the Santhoeck were permitted to retain their houses and properties unless there were prior Dutch claimants who vacated their houses during the Rising administration and decided to return from New Amsterdam and reclaim their properties.

Stuyvesant appointed Captain Dirck Smith (sometimes spelled Smit or Smidt) as provisional commander of New Sweden with his headquarters at Fort Casimir. Smith commanded a company of sixty soldiers during the invasion, but it is not known how many of these men remained with him and how many returned with Stuyvesant to defend New Amsterdam against further Indian attacks. Most of those who remained were stationed at Fort Casimir, with only a few housed at Fort Christina, which the Swedish soldiers had deserted. At this time the directors of the Amsterdam Chamber had a low regard for the old Swedish fort. They instructed Stuyvesant to keep Fort Casimir adequately supplied and armed, "but little attention need to be paid to Fort Christina, where you will leave only three or four men to live there as a garrison and to keep it in our possession . . ."[29]

At the time Fort Christina was besieged by Stuyvesant's forces Rising described it as "a small and feeble work, and lay upon low ground and could be commanded from the surrounding heights . . ."[30] Rising fully understood why the Dutch West India Company selected Fort Casimir at the Santhoeck, instead of Fort Christina, as the center of their activities along the Delaware River. From the very beginning he did his utmost to make it the core of New Sweden's defenses, but the blame for his failure must be shared with many others.

6. JACQUET'S ADMINISTRATION

DIRCK SMITH WAS kept busy trying to put Fort Casimir and Fort Christina in order, keeping peace with the Indians, and encouraging his soldiers at the Santhoeck to assist in planting winter grains. There is no evidence that he kept a journal of his brief military administration, and next to nothing is known of what occurred at Fort Casimir from the time Stuyvesant left for New Amsterdam on September 18, 1655 until December 8, 1655 when the temporary position held by Smith was filled by Jean Paul Jacquet. (The above dates are given according to the Dutch calendar and, unless otherwise noted, will be used in the following chapters while the Dutch were in control.)

The directors of the Amsterdam Chamber wrote Stuyvesant on November 23, 1654 that Jacquet was coming from Holland with his wife and family on the vessel *Groote Christoffel* (*Great Christopher*). They said he had served the West India Company for many years in Brazil and had decided to take up farming in New Netherland. Since Jacquet was unacquainted with New

Amsterdam, and was coming as a freeman, the directors requested Stuyvesant to assist him and allot him as much land as he was able to cultivate.[1] Although he was not of Dutch descent, Jacquet was a Dutch citizen from his youth, and one infers that he must have been held in esteem by influential members of the Amsterdam Chamber. He obviously did not come as a common farmer, but as a land entrepreneur hoping to prosper in the New Netherland.

Jacquet was not in New Amsterdam very long when Stuyvesant and his council, impressed by Jacquet's intelligence, experience, and executive ability, appointed him on November 29, 1655 as Vice Director and Chief Magistrate of Fort Casimir, Fort Christina, and the Swedish settlements north of Fort Christina. Thus Jacquet accepted an administrative position with the West India Company, probably with the understanding that land on the Delaware for his private use would be made available to him. Responsibility was delegated to him for the management and command of the colony and for administering justice to the colonists as well as the Dutch soldiers at the two forts. Of course, Stuyvesant as the Director-General of the New Netherland outranked him and reserved the authority to veto his decisions, and, if it became necessary, to relieve him of his office. Jacquet was assisted in the administration of law and justice by a council, also acting as a law court, consisting of Andries Hudde, Elmerhuysen Cleyn, and two sergeants from the garrison (who initially were Gysbert Bray and Hans Hopman) "if the affair is purely military or concerning the Company properly." If the affair to be decided was a civil one between colonists and Company employes then Jacquet was authorized to select two of the most suitable freemen to take the place on the council of the two sergeants.

Stuyvesant's lengthy instructions and a transcript of Jacquet's oath of office taken December 8, 1655 have been preserved. He swore to advance the service of the Company, and also "maintain and advance as much as I can the Reformed religion, as the

same is taught and preached here and in the Fatherland . . .''
He was instructed to be watchful of the Swedes allowing none
of them to remain in the fort overnight, a precautionary step to
prevent another Swedish coup. If any Swedes were found antagonistic toward the Dutch he ''shall with all possible politeness
make them leave . . .'' Among other things he was also reminded to observe the ordinances prohibiting the sale of brandy
and strong drink to the Indians.[2]

At the time of Jacquet's arrival there were more Swedes and
Finns than Dutch living in the twenty-one or twenty-two houses
that they occupied when the Dutch families returned to New
Amsterdam in the early days of Rising's administration. There
was also a Swedish-Finnish population of perhaps 200 to 300
men, women, and children living on farms between the Christina River and the Schuylkill, an area then devoid of a Dutch
settlement.

Stuyvesant did not relax in his ambition to increase the Dutch
population at the Santhoeck, and he instructed Jacquet to ''clear
a good street behind the houses already built and lay out the
same in convenient order and lots of about forty or fifty feet
width and one hundred feet length, the street to be at least four
to five rods wide.'' (An Amsterdam foot was equal to slightly
more than eleven English inches, and an Amsterdam rod ap-
proximated 12.071 English feet or 3.6807 meters.)

The new street was to be laid out in the area southwest of the
fort where the existing houses were then located. Stuyvesant
cautioned Jacquet not to lay out building lots directly behind the
fort or north of the fort as far as the kill (''ye Little or Towne
Creeke'') because this land was to be reserved for expansion
and outworks of the fort.[3]

The Delaware historian Jeannette Eckman wrote that the new
street became the ''Second Row,'' present Fourth Street which
now borders the Green.[4] There was then no Third Street; in fact,
this was before there were any streets having names. Miss
Eckman believed the houses then standing in the Strand were

Minques Kijlingt Apoque Kema.

Aclans Mamargaä

Taskhaikungh

Tanakonck Sandhoeck
vel titiamnominat
Trefaldighect

Nieuw Carolandh.

Salinge,
Hr Tranen Vdd.

Christina Kijl.

Korsen Revier

Oijtseging Elßborg af
Afamshadling.

Afamhadkings Kijl.

Ocßgrahagijt.

Ramel Kijl.

Bryne Vdd.
Kacki Keniackien.

Copied from a portion of
Lindeström's Map B by
J. J. ALEXANDER

Some Features on Lindeström's Map "B"

(shown on the opposite page)

Several references have been made in the text and chapter notes to two maps of the Delaware River watershed made in 1654-55 by the Swedish engineer Peter Lindeström, identified as Map "A" and Map "B." Some of the same place-names are spelled differently on the two maps, which were drawn at different times. Map "B" gives a detailed representation of the environs of present New Castle including small circles denoting dwellings. A copy of the map is owned by the Historical Society of Pennsylvania, and with the Society's kind permission the Delaware artist J. J. Alexander photographed and enlarged this portion of the map and then made an ink drawing carefully duplicating the handwriting to make a legible rendition of the entries.

South is at the top of the map and north is at the bottom. The names on the west side reading from top to bottom are as follows, with certain Swedish diacritical marks omitted below due to type limitations:

Minquas Kyl [eller?] Apoquekema
On Map "A" Lindeström calls the stream Apoquenema. It is doubtless present Appoquinimink Creek. In Lenape it means "the place where we stayed a long time" (Ah-puk-wen-e-ming). It was also called the Minquas Kyl because it was one of the several streams the Minquas traveled over to reach the Delaware River. (The Christina River was also called the Minquas Kill.)

Ackan Manangaa
Given on Map "A" as Ackan Mamangaha. A Lenape place-name in the Delaware City-Port Penn area, possibly the name for St. Georges Creek. Meaning unknown.

Taskhoikungh
A Lenape word given on Map "A" as Tasckhockung. Possibly Red Lion Creek. Meaning unknown.

Tamakonck Sand Hoeck velutiam nominetz Trefaldighect
The two central words are garbled Latin. Lindeström apparently wanted to convey the thought that the stream was called Tamakonck, but that Tamakonck, Sand Hoeck (Santhoeck), and Trefaldighet were also names for the fort and the Swedish settlement. The tiny drawing of Fort Trinity shows the outer bulwark the Swedes built in front of the fort proper and armed with cannon. Note the position of the sixteen circles representing houses, and the four houses north of the then nameless creek now "the Dyke." These homes were built by the Dutch prior to Rising's arrival, but were vacated and then occupied by Swedes, Finns, and other non-Dutch settlers.

Niew Carolandh

Spelled Niew Claerlandh on Map "A" it means "newly cleared land." After Rising's arrival the Swedes cleared seven tracts here for farms.

Strand Wyk (Strandwyck or Strandwijk)

A Dutch word meaning a shore district in an area bounded by a waterway. The map shows eleven dwellings there, possibly log cabins built by the settlers who arrived with Rising on the *Örn*. These may possibly be the homes in "the second hook" referred to during Jacquet's administration; see chapter 6.

Salunge

The name cannot be translated nor the place precisely identified.

Traner Udd

Given on Map "A" as Traneudden ("the crane point"). Known to the Dutch as Kraenhoek, and later to the English as Crane Hook, its present name.

Christina Kyl (Kill)

The Christina River, but the stream is not visible on this portion of the map; it is shown below the name. The creek immediately above the name has not been identified and has probably been obliterated by topographical alterations.

On the east side of the Delaware River the name Asamhackings Kyl, (shown on Map "A" as Asamohaking) seems to be the Varkens Kill (Salem River), and it may also have been the name of a Lenape village immediately to the south. Meaning unknown, but "haking" or "hocking" is a locative meaning "land of." Elfsborg (Oytsessing, i.e., Watcessing) is also shown, but Lindeström does not pinpoint the site of Fort Elfsborg, which was abandoned before the map was made.

The dots in the river represent shoals near a small island.

arranged in a "First Row." This assumption is supported by Lindeström's Map "B" (1654-55) which designates eight or nine houses in a row, although he also indicates other houses in a haphazard arrangement.[5] Unfortunately there is no contemporary description or drawing of the architecture of these dwellings, but they were probably small, hastily-built frame structures, none of which has survived.

Nothing was said about a "Green" in Stuyvesant's instructions to Jacquet. A historical marker at the corner of the Green and Delaware Street in New Castle bears an inscription that the Green was laid out by Stuyvesant in 1655. The reader has seen that Stuyvesant's invasion in the fall of that year was purely a military coup unrelated to town planning of what was then essentially a Swedish-Finnish community. The "Second Row" was not laid out until after Stuyvesant's return to New Amsterdam where he issued the instructions to Jacquet on December 8, 1655. The assumption that Stuyvesant laid out the Green or instructed Jacquet to do so must be questioned until convincing documentation is produced. The writer has sought in vain for such evidence. Stuyvesant may be considered New Castle's founding father because he built Fort Casimir on his first visit in 1651, but evidence is lacking that he was the architect of the Green.

Scarcely had Jacquet established a residence at the Santhoeck, possibly in a house in the palisaded rear area of the fort, when several Lenape chiefs called to request an audience with him. The chiefs complained that they were not receiving the quantities of trade goods, especially duffel cloth, for their furs that Dirck Smith promised would be given to them. Jacquet answered that he had just arrived at Fort Casimir and was not familiar with Smith's promises, but that he wanted to be fair and live in friendship with the Indians. His answer seemed to satisfy the chiefs, but they then asked if a ratio could be set for bartering; namely, so much cloth for so many pelts. Jacquet dodged the issue by saying he alone did not have the authority to fix prices and the Indians were free to trade with those who made the best offers. The chiefs reluctantly accepted the answers, but then replied that when they previously entered into negotiations with the Dutch, presents were always given to them, and they expected the same generosity at their first meeting with the new commander. Jacquet replied that goods were scarce, but in two or three days he would have presents for them.[6]

Shortly thereafter Jacquet called the residents of the Santhoeck together and explained that the Indians were awaiting the promised gifts, and failure to oblige them might arouse their animosity. He asked each resident to make a contribution to assure friendship with the natives. Jacquet contributed fourteen florins and ten stuivers to the fund, and fourteen others also made contributions of lesser amounts. The amount each contributed is not relevant, but the list of contributors provides the names of some of the residents of the Santhoeck when Jacquet arrived. By no means is this a complete list of the residents occupying the twenty-one or twenty-two houses, but consists of those who could afford to make a contribution, and were willing to do so. There were others living at the Santhoeck who did not have Dutch money to contribute or who opposed subsidizing the Indians. The spellings of the names of the contributors are given as they appear in the original document:[7]

> Andries Hudde
> Dr. Jacop [Jacob Crabbe,
>   a barber-surgeon]
> Elmerhuysen Cleyn
> Thomas Bruyn [Brown]
> Willem Maurits
> Jan Eeckhoff
> Cornelis Maurits
> Harman Jansen
> Sander Boyer
> Jan Flamman

Oloff Steurs
Jan Schaggen
Laurns Bors
Mons Andries

According to the revised regulations of the West India Company all persons were permitted to engage in the Indian fur trade, and heated competition developed for animal pelts. This was to the advantage of the Indians because white buyers bid up the amount of trade goods they would give for furs. Jacquet and his council were obliged to do something about this "whereas some people do not hesitate to ruin the trade with the Indians [for the others] by having already run up the price of deerskins by more than a third and it is apparent that they shall run higher yet to the great and excessive damage of the poor community here . . ."[8]

Jacquet summoned all the members of the community to assemble again at Fort Casimir on January 10, 1657 to discuss the situation and agree on a rate of exchange to be observed. Specie continued to be scarce, and sewant (wampum beads), a medium of exchange with the Indians, was also used for transactions in the Dutch community. The natives, incidentally, would accept only Indian-made sewant; shell beads made by the whites were considered counterfeit.

The exchange rates agreed upon were as follows:

For one merchantable beaver [pelt], two fathoms of sewant [a string of beads about six feet long equalled a fathom].
For one good bearskin, worth a beaver, two fathoms of sewant.
For one elkskin, worth a beaver, two fathoms of sewant; otters in proportion.
For one deerskin, one hundred and twenty sewant [loose beads] foxes, lynxes, raccoons and so forth to be valued in proportion.

At what might be termed "town meetings" Jacquet discussed current issues with the residents, and although their remarks were not inhibited, the final decision rested with him and his council. At this particular meeting a proclamation was read which prohibited any of the residents going into the woods to trade with the Indians at their villages or hunting camps. This practice resulted in disorder, and probably illegal trading with liquor, and the council could not supervise the conduct of persons competing for furs. The proclamation stated that the Indians should be allowed free passage to bring their pelts to Fort Casimir and to trade with residents in the village with whom they desired to barter.[9] No doubt the council believed this was a way to avoid "brokers" from cornering the fur market, and also prevent the use of liquor in the transactions, but it proved to be a vain hope.

A few of the residents of the village owned barks or other small craft which they sailed back and forth to Manhattan Island where they exchanged beaver pelts for gunpowder, gun barrels, cloth, cheese, rum, wine, beer and other commodities. There were close ties between the two settlements since both had a common Director-General, and new residents and soldiers came from New Amsterdam to the Santhoeck to live. The small coastal vessels provided needed transportation for mobility in both settlements. The modern resident of Delaware who takes shopping trips to New York City is following a pattern set by Dutch colonists at New Castle more than 300 years ago, but with faster and more efficient means of transportation.

The proclamation setting the rate of exchange with the Indians was endorsed by thirty-three members of the Fort Casimir community. Twenty-one signed their names, and twelve who were illiterate made their marks.[10] This is more complete than the previous list and provides names of residents at New Castle as of January 10, 1657—the earliest unofficial census. The names of the signatories are given as spelled in the document and asterisks indicate individuals who made their marks. The names are listed in the same order as they were originally recorded:

Jan Pauwl Jaquet
Andries Hudde
Isack Allerton
Zenon [?]
Willem Mouritsen
Alexander Boyer
Thomas Bron *
Gabriel de Haes
Jacob Crabbe
Harman Jansen
Cornelis Mouris
Heyndryck Dybert
Jan Flaman
Constantinus Groenenborch
Isack Mera
Abraham Quyn

Jan Tibout
Herman Heyndrick
Louwern Piters *
Leendert Clasen *
Jan Eechoff
Tymen Stidden
Willem Claessen
Jan Schaggen *
Lucas Piters *
Moens Andris *
Oele Toersen *
Laers Boers *
Heyndrick Vryman
Jurriaen Joesen *
Cornelis Teunissen *
Elmerhuysen Cleyn
Mattison *
[Anders Mattysen?]

The reader may recognize Cornelis Teunissen (also spelled Teunisse, Tonisen) and Cornelis Mouris (also spelled Mauritz, Mourits, Mouritsen, etc.) as two of the freemen in the party that Commandant Bicker sent out from Fort Casimir on May 20, 1654 to board the *Örn*, as related in chapter 4. The individual who signed his name Mattison could have been Anders Mattysen, as indicated, or Mattys Mattysen. One cannot be certain, nor can the individual who signed Zenon be identified.

The above list does not include the names of soldiers stationed at Fort Casimir, and the names of a number of contemporary civilians were not included for unknown reasons. The minutes recorded by Andries Hudde, secretary of the court and council, official surveyor, and deputy prosecutor of the court, include names of other persons who were residents of the village or the immediate environs. Among these were Gerret Abel, Mattys Bussaine, appointed by Stuyvesant as the court messenger or "summoner," Elias Emmens, Reynick Gerritsz, the ex-Swedish Lieutenant Gyllengren, whose name is given as Elias Guldengreyn (the council granted him land for a house below the fort), Peter Harmensen, Jan Jacobsen Constapel, Claes Janse, a carpenter, Niles Larsen, Robert Marthyn, Marten Roseman, Claes [Pietersen?] de Smit, Mattys de Vogel, and many others. Some names appear in more than one spelling making it difficult to identify the individual with certainty.

The nationalities of these residents cannot be determined by their names; some Dutchmen bore names that appear to be Scandinavian; some Swedish names sound Dutch; and as previously pointed out Finns usually had Swedish names. From their names alone one would not suspect that Peter Trotzig, an executive in the New Sweden Company, was a native-born Swede, as was Harald Appelbom, a diplomat who represented the Swedish court in Holland. Hendrick van Elswick (also given as von Elswick), although born in Lubeck in Germany, lived in Stockholm, once commanded a Swedish vessel on a voyage to America, and became a lieutenant in the Swedish garrison at Fort Christina. On at least one occasion he signed his name "Henrich von Elsswich," and this kind of inconsistency tends to confuse the issue of identities. Harman Jansen, despite a Swedish-sounding name, was Dutch or German, probably the latter; Sander Leendertsen was Scotch; and Jan Flamman (or Flaman) was a Frenchman. Flaman was the captain of a French privateer *L'Esperance* (*Hope*) one of the vessels Stuyvesant impressed into Dutch service at New Amsterdam for his invasion forces of 1655. Flaman must have been impressed with the commercial opportunities at the Santhoeck for he returned there to live and engage in the coastal trade, especially between Fort Casimir and New Amsterdam.

Since all of the thirty-three signatories on the above list dated

January 10, 1657 are specifically named as "members of the community" at Fort Casimir their nationalities are of particular interest. Nine or ten of these men, about 35%, appear to have been Swedes or Finns so far as the writer can determine from entries in other sources. There is little doubt that Jan Eechoff, Tymen Stidden (Stiddem), Jan Schaggen, Lucas Piters, Moens Andris, Laers Boers, Heyndrick Vryman, Jurriaen Joesen, and Anders Mattysen (Mattison) were Scandinavians. There is some question about Constantinus Groenenborch, often referred to as Swedish because he was a soldier in the original Swedish garrison at Fort Elfsborg, and served elsewhere in New Sweden. The question arises because his name is entered in the *Monatgelder Buch* (*Monthly Account Book*) of salaried Swedish employes, 1642 to 1663, as "Constantinus Groneberg of Mark Brandenburgh," which suggests he may have been born in Germany. His name was also recorded in New Sweden as Groenenbeurch, Gronenbergk, and in other spellings.

Among the other non-Dutch on the January 10 list are Isack Allerton, Gabriel de Haes, Jan Flaman, Alexander Boyer, and possibly Willem Mouritsen. Jeannette Eckman believed that the latter was an Englishman named Morris whose name was Dutchified, which is possible, although positive proof is lacking. The seventeen remaining names may have been those of Dutchmen, although the records leave doubt about some of them. Even if one assumes that all seventeen were Hollanders the reality is that New Castle's known male residents under the government of the Dutch West India Company in 1656-57 were approximately 50% non-Dutch, and most of these were Swedes or Finns. The administration may have been essentially Dutch, but the illusion of "the little Dutch town" becomes questionable in terms of the male residents.

One should not lose sight of the fact that many of the residents of Holland were not native-born Dutch. As a center for textile manufacturing, shipbuilding, brewing, distilling, salt refining, and other industries many aliens were attracted to live in the Netherlands. Amsterdam was a cosmopolitan city having in its population unknown numbers of foreign-born Norwegians, Danes, Germans, French, Swedes, English, and others. The reader may recall that the English Pilgrims spent almost twelve years in Leyden before they came to America; the religious tolerance in Holland rather than economic factors was their principal motive. Other Englishmen moved to Holland for commercial reasons, and some of them, as well as other aliens, became employes or soldiers of the West India Company.

The pluralistic society that developed at the Santhoeck was further extended by a number of marriages of mixed nationals, which were recorded. Sander Boyer, who interpreted the Dutch language to the Indians, was neither Dutch nor Swedish, and although his nationality has not been conclusively established, he married a Swedish wife. The children of this marriage, John, Josyn, and Thomas, were apparently raised under the influence of their Swedish mother, but how can one accurately classify them other than to call them Americans? During Jacquet's administration Louwern Pieters, who came from Leyden (a servant of the Englishman Thomas Brown), married Catryn Jans, a nineteen-year-old lass from Gothenburg, Sweden. Another female from Gothenburg, named Endel Melis, married Jurriaen Hanouw from Greater Poland. Thomas Brown's sixteen-year-old daughter Jannitien, born in New Netherland, married the aforementioned Willem Maurits (Mouritsen), a thirty-three-year-old bachelor.[11] Other examples could be cited, but these will illustrate the point.

The West India Company granted Dutch citizenship to persons of all nationalities who settled on the Delaware (also elsewhere in the New Netherland) and swore allegiance to the Dutch government—Danes, Norwegians, Holsteiners, Scotch, English, and French, as well as Swedes, Finns, and one Pole. At least two Jews, Isack Israel and Isack Cardosa, were engaged in commerce between Fort Casimir and New Amsterdam. Isack Allerton, whose name is on the above list as a resident of Fort

Casimir, was an Englishman who came to America with the Pilgrims on the *Mayflower*. He was engaged for many years in fishing and commercial ventures in coastal waters.[12]

Allerton, who was in his seventies during Jacquet's administration, had a ketch at Fort Casimir that he used for trading purposes. He imported a variety of products, which he sold on credit terms to the residents on the Delaware. In 1657 he complained to the council that 12,000 guilders were owed to him, and some of these debts had been outstanding on his books for as long as eight years.[13] Allerton's English identity has been well established, but to identify the nationality of all of the individuals cited in the early Fort Casimir records requires genealogical research beyond the purview of the present study.[14]

A roster of the soldiers assigned to the garrison at Fort Casimir is not available, and some of them apparently moved back and forth to New Amsterdam and other places. By sieving Andries Hudde's minutes of the court sessions, and applying personal judgment, an incomplete list has been compiled. Some of these men may have been soldiers at one time and civilians at another; for example, Sergeant Luycas Dircksen, who was in the West India Company's employ for four years, bought a house at the Santhoeck, and on February 15, 1656 he petitioned Governor Stuyvesant for a discharge and permission to transport himself and family from New Amsterdam to the Delaware permanently. Permission was granted and he and his family arrived on the bark *de Fenix* (the *Phoenix*?) in the spring.[15]

The following list contains the names of some of the soldiers at Fort Casimir during Jacquet's administration. The spellings conform to the entries in Hudde's minutes:[16]

> Corporal Heyndrick van Bilevelt
> Frederick Bitter
> Jan Emans (Johannes Eymans),
>   lance corporal, also a cooper
> Laurns Hansen, quartermaster

Frederic Harmanse, cadet
Engel Cornelisen Hoogenburgh
Peter Jansz
Sergeant Paulus Jansen
Philip Jansen
Jan Justen, gunner
Adam Onkelbach
Elias Roews
Jacob Vis van Rotterdam
Jan Swart, also a carpenter

Several men formerly associated with the Swedish military forces remained at the Santhoeck as civilians during the period Dirck Smith was in command. Reference has already been made to ex-Lieutenant Gyllengren who, with several others, were still there when Jacquet arrived. Jan Stalcop, former Swedish gunnery sergeant was one of these; also known as John Anderson Stalcop, he later owned extensive lands where Wilmington is now located.

Upon his arrival Jacquet admired a table and wardrobe used by Dirck Smith, which he may have assumed belonged to the Company and would be turned over to him while he was in command. Smith insisted the furniture was his personal property, which he had purchased from Sergeant Stalcop when he took command. On December 18, 1655, Stalcop testified before Jacquet that he had, in fact, sold the articles to Smith, which settled the question of ownership. Jacquet's only recourse was to offer to buy the furniture from Smith, but Smith wouldn't relinquish his property and refused to sell.[17] The vessel that took Smith back to New Amsterdam for a new assignment probably also transported Smith's table and wardrobe. The descendants of Jan Stalcop would probably like to know what happened to these family heirlooms.

Tymen Stidden, a barber-surgeon of Swedish or Danish descent, who spelled his name Stiddem, rendered medical service to some of the Dutch soldiers at Fort Casimir on Commandant Smith's orders. Stidden is named as a resident of the Santhoeck community during the Jacquet administration where he probably practiced medicine. There is no indication that Stidden ever graduated from a university, and it is not certain that he served an apprenticeship in a barber-surgeon guild. He may have been self-taught, acquiring a rudimentary knowledge of medicine, and could provide basic dental and surgical care as well as cutting hair, trimming beards, and shaving his customers. He doubtless could set bones, amputate wounded or diseased limbs, draw blood through venesection, and prescribe a large variety of herbal medicines. A volume of herb cures that belonged to New Castle's first physician has been preserved in the collections of the Historical Society of Delaware. Dr. Stidden, whose name was later spelled Stidham, became the owner of extensive property within the limits of present Wilmington.

Jan Justen (Johan Gustafsson), referred to as a gunner at Fort Casimir during the Jacquet administration, was one of the signers of the oath of allegiance to the Dutch government following Stuyvesant's invasion of 1655. He was undoubtedly a Swede or Finn, but he seems to have served in the Dutch garrison at the fort. In 1656 Jacquet and the council granted his request to make a plantation on the Christina River, and he seems to have been the ancestor of the Justis family of Delaware.

Sergeant Sven Skute, who returned to the Santhoeck after the court martial proceedings, instead of going back to Sweden with Rising, was a resident while Dirck Smith was in command. He was living in the community when Jacquet arrived, but he had little affection for the Dutch and probably harbored resentment toward Stuyvesant who had tricked him in the surrender terms. At his first meeting with Jacquet, Skute claimed that Dirck Smith owed him for approximately seven and one-half bushels of rye, and four and one-half bushels of peas, which Skute delivered to the fort, as well as four sill beams used to repair the guardhouse. Skute also said he personally owned a badstu, or bathhouse, behind the fort, which the Dutch confiscated, and he claimed the Company owed him 100 florins for it. It seems ironic that Skute, who surrendered the fort to the Dutch, returned as a private landowner and householder and sold victuals presumably for consumption by the Dutch garrison. Skute was more of an opportunist than a collaborator in the strict sense of the word, because he was openly critical of the Stuyvesant government, and Jacquet considered him a troublemaker.

On December 20, 1655, only two days after he arrived at Fort Casimir, Jacquet ordered Skute put in confinement because of "improper utterances disseminated by him." Jacquet threatened to send him to New Amsterdam to answer for his objectionable behavior unless he turned over a new leaf. The threat must have been effective because the following March, Jacquet purchased barley and rye from him, which were harvested in three fields, a burnt clearing in the second row, on a second plot above the second row, and on a plantation north of "the public road." This road, possibly an Indian path made wide enough for a horse cart, was the route to a fording place on the Christina River where Wilmington's Third Street Bridge is now located. This was the route connecting Fort Casimir with Fort Christina, to which the Dutch gave a new name, Fort Altena or Altenae. A town in western Germany bore this name, and it was also a place in the Netherlands.[18] Who decided on the name change is not known, but obviously Stuyvesant did not relish perpetuating the name of the abdicated Swedish queen in New Netherland territory.

Reference has been made to the two Dutch sergeants, Gysbert Bray and Hans Hopman, who served as members of the council when military affairs were considered. Sergeant Hopman became involved in an incident that reflected unfavorably on his integrity as a municipal official. On the evening of September 20, 1656, Jacquet gave him orders to be transmitted to Corporal van Bilevelt (also spelled Bylvelt) who was on duty in the guardhouse. The sergeant later testified that he found the corporal drunk and unfit for duty. When the sergeant gave him the orders Bilevelt drew his sword and said he would no longer obey him. While the men were arguing Jacquet appeared and Bilevelt said to him, "I will gladly be commanded by you, but not by a scoundrel." He forthwith punched Sergeant Hopman with his fist, and the sergeant struck him back with his cane.

A hearing was subsequently held, and Jan Emans, a lance corporal, testified that the friction between the corporal and the sergeant was due to a misdemeanor committed by another soldier, Adam Onkelbach "from Rowan." Onkelbach was accused of illegally entering Cornelis Mouris's property at night and stealing cabbages. Mouris, looking for his stolen vegetables, went to the soldiers' quarters at the fort on September 19 where he saw Onkelbach cutting up cabbages in his kettle. He then entered a formal complaint and Jacquet ordered Onkelbach to be locked up in the guardhouse.

During his hearing Onkelbach blurted out, "Petty criminals are hanged while the big ones who steal the Company's guns and sell them are allowed to run free." When pressed to explain what he meant he accused Sergeant Hopman of selling his musket to the Indians for three and one-half beaver pelts, probably worth more than the sergeant's monthly pay. The musket was non-transferrable Company property as all the soldiers knew, and thereafter several cadets and other soldiers showed their contempt for Sergeant Hopman by refusing to obey his orders. What worsened their resentment was that Hopman took another musket from the Company's store of weapons to replace the one he had sold.

Recognizing that Sergeant Hopman's usefulness to the Company depended upon his having the confidence and support of his troops, the council agreed that his fate should be decided by Stuyvesant's council at Manhattan. Sergeant Hopman and Private Onkelbach were taken to New Amsterdam in Isack Allerton's ketch. Before boarding the vessel both were shackled "since they are enemies and might otherwise do injury to each other during the voyage.'' Neither man is heard of again on the Delaware during the Jacquet administration and Sergeant Paulus Jansen replaced Hopman as a member of the council.

During Jacquet's administration Stuyvesant issued land patents at the Santhoeck on behalf of the West India Company to a number of individuals, some of whom are named in this chapter; others seem to have been absentee landowners. Perhaps they may have intended to build domiciles, but something interfered with their coming to the Santhoeck to live. Others may have been residents of New Amsterdam who came to the Delaware for a short time and then returned; others may have migrated to Maryland.

Some of the patents were for numbered lots in the two rows surveyed by Hudde, and others were for ''larger'' plantations beyond the town limits. A few patents covered land at Fort Altena. It would be an interesting but laborious exercise to make a drawing to scale showing the bounds of the lots and the names of the original grantees, which could be done from the sources cited in the notes.[19] This would be a worthy task for a student of New Castle's early land records despite the fact that thirteen pages are missing from the Dutch land title book.

The village at Fort Casimir had an active local government and a court of law before it had a name of its own. In contemporary records the name Fort Casimir is used to refer both to the fort and the adjacent community, although the term Santhoeck continued to be used. There were no schools or churches and no courthouse in the village; the court still met in an upper room in a building within the fort. The village continued to grow slowly, and early in March of 1656 the ''Second Row'' was taking shape.[20] No population figures are on record during the Jacquet administration, but one gathers the impression the population may have peaked at about 125 or 150 men, women, and children, including soldiers and their families. But before Jacquet was replaced in April of 1657 there had been a sharp decline, which will be discussed in the next chapter. During Jacquet's administration men outnumbered women and marriageable females continued to be scarce. Single girls usually married in their teens, and widows did not remain unmarried very long. Jacob Crabbe, another barber-surgeon, a bachelor born in Holland, married Gertrude Jacobs, widow of Roeloff Janssen de Haes, probably a Scandinavian, who had three children, a son Johannes, aged ten, and two daughters Marrities (Maria), aged nine, and Annitien (Anna), aged three.[21] Johannes later became a prosperous New Castle merchant, a magistrate, and a member of the William Penn assembly and council.

The court met more than fifty times from December 18, 1655 until April of 1657 when Jacob Alrichs arrived to succeed Jacquet. The minutes kept by Hudde contain a number of human interest stories that illustrate the variety of subjects under the court's jurisdiction. For all practical purposes the court and council functioned as a single entity and decisions were rendered without benefit of a jury. None of the litigants were represented by lawyers, but pled their own cases. The court adjudicated disputes over debts, sentenced those guilty of petty thefts, recorded marital engagements, posted wedding bans on three successive Sundays, disciplined unruly soldiers and civilians who got into brawls due to drunkenness (which was common), controlled the Company's property, occasionally granted small parcels of land to residents, and collected a moderate land tax annually of twelve stivers for each morgen of land. Major disputes and serious infractions of the law were normally referred to New Amsterdam for Stuyvesant and his council to settle, although there is no record in Jacquet's court of cases of murder or manslaughter.

The court minutes do not specifically mention a tavern at the Santhoeck at this time, but there was no difficulty obtaining alcoholic beverages at certain private homes where the residents sold beer and liquor. These quasi-taverns were numerous in New Amsterdam where there were also licensed taverns that provided overnight lodging. The licensed taverns offered tapping, bed and board, dicing, card-playing, and other forms of conviviality. Numerous rules and regulations governed the conduct of the tavern keeper, such as guarantees for fair measure, discouraging rowdyism from overindulgence, prohibiting the sale of liquor during Sunday church services, paying excise taxes, etc. The quasi-taverns were operated by colonists having other trades or professions who served intoxicants in their homes, but did not offer lodging.[22]

At the Santhoeck, where there were no licensed taverns, both soldiers and civilians came to Reynick Gerritsz's house to socialize and tipple. On one occasion Gerritsz resorted to subterfuge to sell brandy to Indians, which was a serious offense punishable by a fine of 500 florins plus corporal punishment determined by the court. A number of thirsty Indians came to his house and Moens Andris, who was there, asked Gerritsz whether he was willing to accommodate them with brandy. Gerritsz agreed to do so, according to testimony given by Andris, provided Andris would collect the money for the liquor from the Indians. Andris apparently did so, but when he tried to give the money to Gerritsz, the latter said "Throw it into the cap." Andris did so and said to Gerritsz, "You can count it yourself," which he must have believed exempted him from being a participant in an illegal transaction.

When Gerritsz was taken to court for violating the law his defense was that he had sold the brandy to Andris, and had no knowledge of what Andris did with it! The court rejected this defense and seized Gerritsz's sloop and goods until further disposition of the case.

Cornelis Mouris (Maurits) was accused of selling pails of beer at his house, which were delivered to Louwern Piters' house where the beer was drunk by "five Indian men, three women, a big boy, and a child." This off-the-premise sale and consumption caused Louwern Piters to inform Jacquet, because he did not want to be involved in an illegal transaction, particularly since the Indians became drunk and insolent.

The court read Stuyvesant's proclamation to Cornelis Mouris prohibiting the sale of liquor to the Indians, but after learning that this was his first offense the court did not fine him but ordered him to cease vending alcoholic beverages for six months. The sentence intimates that his residence may also have been a semi-tavern. About a week later Mouris petitioned the court requesting "that he be allowed to tap again, complaining vigorously that he has nothing to live on, and without the same he would have to suffer deprivation with his wife and children." The court decided to be lenient and granted him a pardon provided he pay twenty-five florins to the poor fund. The reference to the poor fund suggests there may have been residents on welfare in Delaware as early as 1657!

Early in Jacquet's administration the council imposed an excise tax on the consumption of French wine, brandy, Dutch or foreign beer, and other alcoholic beverages "for the maintenance of the fort and other unavoidable expenses." This income was badly needed to repair the fort which Jacquet and the council found "completely decayed in its walls and batteries" in their first inspection tour, "and must be rebuilt from the ground up since the outer work has for the most part already fallen down and that which still stands must necessarily fall since it has been torn open and dislocated as a result."

At a "town meeting" on November 8, 1656 the council requested the men in the community to cut palisades to cover the outside of the fort for the common defense. The community was also informed that it was necessary for the men to assist in building a bridge over the creek because the route was impassable and should be kept open for an emergency.[23] This undoubtedly was "the public road" previously mentioned leading to the Christina River. One should keep in mind that Jacquet's concern for the defense of the Santhoeck was not only due to the fear of an English attack, or a Swedish mutiny, but he did not trust either the Minquas or the local Lenape.

The excise tax levied on liquor did not apply to private

persons "who wish to lay in some for their own provision," but only to those engaged in buying and selling. Harman Jansen, having brewed beer for his own consumption (so he said) was exempt from the tax, but when he began to sell the beer at his home he was hailed into court for tapping without paying the excise tax. His defense was that it was not very good beer, and he sold it at low price just to get rid of it. The court was unconvinced and ruled that he should pay a tax on the beer he sold, and he was fined twenty-five guilders, one-third of which went into the poor fund.

The function of the court in approving (or disapproving) marital engagements is illustrated in the case of Jan Picolet, a native of Bruylet in France, and Catryn Jans who was born in Sweden. The couple appeared before Secretary Hudde on January 24, 1656, and requested permission to become engaged to marry. In the presence of witnesses, permission was granted and a paper signed, but the marriage had to be delayed until a minister was available. There was then no resident minister at Fort Casimir, although the colonists were of two denominations— the Dutch were members of the Dutch Reformed Church and the Swedes and Finns were Lutherans.

The only minister on the Delaware at the time was the Lutheran Lars Carlsson Lock, which he Latinized to Laurentius Carolus Loeckenius. He was sometimes called Pastor Lock, but Hudde refers to him in the court minutes as "the honorable Mr. Laers, minister." After Nertunius and Hiört returned to Sweden with Rising in 1655, Lock was the only remaining pastor in the colony. He lived for a while at Fort Christina and then at Upland (present Chester) where he ministered to the Swedes at the church on Tinicum Island. From time to time he came to Fort Casimir to conduct weddings, baptisms, and other services for the Swedes and Finns living at the Santhoeck and environs. Of course, no devout member of the Dutch Reformed Church would attend Lutheran services or be married or baptized by a Lutheran pastor.

As a Swede, Catryn Jans would have had no objection to being married by him, and since Jan was a Frenchman he probably would not have insisted upon a Dutch Reformed wedding service. Thus, they waited impatiently for the arrival of either Pastor Lock from Upland, or a Dutch Reformed minister from New Amsterdam; in the bliss of their love either would probably have sufficed. Meanwhile, the couple agreed to observe their pre-matrimonial promise to refrain from sexual intimacy in the knowledge they would be punished as adulterers, if they sinned.

On May 24, Jan Picolet appeared before the court and by petition both verbally and in writing requested that his engagement of marriage to Catryn be declared null and void. He said that about a month after the engagement contract was drawn up and signed he asked Catryn whether she had any obligation to any other man, and she replied negatively. He said he would have married her then and there if a minister had been present. "Afterwards," he said, as recorded verbatim by Hudde, "everyone began to notice that his fiancee, the defendant here present, was pregnant. Whereupon he, as an honest man, availed himself of the opportunity to keep himself from her, the defendant, because he could not understand how such obvious signs of pregnancy could appear in an honest woman in such a short time . . ."

Catryn said she was willing to join him in matrimony, but confessed that in the fall of 1655 she was betrothed to a sailor named Willem, a member of the *Wagh's* crew, "and to have had carnal intercourse with him at different times and places from which she became pregnant." She said she repented not having told Picolet of her indiscretions, but the court ruled she misled and deceived him and released Picolet from his promise of marriage. Catryn, big with child, was sentenced to beg God and the court for forgiveness on bended knee, promising to behave herself honestly in the future. If she transgressed again the court said she would be disciplined and punished according to the prescribed laws of the fatherland. At this point the romance between Jan and Catryn ended, but the scarcity of females in the colony was in her favor. The following November, Catryn married Louwern Piters from Leyden as previously noted. The court records do not reveal whether or not Jan Picolet found a wife worthy of his devotion.

Today's residents of New Castle, and visitors to the town, may not realize that tobacco once held promise of becoming an important crop. As early as 1656 in the Jacquet administration tobacco was being raised in town gardens and in larger quantities on outlying farms. Before the year was over the first tobacco inspectors took their official oaths. In a quasi-democratic process the town nominated four candidates, and Jacquet selected two for the job, Moens Andris and Willem Mouritsen. They took the following oath:.

> We the undersigned promise and swear that we shall act to the best of our knowledge in inspecting tobacco, not allowing ourselves to be misled by cunning or craft *or gifts*, but to conduct ourselves equally and just to everyone, the buyer as well as the seller. So help us God Almighty.

The added italics suggest that Jacquet's council was not unaware of the possibility of improper conduct on the part of the appointees.

The tobacco inspectors examined all tobacco before it was delivered to a local resident or exported, and satisfied themselves it was of good quality. The intent was to prevent unprincipled marketers from deceiving their customers by concealing inferior or blighted leaves by covering them in their casks with first-grade tobacco. Not only did Jacquet want to protect customers from fraud, but he wanted the colony to acquire a reputation as a producer of fine quality tobacco. The inspectors were paid ten stivers per hundred pounds of tobacco by the parties to the transactions who were given a certificate that the tobacco was in good condition. (One guilder was worth twenty stivers).

Due to the shortage of Dutch money some debts were contracted in pounds of tobacco, and other debts contracted in guilders were paid off in tobacco. Captain Jan Flaman appeared in court February 23, 1656 to get satisfaction for 515 pounds of tobacco owed him by Thomas Brown and Willem Mouritsen; 546 pounds owed by Jan Schaggen, and 206 pounds owed by Moens Andris. Debts were also paid off in beaver pelts or rum when available, and cattle was sometimes used as security for a loan.

The available records, which are all too brief, give the impression that life was hard and luxuries were lacking in the little village. The income of the freemen was largely derived from growing tobacco, corn, wheat, rye, barley and peas, and raising hogs, pigs, and goats. Milk cows were scarce, and cheese, other than that made from goat milk, had to be imported from New Amsterdam at a relatively high price, which many could not afford. The freemen could sell their farm products to the Company or to other buyers, although it was necessary to retain some for their own survival.

Jacquet's responsibility for the welfare of the colony and the advancement of the Company's interests meant returning a profit, and that was not easy to do. He could not conscript Swedish and Finnish farmers, nor Dutch freemen, into the Company's service, and he had to rely upon soldiers and other Company employes to work the Company's land. Sometimes he was able to engage freemen to work in the Company's fields for a specified share of the crop. For example, he engaged Pouwl Jansz (Paulus Jansen) to sow seeds on the Company's land for one-half the crop; the Company supplied one ox for the plowing and Jansen supplied the second one.

Unattended goats and hogs running loose in the cultivated fields ruined some of the crops, which prompted the council to issue a proclamation on February 23, 1656 ordering owners of farms and plantations to enclose their properties with fences. A moderate fine was set for persons who ignored the regulation. Apparently those living on lots in the two rows did not feel the proclamation applied to them, and they were in no hurry to fence in their goats and hogs. On May 22 the council ordered "each and every inhabitant residing near Fort Casimier" who owned hogs to put yokes on the animals' necks within twenty-four hours to keep them from devouring the Company's grain. Owners were put on notice that if any hogs were found henceforth in the grain that the soldiers would kill them.

Neither of the two regulations seemed to have corrected the situation, and those who continued to suffer damage to their crops protested to the council for relief. A third proclamation issued on November 27 warned all owners of "plantations or lots" to enclose their properties "with a good solid fence." Those who failed to do so within three months were subject to heavy fines, and anyone found guilty of non-compliance twice would be considered "to have an obstinate disposition," and the Company would confiscate his property.

Two "overseers and inspectors of fences," Herman Jansz (Harman Jansen) and Jan Eechoff (Eckhoff) were appointed at this time to make certain that all residents complied. No specific description of the early fences at New Castle is on record, but from sources relating to other parts of the New Netherland it is known that Dutch farmers erected post and rail fences, and paled fences made of clapboards or slabs of wood.[24] The Swedes and Finns were also skilled in making rail fences of split logs, and inasmuch as there is no record of a sawmill at the Santhoeck during this period it seems likely that rail fences were common.

A study of the council minutes during Jacquet's administration leaves no doubt that many men owning next to nothing who settled at or near Fort Casimir had the opportunity to become landowners irrespective of their nationalities. Servants could climb the social ladder, slowly to be sure, and become freemen; some freemen participated in government functions such as tobacco inspection and fence inspection, and the regulations provided for two civilians selected by the Vice-Director to sit on the council to judge civil cases. The vice-director and his council were responsive to the needs of freemen, servants, and soldiers, all of whom were entitled to have their day in court if they felt it necessary. This should not be construed to mean that there was no contention in the colony; nationalistic ties, religious differences, and languages that were not mutually comprehensible tended to make a divisive society. It can be inferred from the court records that there was often friction between the Dutch colonists and the Swedes and Finns. It was probably not easy for the latter to forget Dutch plundering of the farms of their fellowmen north of the Christina during Stuyvesant's invasion.

Stuyvesant visualized the colony on the Delaware consisting of "16 or 20 persons or families together" in a number of hamlets, dominated by the seat of justice and center of population at the Santhoeck. His rationale was that small self-contained communities could be more readily policed than a scattered population, but this concept was not then readily accepted by the Scandinavians. In compliance with Stuyvesant's instructions Jacquet attempted to persuade the Swedes "living at the second hook above Fort Casemier" (possibly the Strand Wyck near present Swanwyck) to form a village and become town dwellers. In the articles of capitulation between Stuyvesant and Rising, section 6 gave the Swedish freemen one year and six months to dispose of their property if they were unprepared to leave the colony. Accordingly these Swedes living at the second hook petitioned the council that they be permitted to remain on their farms for that period of time. They said that they would then resolve what to do, but for the present "are not of the mind to change their dwelling places or build in the village which is to be established . . ."[25] Jacquet wisely did not pursue the issue, but allowed the Swedish and Finnish families at the second hook, as well as those living on the scattered farms between Fort Christina and the Schuylkill, to remain undisturbed.

Jacquet's tenure on the Delaware was too limited to enable him to understand fully the nuances in Dutch-Swedish relations, but he was aware that he could not ignore Swedish provincialism. He knew the Swedes had taken oaths of allegiance to the Dutch, but they wanted officials to be selected from among their own people. This was a peculiar situation because their political ties with Sweden were broken when Governor Rising surrendered and left the colony. The several hundred Scandinavians living in the area north of the Santhoeck, with their principal house of worship on Tinicum Island, did not want their political and judicial affairs handled by a Dutch Vice-Director and council at Fort Casimir who did not even converse in their language.

In the capitulation terms, as previously pointed out, Stuyvesant agreed that the Swedes and Finns who remained on the Delaware were permitted to enjoy the Augsburg Confession and have their own minister. American officials of the West India Company were generally prejudiced against those who were not members of the Dutch Reformed Church, despite the religious tolerance that existed in Holland. Stuyvesant's conciliatory gesture toward the Swedish Lutherans was a significant step toward coexistence. In a further attempt to placate the Swedes, Stuyvesant and his council decided to allow them to have their own deputy schout (a combination sheriff and prosecuting attorney), and also magistrates selected from among their people.

On August 14, 1656, Jacquet summoned Gregory van Dyck to Fort Casimir and notified him that Stuyvesant had named him the first deputy schout "among the Swedish nation." Swedish magistrates were also appointed although Hudde's brief minutes do not reveal the number nor their names. Gregory (also spelled Gregorius) van Dyck was a native of the Hague, but the contemporary accounts indicate his unswerving loyalty was to Sweden. He accompanied Ridder to New Sweden in 1640 as assistant commissary at Fort Christina; he served as head guard at Fort Elfsborg during Printz's administration; and he was a sergeant at Fort Trinity under Governor Rising.

Little is known about the activities of Schout van Dyck and the Swedish magistrates during the remainder of Jacquet's administration except, when Isaac Allerton attempted to collect delinquent accounts, the court at Fort Casimir informed him on January 31, 1657 that two of his debtors "belong to the jurisdiction of Tinnekonck. He was therefore referred to the court there."[26] This entry indicates that the Swedish magistrates appointed by Stuyvesant to serve their people had their judicial seat on Tinicum Island where Governor Printz built his gubernatorial mansion and held court almost fifteen years earlier. According to Governor Rising's journal he also held a court at Tinicum, as well as at Fort Trinity and Fort Christina—the earliest circuit court in the Delaware Valley.

During the closing days of his administration Jacquet was accused of misconduct by several colonists; Jan Schaggen claimed Jacquet seized land that belonged to him and drove him from his house; David Wessels claimed Jacquet tore down his house and used the wood to build a barn; Isack Allerton also complained against the Vice-Director. Formal charges were brought against him before the council at New Amsterdam alleging that "he conducted himself very unbecomingly there in vexing the community, prosecuting with violence the inhabitants, tyrannising over the soldiers, diminishing and destroying the Company's property, etc."[27]

In preparation for his defense Jacquet brought with him the financial records of his administration and voluntarily turned them over to the Council with the request that his accounts be carefully audited. After listening to his defense at a hearing, the Council excused him and allowed him to return to Fort Casimir with the understanding that he would be held responsible for any irregularities found in his accounts.

When the city of Amsterdam came into possession of Fort Casimir, to be discussed in the next chapter, Jacob Alrichs wrote Stuyvesant that he investigated the charges brought against Jacquet and found they were based on "more passion than reason" and he had arbitrated all the complaints.[28] When Jacquet left the employ of the Dutch West India Company he did not return to New Amsterdam but acquired a large tract on the south side of the Christina River. He kept a ferry there over the river for many years near the location the present Third Street Bridge, and he also achieved his ambition to be a farm proprietor during the years before his death in 1685.[29]

7. THE CITY'S COLONY

NOTHING LIKE IT has ever happened before or since in American history—a European city acquired ownership of an American colony. The city of Amsterdam in Holland (hereafter called the City) took over the governance of what is now New Castle, a turn of events that changed the economic, political, and social dimensions of the Dutch colony on the Delaware.

Stuyvesant's efforts to dominate New Sweden, as discussed in the previous chapter, resulted in military success but financial disaster. The expenses incurred in razing Fort Nassau and building Fort Casimir in the invasion of 1651, and recapturing it in the second invasion of 1655, were a drain on the West India Company's treasury. The Dutch failure to convert the colony into a self-sufficient community caused additional losses. The City's loan of the *Wagh* to Stuyvesant with the expenses of supporting its crew of more than 200 men and officers put the Company in debt to the City. The Company's losses were worsened by unsuccessful attempts to establish commercial settlements in Brazil and on the Guinea coast of Africa, and a combination of all of these reverses caused the Company's stock to plunge to a new low in 1654-55.

The Company lacked funds to expand its position on the Delaware River, which meant that the area was in danger of falling into English hands. This would jeopardize the entire New Netherland because New Amsterdam could not withstand an English vise exerting pressure from the north, south, and west. How could the Company meet this crisis, a matter of national pride? Fortunately several of the directors of the Amsterdam Chamber were also active in municipal affairs in Amsterdam, and they exerted a strong influence on the City's lord-mayors or burgomasters. A number of the burgomasters also owned large blocks of stock in the Company, and there were other interpersonal relations between City, Company, and the States General that time has obscured. What is known from existing records is that a proposition was made that the City take over Fort Casimir and the Santhoeck, which was discussed at length, and finally approved by committees representing both the Company and City. The negotiation became official on August 16, 1656 when it was ratified by the States General. The interlocking interest left no doubt that the City would have the Company's full cooperation and no rivalry was then anticipated even though the New Netherland would be divided into two parts. It was agreed that Peter Stuyvesant and other Company officials who continued to retain their posts at New Amsterdam would give their full cooperation to personnel sent by the City, and the City understood that its officials would be beholden to the Company in a number of ways which will be discussed.

The burgomasters decided that Fort Casimir would be renamed Fort Amstel, and the colony would be known as New Amstel (*Nieuwer Amstel*), the name of a village and country district then adjoining Amsterdam. Six of the burgomasters were selected to serve as the commissioners of New Amstel, prepare rules and regulations for its colonization, and act as a sort of absentee board of directors. The "conditions" offered by the City to attract colonists were jointly written by the commissioners and Company representatives, and publicized in placards and handbills widely distributed in the Netherlands.

Why did the burgomasters want to take over a withering Delaware colony? How could they justify expending the City's funds on a venture that had practically bankrupted the Company? The expressed reason for the City's investment was based on economics, and this was clearly stated; namely, the burgomasters "hath no intention to extend any authority or power abroad, but merely design *to promote commerce which is the soul of this city* . . ."[1] Italics added.

Amsterdam with its 200,000 people was a thriving commercial center, but its life blood was in its imports. Sugar, tobacco, and furs came from America; silks, porcelains, spices, perfumes, and other products were shipped from the East Indies; rye, wheat, barley, and other grains were imported from the Baltic, because the low-lying Dutch soil was not conducive to raising large grain crops. Amsterdam had few trees, and its shipbuilding industries depended upon oak and other hardwood from the Rhine countries, and the fir and pine used for decks, masts, and ships' stores came from Scandinavia.

In the judgement of the burgomasters a City-owned New World colony that supplied grains and lumber would relieve the City from its dependence on the Baltic and other European countries. It seemed reasonable to them to control as far as possible the source of these commodities critically needed in its industrial life. Recognizing that the Company erred in overextending itself, the burgomasters agreed to concentrate in a limited area of the New Netherland and encourage its representatives to focus on certain specific goals in the colony itself and to establish trade relations with the Indians, as well as English merchants in Maryland and Virginia.

The commissioners engaged Jacob Alrichs as the Director or Commissary General of New Amstel reporting directly to them. Alrichs had been in the Company's employ in Brazil and came highly recommended as an intelligent, resourceful business executive. Martin Crieger (sometimes spelled Kreyger or Krijger) who had returned home from New Amsterdam where he held several important positions in the Company's employ, was hired as the captain in command of fifty soldiers to be sent to protect the colonists and also act as a police force within the colony. Alexander d'Hinoyossa, who had served the Company as a military officer in Brazil and elsewhere, was employed as a lieutenant under Captain Crieger. Probably Alrichs, Crieger, and d'Hinoyossa all played a part in selecting the soldiers who became City employes and were paid stipulated wages and subsistence expenses.

The Company deeded to the City the land from the west side of the Christina River running south along the Delaware to Bombay Hook. The City accepted the Indian deeds negotiated by Stuyvesant in 1651 when he built Fort Casimir as valid evidence of the Company's unencumbered ownership of this territory. Fort Altena on the east side of the Christina River remained in the Company's control, and the Company's soldiers stationed there continued to take their orders from Stuyvesant at New Amsterdam. Conversely, the City's soldiers to be billeted at New Amstel would be under the jurisdiction of Alrichs, Crieger, and d'Hinoyossa.

The burgomasters made terms very attractive to potential colonists because they were well aware of the difficulties the Company had in inducing Dutch families to go to America. The colonists were not generally employed by the City, but were considered individual entrepreneurs with no limit on their earnings. The City agreed to buy all the grain they raised, the lumber they felled and sawed, the animal pelts they obtained from the Indians, the fish they dried and salted, or any other products marketable in the Netherlands.

The colonists, their families, and their furniture and household goods would be transported at the City's expense, and when their income permitted they would reimburse the City.

Tools and farming implements belonging to the colonists would be transported free of charge and no reimbursement was necessary. The City agreed to furnish food, clothing, and seed grain free of charge for a year, and to provide suitable land free of taxes for ten years. The colonists could cut timber without charge, and hunting and fishing were free. If a colonist discovered minerals, crystals, or precious stones he could possess his findings during his first ten years in America; after ten years he was required to pay 10% of the proceeds to the West India Company. In this way the Company still had an opportunity to benefit from any gold, silver, or copper mines it was rumored could be found in the New Netherland.

The City would transport grain, seed, timber, and other marketable products back to Amsterdam at no cost to the colonists. There the city would maintain a warehouse for New Amstel imports and sell the merchandise on behalf of the owner, deducting 2% commission and applying 10% of the net proceeds to cover the cost of the colonist's passage to America until such expense was liquidated. The remaining proceeds would be credited to the colonist's account. Colonists were obliged to remain in America four years unless given special permission to leave.

The City agreed to lay out streets and lots in New Amstel and to divide the land beyond the town into farm fields and pastures. The City would maintain a storehouse stocked with a variety of merchandise that the colonists would purchase on credit at the same prices prevailing in Amsterdam, with one exception. Since the City was obliged to pay custom duties to the Company on both exports and imports into the City's colony, that duty would be added to the price of merchandise purchased by the colonists. This is another example of how the company received benefits from the colony—although it was agreed that the custom duties would be used to build and maintain public works in New Netherland jointly approved by Company and City. Finally, a smithy, a wheelwright, a carpenter, a minister, and a schoolmas-

ter would be provided at the City's expense for the convenience
and service of the colonists.

The economic incentives were liberal and attractive, and the
colonists were also assured of enjoying the same administration
of justice and the same political rights they had in the Netherlands. A schout was to be named by the City's commissioners
in Holland, but three burgomasters to officiate in New Amstel
were supposed to be appointed by the burghers or citizens of
New Amstel from "the honestest, fittest, and richest." The
City's commissioners were to appoint from five to seven schepens
(magistrates) from a list submitted by the citizens. The City's
commissioners elected to delegate to Director Alrichs the right,
through a power of attorney, to make the appointments of the
schout and schepens. When New Amstel's population reached
200 families the citizens would elect a common, self-supporting
council of twenty-one men who would meet with the three
burgomasters and resolve matters relating to the town government.

The political and judicial structure seems to have been quite
complicated, but the intent was to introduce elements of democ-
racy without sacrificing the authority of Director Alrichs or of
the commissioners. In actual practice Alrichs had to use his own
judgement in organizing a government because the theoretical
structure didn't fit the circumstances; for example, during his
administration the number of families didn't reach 200. There
was also a lack of competent persons to serve all the positions
envisioned by the commissioners, and the best alternative Alrichs
could find was to establish a council of from three to six
members selected by him from the most prominent residents.
The council functioned as an executive, legislative, and judicial
body much the same as Jacquet's council had functioned and
similar to the way Stuyvesant and his council operated.

Stuyvesant and his council also kept abreast of what was
going on in New Amstel, and were able to exercise restraints on
Alrichs when they felt it was necessary. Although New Amstel
ostensibly belonged to the City, the Company did not com-

pletely relinquish all rights and powers. For instance, the schepens at New Amstel had the authority to pronounce sentences in criminal cases and civil suits involving judgements of less than 100 guilders, later increased to 600 guilders. However, a litigant could appeal their decision to Stuyvesant and his council in New Amsterdam. This was a curious situation—the court of appeals from the City's municipal court consisted of executives in the employ of the West India Company! This intertwining of City and Company was also manifest in other ways, which seems to have been a deliberate duality to capitalize on Stuyvesant's valuable experience and to create checks and balances.

Jacob Alrichs and his wife left the Netherlands on December 25, 1656 on the largest of four vessels in the flotilla; the *Prins Maurits* (*Prince Maurice*) manned by a crew of sixteen sailors, carrying 112 persons, including fifty soldiers with Captain Crieger, Lieutenant d'Hinoyossa and their families. The *Beer* (*Bear*), conveyed thirty-three colonists, the *Bever* (*Beaver*) carried eleven, and the *Gelderse Blom* (*Flower of Guilderland*) also brought eleven—a grand total of 167. As they neared the American coast the ships were separated by a storm, but the three smaller vessels arrived safely at New Amsterdam. The *Prins Maurits*, commanded by a skipper and officers unfamiliar with American waters, ran aground on Long Island. Most of the cargo was salvaged before the waves tore the vessel apart, but some of the material intended for building purposes was lost.

With considerable difficulty and inconvenience, the colonists and soldiers finally converged at New Amstel in the spring of 1657. Gerrit van Sweringen, the former supercargo on the *Prins Maurits*, and a Company employe, asked for a discharge and was given permission to remain in New Amsterdam as a freeman. On Stuyvesant's orders the bronze and iron cannon belonging to the Company at Fort Casimir were sold to the City, although some of the Company's property was either transferred to Fort Altena or shipped to New Amsterdam. The Company's

soldiers also vacated Fort Casimir, and a few of them were left
in a small garrison stationed at Fort Altena.

Evert Pietersen who came with Alrichs as a combination
schoolmaster and sieckentrooster, or "comforter of the sick"
(there was no minister in the first expedition), wrote that when
they arrived at New Amstel on April 25, 1657 they found
"twenty families there, mostly Swedes, not more than five or
six families belonging to our nation." He started a school
promptly in one of the houses and soon had twenty-five pupils.
He lacked paper, pens, slates, and pencils, but somehow managed to teach reading, writing, and arithmetic in New Castle's
first school.[2] If there were Swedish or Finnish pupils enrolled
in the school they were taught in the Dutch language.

Alrichs wrote in one of his letters that there were twenty
families living in the houses near the fort at the time he arrived,
but in another letter he said the inhabitants consisted of only
twelve or thirteen families. He did not indicate how many were
Dutch and how many were Swedes or Finns, but Pietersen
clearly states the latter outnumbered the Dutch. The small population, reported by both men, indicates that in the latter days of
the Jacquet administration many families vacated the town.
Some may have left when they learned that the City was taking
over, and others because they had grown to resent Jacquet who
had become harsh and dictatorial. Some of these Dutch emigrés
may have gone either to New Amsterdam or to Maryland to live,
and some of the Swedes and Finns joined their countrymen in
the farming communities lying between the Christina and the
Schuylkill.

About a month after his arrival, Alrichs wrote to the commissioners in Amsterdam stating that, "The Colonists, free me-
chanics, civil servants, with the freemen who were here before
our arrival, and some few who have come and settled here since
may amount to about sixty men capable of bearing arms." His
figures do not include the approximately fifty soldiers, many
with wives and children, as well as maid servants, who were

entitled to receive subsistence as well as the soldiers and their families. The number of females and children accompanying the soldiers is not known. It would appear that at the outset the total population of New Amstel—military, civil, and administrative—probably amounted to 300 or 400 people, but it was an unstable population.

When Jacquet turned the keys of the fort over to Alrichs the latter immediately recognized a serious problem he had not anticipated. He had been led to believe that the officers, soldiers, and their families would be able to dwell in the barracks in the fort where he had been told there were residences, a bake house, a guardhouse, a powder magazine, and facilities for the storage of food and supplies. What he saw was the ruins of a structure having little value either for military or residential use. The gun carriages and platforms were in such a ruinous condition that they could not accomodate gunners or armaments. The front of the fort had washed away in the river, and the barracks and other buildings were so decayed that their roofs leaked, and their walls offered little protection against the weather.

While Crieger and d'Hinoyossa were in New Amsterdam before coming to New Amstel they apparently learned from Company soldiers who had returned from the Delaware that Fort Casimir was in disrepair and was not a suitable place to house their families. Before leaving they found owners of two of the existing houses at the Santhoeck who had moved to New Amsterdam and they made arrangements either to purchase or rent their former dwellings. When they arrived at New Amstel they were able to house their families in comfort, but when the soldiers saw the condition of the fort compared to the officers' homes they insisted upon more suitable living quarters. Temporary shelters had to be built to protect them from the weather while the fort was being rebuilt.

Lacking storage facilities Alrichs was forced to construct a makeshift shelter of boards and timbers covered with old canvas sails to protect the food, clothing, tools, and other supplies intended for use by the colonists. Rebuilding the fort was a major undertaking requiring palisades, timbers, planks, bricks, tiles, hardware, nails, tar, and other building material, as well as horses and oxen to haul the building supplies. The materials his vessels brought from Holland were inadequate to meet the needs.

Stuyvesant provided as much assistance as he could, charging the City for livestock, carpenters' tools, nails, clapboards, bricks, tiles, lime, and other supplies, as well as the cost of transporting the goods to New Amstel from Fort Orange (present Albany) or New Amsterdam. Bricks, incidentally, were primarily used for ovens, chimneys, and fireplaces; they were too scarce for use in building brick houses. A brick kiln was later erected at New Amstel in 1659, but production was limited, and most of the bricks came initially from brickmakers at Fort Orange or were imported from Holland. Alrichs's letters to the commissioners, which are on record, emphasize the critical need for skilled carpenters, iron padlocks, knives, adzes, crosscut saws, picks, sickles, augers, iron pots and kettles, nails, and other materials.

Alrichs knew that winter would bring additional problems, and he lost no time in conveying building lots to the colonists, instructing each owner to plant vegetable gardens and encircle his property with a fence. The colonists were also encouraged to plant winter grains in the farmland beyond the town. He aided the colonists in erecting makeshift shelters to lodge their families while they awaited the availability of building materials. He hired Andries Hudde, who still lived at New Amstel, to survey the home lots one adjacent to another with common fences between them, and he also engaged Hudde as a combination clerk-secretary-deputy sheriff, the same position he held during the Jacquet administration. Hudde sold his house on the Strand to Alrichs for use as a church, and when the first clergyman, Evardus Welius, arrived in the City's colony he conducted Dutch Reformed services there.

Welius served as the town's pastor for only two years, and in

1659, the year of his death, membership had grown to the point that the church-house had to be enlarged. The commissioners sent a bell from Holland, but whether this was mounted on a pole in front of the church or in some kind of belfry is not known. The contemporary records indicate that the commissioners instructed Alrichs that no religion except the Reformed Church should be tolerated at New Amstel, and under no circumstances was a Swedish minister allowed to teach Lutheran theology.

Although the church did not have a pastor after Welius's death, and for unknown reasons he was never replaced, services of prayer, sermon reading, and psalm-singing were conducted by lay readers and comforters of the sick during the period the City owned the colony. Four years after Welius's death, a young Lutheran minister named Abelius Zetskoorn arrived from Holland to become the schoolmaster in New Amstel. He never performed the duties of a minister in the town, but since he was conversant in Swedish he once preached a sermon to the Swedish congregation at the church on Tinicum Island. The Swedes wanted him to stay as a combination teacher-preacher, but the Dutch residents of New Amstel insisted upon his return to teach their children, which he did. But they wanted no part of his religion.[3]

Alrichs was a persistent and conscientious director, and despite adversity of many kinds he was able to report in 1659 that the community consisted of 110 houses, the fort had been renovated and contained new barracks for the soldiers, a new guardhouse, a new bakery, a forge, and a number of renovated dwellings within the perimeter of the fort. Alrichs and his wife lived for a while in one of these houses which he patiently restored, but he later built a new dwelling on the Strand, also large enough to accommodate his servants. At this time New Castle had a full-fledged tavern, also on the Strand, operated by Foppe Jansen Outhout. The quasi-resident tavern keepers of the Jacquet administration were now replaced by a professional, and there was no decline in the substantial consumption of beer, wine, and other alcoholic beverages by soldiers and civilians previously discussed.

The Santhoeck had no fast-flowing streams suitable to turn grist and saw mills, which was also true of the majority of the cities in Holland where windmills provided a source of power. Thousands of pounds of flour had to be imported to feed the colonists, and Alrichs's solution was to build a horsemill, which was under construction in 1658, but due to the death of the builder the mill was not completed and in operation until 1662.[4]

This horsemill which accommodated the townsfolk and nearby farmers for at least a decade is believed to have been located near the river at the south end of present Fourth Street, but no contemporary description of it remains. In the horsemills built in the Netherlands an upright shaft was turned by the traction of one or more horses harnessed to it on the ground floor. At the top of the shaft near the ceiling a large wheel was attached, which revolved as the horses began their circular route. The wheel was connected to shafting and other mechanical linkage which caused the millstones to revolve. In 1681-82 a windmill was built at New Castle but this was in the English period, which is beyond the purview of the present account.[5]

New Amstel continued to grow; the First Row had been extended and became part of the Strand; the Second Row became Beaver Street as additional houses were built. Apparently all the houses faced the river, the gardens in the back. Between them was an area later called the "Market plaine," the present Green, although the latter term was not used during the City's period of ownership. Nevertheless, despite the town's physical growth, Alrichs was hampered and inhibited by many things beyond his control which prevented achieving the success the burgomasters were looking for. The colonists who arrived with him, and those subsequently sent by the City, could not raise enough food to support themselves. There were too many artisans, clerks, and craftsmen such as weavers, shoemakers, button makers, tailors, and the like, and not enough dirt farmers to accomodate those who had no experience in farming and lumbering and had to be fed at the City's expense.

Not only were there too few farmers, but spells of unfavorable weather reduced the yield from the fields. Heavy rains and droughts ruined the limited grain crops, and severe winter weather made life an ordeal for the whole community. In his letters Alrichs also speaks of "a worm" which destroyed grains and vegetables in the fields during favorable weather. This was in an era long before biological sprays and there was no way to combat this destructive parasite.

The worst tragedy came in the form of an epidemic characterized by general sickness and burning fevers that spread through the town. During the second year of New Amstel's existence more than a hundred men, women, and children died, including Alrichs's wife. Those who survived were left weak and undernourished and many were unable to work. Malnutrition caused by a scarcity of grain and fodder resulted in the deaths of many animals. The town became a place of misfortune and sadness, and dissatisfaction, hunger, and pestilence brought the colony to the edge of ruin.

Some families wanted to leave and reside in New Amsterdam or in the Company's jurisdiction north of New Amstel. Alrichs insisted that they remain and serve the full four years they had agreed to live in New Amstel. He claimed they wanted to leave in order to evade their indebtedness to the City. Some probably slipped away without his consent for this reason, whereas others who offered to discharge their debts were not permitted to leave. Alrichs was so exacting in following the rules and regulations laid down by the commissioners that his inflexibility caused him to be resented by some and hated by others. When he had to ration food, and reduce the quantities, it caused further dissatisfaction.

In 1659 six enlisted soldiers deserted their command and fled to Maryland—Hans Roeloff of Stockholm, Andries Thomasen of Jutland in Denmark, Cornelis Jurriaensen of Winseren in Sweden, Jacob Jansen of Antwerp, Jan Hinger of Utrecht, and Evert Brants of Amesfort. They took their families and maid servants with them.[6]

The burgomasters in Amsterdam were painfully disappointed because they were not enjoying the profitable imports they expected, and the City was going deeper into debt to support the colony. No grain shipments had been received from New Amstel because the colonists were unable to raise enough to feed themselves and their livestock. The epidemic left too few able-bodied men to engage in lumbering, and the fur trade was practically at a standstill. There was so much to do, and not enough competent people to do it. The City initially invested 30,000 guilders to start the colony, but the need to supply foodstuffs and larger quantities of supplies, and to finance ships' voyages necessitated borrowing money from private sources, plus interest. Within a short time, at least 150,000 guilders were invested in the colony, an enormous sum for the time, having the purchasing power of several millions of dollars today—and the returns were negligible.

To make matters worse relations between the Company and City officials in the New Netherland began to deteriorate. Alrichs became embroiled in a number of disputes not only with the Company, but with one of his key officers, Captain Martin Crieger, whose commission from the burgomasters gave him full authority over officers and soldiers "to obey all and whatsoever he may command them." Crieger claimed Alrichs admonished the soldiers for minor offenses instead of delegating the authority to him. They also had other differences which led Crieger to submit his resignation to the City and return to New Amsterdam with his family where he was re-employed by the Company.

Company officials accused shippers of surreptitiously unloading merchandise at New Amstel without having paid the duties they were required to pay the Company in Holland before sailing.[7] The Company's representatives inspected the exports in the home port and stamped their approval directly on the shipments, but some shippers whose vessels were chartered by the City smuggled merchandise out of the country and then smuggled it into New Amstel. Shippers were also required to pay an ad valorem duty on products obtained in the New Netherland for shipment to Holland, and some also evaded this tariff. The consequence of the smuggling was that merchants at New Amstel could undersell those at New Amsterdam who observed the regulations and paid duties to the Company. The Company expected Alrichs to cooperate and make certain no contraband came in or out of the town, but the City did not provide him with a customs inspector. He did what he could, and on one occasion seized a shipment of thirty-five muskets smuggled ashore, but time did not allow him to undertake a responsibility that rested with the Company. He recommended that Gerrit van Sweringen, the former supercargo on the *Prins Maurits*, be sent to New Amstel from New Amsterdam as a commissary with the responsibility of a customs inspector.[8]

In the spring of 1658 Stuyvesant personally visited the settlements on the Delaware—his third visit to New Castle. He carefully examined the procedures in handling cargoes, and he also visited Fort Altena and laid out some lots there to be sold to colonists. He also sailed up to Tinicum Island, the heart of the Swedish community, and there he reappointed the Swedish officials, Sheriff Gregorius van Dyck, and the magistrates (also known as commissioners) Olof Stille, Mathys Hanson, Peter Rambo, and Peter Cock who functioned as a council. He also permitted the Swedes to form a militia under their own officers, Captain Sven Skute, Lieutenant Andries Dalbo, and Ensign Jacob Swensen.[9] These three officers were no strangers to Stuyvesant; they all held commands at the former Fort Trinity when he forced its surrender. In the meantime they had sworn allegiance to Holland and the West India Company, and Stuyvesant as the Director was their commander-in-chief.

Stuyvesant believed that by allowing the Swedes local auton-
omy with their own political and military leaders that there was
less chance of resistance to the Dutch that might result in
mutiny. When the directors in Amsterdam learned what he had
done they strongly opposed allowing the Swedes to have their
own local government, and especially a militia. They did not
trust the Swedes, and instructed Stuyvesant that when the terms
of the Swedish officers expired they must be replaced with
Dutchmen. In addition the directors ordered that he should
prevent any concentrated Swedish settlements from forming, but
that he should scatter the families.[10]

Upon his return from the Delaware, Stuyvesant and his council decided that a Company employe should be sent to New
Amstel, not only as a customs inspector, but also to administer
the Company's economic and political affairs as Jacquet had
done. If Jacquet had not left office under a cloud he would have
been a suitable candidate for the position, but Willem Beeckman,
a schepen and elder in New Amsterdam, was appointed as
Commissary and Vice Director of the Company's Delaware
colony. He was instructed to supervise the Company's soldiers
and freemen, administer law and justice in both civil and military cases, as well as minor criminal cases, maintain the Dutch
Reformed Church, and to make certain that no goods were laden
or unladen without paying tariffs to the Company.[11]

Beeckman was invested with authority at Fort Altena and the
land northward to the Schuylkill, but was instructed to allow the
Swedes to administer justice through their own officers until
such time as the circumstances required a change. Alrichs remained in charge of New Amstel and the land southward to
Bombay Hook. Beeckman moved his family to a house at Fort
Altena with the intention of renting a house in New Amstel at
Company's expense when he found a suitable dwelling, according to his instructions. Beeckman was paid fifty guilders per
month salary and 200 guilders annually for commutation of
rations, the same remuneration paid Jacquet. However, Beeckman

was also entitled to share, at the Company's discretion, in the value of any smuggled goods he confiscated.

One of the first assignments Stuyvesant gave Beeckman was to purchase the land from the Indians south of Bombay Hook to Cape Henlopen. This may seem peculiar since the Company had divested most of the colony to the City, but the plans were that after Beeckman made the purchase the land would then be transferred to the City.[12] This arrangement had been approved in Amsterdam by the Company and City executives because they all feared that the English were planning to make a settlement at the mouth of the bay. This apprehension was confirmed when two small boats with fourteen Englishmen from Virginia were cast ashore at Cape Henlopen where they were captured by the Indians. Learning of the incident, Stuyvesant recommended that Alrichs take the English into custody. Alrichs sent a vessel to Cape Henlopen authorizing the captain to pay a ransom to the Indians to free the English and bring them to New Amstel. The Company sharply criticized Alrichs for allowing these intruders to come to New Amstel and ordered that they should be returned to Virginia, "and under no circumstances ever to admit anyone of the English nation there again, much less encourage them to come there."[13]

Following instructions received from Amsterdam, Alrichs and Stuyvesant jointly planned for two negotiators to go to the Hoerekil and buy land from the Indians—Beeckman representing the Company and d'Hinoyossa representing the City. Twenty of the City's soldiers were sent under d'Hinoyossa's command, which practically stripped New Amstel of its defenders, and Beeckman took a number of the Company's soldiers with him. Evidently the Dutch thought that the uniformed men bearing arms would impress the Indians with their military strength, although no doubt messengers were sent in advance to assure the Indians that the soldiers came in peace. On June 7, 1659 a deed of sale was signed by sixteen Indian chiefs and great men in exchange for kettles, mirrors, knives, beads, duffel cloth, and other merchandise. The witnesses as their names were spelled in the document were Alixander Boeyer (Sander Boyer), who acted as interpreter, Michel Poulussen, Jan Broersen, Hendrick van Bylevelts, Jacob Jacobsen, and Pieter Alrichs who was Jacob Alrichs's nephew.[14] This is the earliest reference the writer has found to Peter Alrichs who later figured prominently in the City's colony, but at this time the records are not clear whether he was employed by the City or the Company.

After the deed was signed the soldiers built a fort, which became known as "the Company's fort," although d'Hinoyossa remained there on behalf of the City in command of the City's soldiers.[15] The Company's soldiers returned to Fort Altena with Beeckman. The City now owned the land from the Christina River as far south as Cape Henlopen, and the entire area was under Alrichs's direction.

Unknown to Alrichs, Stuyvesant was reporting to the directors in Holland that the City's colony was "in a very deplorable state," and soldiers and their families and colonists with their families were fleeing to Virginia and Maryland. On September 17, 1659, Stuyvesant wrote that hardly thirty families remained at New Amstel, and the original contingent of fifty soldiers was reduced to one-half, and of these the majority were stationed at the fort at the Hoerekil. He warned that action should be taken at once before a calamity occurred such as an attack by Indians, or an invasion by Swedes or English.[16]

Stuyvesant had good reasons to suspect the English, especially those in Maryland. A new governor, Josias Fendall, appointed by Cecil Calvert, had taken office, and the news spread that Fendall intended to enforce Lord Baltimore's rights under the terms of the Maryland Charter. According to his interpretation, all the territory now comprising the state of Delaware was included in the grant James I made to the Calverts. Thus, the City's colony at New Amstel, the fort at the Hoerekil, and the Company's Fort Altena were all on Maryland territory. The Maryland Council ordered Colonel Nathaniel Utie, a bold and arrogant officer, to go to New Amstel and persuade the Dutch to become Maryland subjects or vacate Lord Baltimore's property.

Colonel Utie was accompanied by his brother George, his cousin, Major Samuel Goldsmith, Jacob de Vrint (alias Young), and a servant. One can imagine how the officers resplendent in their uniforms, swords at their sides, marched into Foppe Outhout's hostelry to demand the best accomodations available to officers in the services of the King of England and Lord Baltimore's personal emissaries. With de Vrint as his Dutch interpreter, Utie accosted the townsfolk, threatening to drive them away and plunder their homes if they did not acknowledge Lord Baltimore's sovereignty.

Utie demanded an official audience with Director Alrichs, who hurriedly sent a messenger to Fort Altena urging Beeckman to come at once. In the transfer of New Amstel to the City the West India Company was a guarantor of any loss suffered by the City due to encumbered deeds, and Alrichs knew that Beeckman as a Company official was obliged to come to his assistance. In the conference that ensued Utie repeated his warnings and added if the Dutch leaders refused him he would not be responsible for any spilled blood, because the charter empowered Lord Baltimore to make war against trespassers.

Alrichs's military forces at New Amstel then consisted of eight soldiers, two cadets, and one sergeant; Beeckman's defenses at Fort Altena amounted to twenty-one soldiers—an insignificant army to protect the colony against an invasion of a rumored Maryland army of 500 soldiers, a much exaggerated figure. Beeckman and Alrichs asked for three weeks grace to consult with Stuyvesant, and Colonel Utie reluctantly granted the delay, threatening them that if acquiesence was not forthcoming in three weeks he would return with the Maryland army.

When Stuyvesant received the news he was furious, and addressed a reply jointly to Alrichs and Beeckman stating they had given a "stupid answer" to the "frivolous demands of

Colonel Utie." He said they should have arrested him as a spy and sent him in chains to New Amsterdam to be tried. He added he was sending Captain Martin Crieger, then a burgomaster at New Amsterdam, and Cornelis van Ruyven, secretary, with sixty soldiers to reinforce the garrisons at New Amstel and Fort Altena, and when and if the English came the Dutch would be prepared to repel the invaders. Crieger's instructions from Stuyvesant, which must have irritated Alrichs because no love was lost between the two men, stated that "the brave Martin Crieger, mayor of the City of Amsterdam in the New Netherland" must be obeyed by "all major and minor officers and soldiers."[17]

Crieger informed Alrichs that he must take drastic steps to keep up the City's forces by conscripting fifty townsmen and arming them to defend the town. Alrichs took the position that it was the West India Company's duty to protect the City's colony against the English because the Company had guaranteed clear title to the land conveyed to the City. Alrichs had always maintained the City's troops were there to protect against a possible Indian attack and to function as a police force in maintaining order in New Amstel, but not to repel European invaders.

Colonel Utie did not show up on the designated day, nor thereafter, and no English troops marched against New Amstel. In due time Ruyven, Crieger, and their men returned to Manhattan, and Stuyvesant resorted to diplomatic means by sending representatives from New Amsterdam to meet with the Maryland authorities. This is another story which has been told elsewhere.[18]

As a result of reports Stuyvesant sent to Amsterdam, Alrichs was sharply reprimanded in a letter signed by two members of the Amsterdam Chamber. They told him flatly "the Company has reserved for itself supreme authority and supervision. Consequently, the aforesaid colony cannot be considered anything else but a subordinate colony under the West India Company. . ."[19]

This also upset Alrichs, because his instructions and financial support came from the City. Now the Company clearly indicated he was expected to serve two masters, which meant subservience to the Company's officials in the New Netherland, and the possibility he would soon be expected to take orders from Crieger and Beeckman, as well as Stuyvesant. About this time rumors were heard in America that the City's colony would soon be returned to the Company because the venture had been a costly failure.

No objective account of Alrichs's administration was written by a contemporary observer. There is no series of court records such as occurred during the Jacquet administration discussed in the previous chapter. It is not clear how his council functioned, and one cannot be certain of the persons on the council except that Andries Hudde, Gerrit van Sweringen, Abraham van Rynevelt, and Alexander d'Hinoyossa seem to have held positions of authority delegated by the director. Stuyvesant's copybooks containing his letters to Alrichs have not survived, although a number of Alrichs's letters to Stuyvesant have been preserved, and this one-way correspondence gives the historian some insight of Alrichs's character. His administration lasted a little more than two years, a disappointing, frustrating experience for an intelligent, honest, and conscientious business executive.

Alrichs's main personality weakness was that he was inflexible and unswervingly followed his instructions to the letter. This resulted in his unpopularity with colonists living off the City's limited stores. He was plagued by his superiors who expected instant results, and in carrying out his orders he was accused by Stuyvesant of "too great preciseness," which caused colonists and soldiers to desert the colony.

Alrichs fell ill with the same undiagnosed illness that had taken the lives of his wife and hundreds of others, and he died at New Amstel on December 20, 1659.

8. THE ENGLISH CONQUEST

JACOB ALRICHS STATED in a clause in his will that
Lieutenant Alexander d'Hinoyossa was his choice to succeed
him as Director and Commissary General of the City's colony.
He doubtless would have been less supportive of d'Hinoyossa if
he knew that the lieutenant (also referred to as captain-lieutenant)
had been writing letters behind his back to the burgomasters in
Amsterdam criticizing him on many counts, including nepotism
for appointing one of his nephews, Cornelis van Gezel, as
secretary of the council. Of course, the authority to appoint his
successor did not rest with Alrichs, but with the burgomasters.
Nevertheless, d'Hinoyossa as the second in command assumed
they would accept Alrichs's recommendation, and immediately
following the latter's death he took over, giving himself the title
of "president." He unseated van Gezel whom he disliked, and
selected Johan Crato to take his place on the council. He named
one of his cronies, the schout Gerrit van Sweringen as secretary
of the council, and appointed Dr. Jan Willemsen the surgeon,
and Hans Block, a constable, to sit on the council as magistrates
when certain matters were under discussion.[1]

D'Hinoyossa's council, like Jacquet's and Alrichs's, constituted New Amstel's legislative and executive branches, but at
times some members functioned as a court of law in the role of
magistrates. Legal matters continued to be adjudicated in a
courtroom upstairs in the fort, and the somewhat unorthodox
court was dominated by d'Hinoyossa. New members took their
place on the council as needed; when Jan Willemsen died Pieter
Pietersz was appointed. Joost de La Grange became a member,
and Hendrick Kip, Jacob Crabbe, Baes Joosten, Henri Couturier,
and others also served at various times. All the decisions were
subject to reversal by the commissioners in Amsterdam, but this
rarely occurred. They were too far removed from the colony to
keep abreast of all the details, and d'Hinoyossa was the main
decision-maker. Since there was an official secretary, minutes
must have been kept of the proceedings of the council and
decisions of the court, but if they have survived their whereabouts is not known. Practically all that is known about the
business of the court and council is found in Beeckman's gos-
sipy letters to Stuyvesant. Since Beeckman was employed by
the Company and was not a member of the council, what he
wrote must be regarded as unofficial and cannot be characterized as council or court records.

It is also regrettable that little is known of d'Hinoyossa's
background; his surname suggests non-Dutch ancestry, probably
Italian or Spanish, but it is believed he was a member of an
aristocratic family that came to the Netherlands and became
influential in Amsterdam. His haughty manners and arbitrary
methods caused some of the colonists in New Amstel to refer to
him as "the little prince," suggesting he was not a tall man. At
this time he was still in his late twenties. He antagonized many
with whom he had dealings, including Peter Stuyvesant and
Willem Beeckman.

Beeckman, who lived alternately at Fort Altena, and in a
rented house at New Amstel where he could check the incoming
and outgoing cargoes and collect duties for the Company, was

in close contact with d'Hinoyossa, and both men resented each other. Beeckman's letters to Stuyvesant are full of complaints about d'Hinoyossa. Neither Beeckman nor Stuyvesant were impartial in their judgements because both were devoted employes of the West India Company, and anyone who criticized or questioned their actions risked their displeasure. Beeckman said that d'Hinoyossa threatened to fine anyone under his jurisdiction who did not speak well of him, which may have been true, and there is no question that d'Hinoyossa was resentful of the Company's interference, and it irked him that an official over whom he had no authority was the customs collector in the City's colony.

There are many examples in the records of d'Hinoyossa's vindictiveness, such as his treatment of Sergeant Willem van Dieman, a soldier who had served under him at New Amstel. Something happened that caused him to bear a grudge against the sergeant, and Dieman's wife claimed he confiscated their plow, ox, canoe, and otherwise harassed them; other complaints were made against d'Hinoyossa.[2]

The burgomasters in Amsterdam and their commissioners for the colony, astute politico-merchants, saw d'Hinoyossa from another light. He was descended from a family having influence; he had originally been recommended by the Company because of his military service in Brazil; and Alrichs reported favorably on his loyalty to the City even recommending him as his successor. Thus, when the burgomasters finally resolved on August 27, 1660, about eight months after Alrichs's death, to continue to support the colony, and not return it to the Company, they appointed d'Hinoyossa as the new Director and Commissary General. This left no doubt that they held him in high regard, and as a further vote of confidence confirmed his appointment of Johan Crato and Gerrit van Sweringen as assistants and councillors. When d'Hinoyossa opened the letter from Holland giving him the good news he jubilantly ordered that three shots be fired from the cannon at the fort.[3]

Some historians are inclined to consider d'Hinoyossa as a scoundrel, and there is little doubt that there was some rascality in his behavior, but probably not to the extent blamed on him. One must not overlook that he inherited a deteriorating colony that the City was on the verge of giving up, and his administration should be viewed in that context. New Amstel was in a sorry financial condition, its population at an all-time low, and none of the burgomasters' objectives had been attained. A firm hand and innovative action were needed to correct the problems. Much has been made of a letter that Hudde wrote to Stuyvesant alleging that d'Hinoyossa sold the City's property, including a pair of millstones, a brewing kettle, smith's bellows, linens, and sundry other goods to the English in Maryland for his own personal gain.[4] Proof is lacking to support these accusations, nor were any official charges brought against d'Hinoyossa, and at this late date it is impossible to separate fact from hearsay.

On the other hand, there is documented evidence that Hudde may have had motives for dishonoring d'Hinoyossa. The City still owed money to him for the house in New Amstel that he sold to Jacob Alrichs for use as a church, which was still in use during d'Hinoyossa's administration. Hudde wrote that when he repeatedly tried to collect the balance due him that d'Hinoyossa turned him away with evasive answers. There is no doubt that Hudde was an opportunist and he worked at one time for the Company and at another for the City when it suited his best interests. When d'Hinoyossa took office he discharged Hudde as a City employe which did not contribute to good relations between the two men. Hudde then moved from New Amstel to Fort Altena where he rejoined the Company as a "Clerk and Reader" assisting Beeckman. Evidently he read church services at the fort and assisted Beeckman with clerical matters. Hudde was advised, "That if he conducts himself in this position as is proper, his further advancement will be considered in due time."[5] Obviously it was to Hudde's advantage to side with Beeckman against "the little prince."

In January of 1660, d'Hinoyossa brought Peter Alrichs into the executive circle by naming him commander of the little fort at the Hoerekil.[6] Peter was a personable, intelligent Dutchman of unusual competency. He spoke English and was familiar with some of the Indian dialects. He served the colony as a military officer, Indian trader, planter, merchant, and later became a justice in the William Penn government and a member of the Provincial Council of Pennsylvania.

On March 29, 1662 d'Hinoyossa issued a proclamation forbidding anyone to trade with the Indians in the area between Bombay Hook and Cape Henlopen except Peter Alrichs.[7] The records do not clarify why d'Hinoyossa took this action nor what kind of financial arrangement was made with Alrichs. Since it was a public proclamation it is a reasonable guess that he was trying to monopolize the fur trade for the City, and the likelihood is that the City paid Alrichs a commission on the pelts he bartered for the City's goods. This is another example where Beeckman criticized d'Hinoyossa in a letter to Stuyvesant, but he failed to obtain a copy of the proclamation, and its contents remain unknown. Beeckman was not malicious—Joost de la Grange found him "an honest and civil man,"—but in his efforts to keep Stuyvesant informed we have only a one-sided view. No letters or reports written by d'Hinoyossa are available to explain why he made certain decisions, and some may have been made on orders from his superiors in Amsterdam.

What is certain is that d'Hinoyossa's appointment as Director resulted in a renaissance in the City's colony. Instead of squabbling with the English in Maryland over land ownership and boundaries d'Hinoyossa invited Governor Philip Calvert to participate in trade relations, which would be beneficial to both the English and the Dutch. The so-called Navigation Acts passed by Parliament were designed to enable England to triumph over France, Spain, and especially Holland in the struggle for world power. Among other things, Parliament declared that no products originating in Asia, Africa, or America could be carried to

England, Ireland, or the English colonies except in English, Irish, or colonial ships, manned by sailors who, for the most part, were British subjects.

A modification of the legislation—the Navigation Act of 1660—prescribed that no foreign ships could import any of the products of the English colonies into England. By restricting commerce from the colonies to English vessels, the English merchant marine was bolstered, and rigid control was placed on the custom duties collected on the shipments. This legislation was not popular in Maryland where planters and merchants preferred open trade to avoid taxes.

By purchasing tobacco direct from Maryland merchants d'Hinoyossa was able to assist them in circumventing English duties. The merchants brought the tobacco to him in New Amstel, or he sent carriers to Maryland to pick it up. He then shipped the tobacco to Holland in Dutch vessels where it was in demand. In fact, the small amounts of tobacco raised on the Delaware were insignificant in terms of the total market in the United Netherlands.

To pay the English for the tobacco they sold duty-free to the Dutch, the City's colony could supply two products much in demand in Maryland: (a) strong Dutch beer, which was brewed in New Amstel and could be purchased duty-free (b) black slaves needed to work in the tobacco fields. The slave trade at this time was dominated by the Dutch, and Negroes seized in Africa could be shipped to New Amstel and then sold to the English planters at negotiated prices per head. D'Hinoyossa was not engaged in anything illegal from a Dutch viewpoint; Maryland was violating the English Navigation Acts, but that was no concern of his.

To facilitate commerce with Maryland, d'Hinoyossa decided on a midway point to avoid long, time-consuming voyages from Delaware Bay to Chesapeake Bay, and he selected a place called by the Indians Appoquinimink which my late Lenape informant, Touching Leaves, translated as "the place where we stayed a long time.'' She pronounced it *ah-puk-wen-e-ming*, and she should know—her forbears lived there a long time before the white man came. This place was at the head of Appoquinimink Creek where the town of Odessa, Delaware is now located. Vessels from New Amstel could sail to this point—the cargoes could then be transported overland to the headwaters of the Bohemia River, a tributary of the Chesapeake, and there loaded aboard other vessels to dock at St. Marys and other Maryland ports on both western and eastern shores.

This route was used before d'Hinoyossa came to New Amstel; it was one of several used by the Minquas trading parties to come to the Delaware River from the Susquehanna River. But with a trading center at Appoquinimink, which d'Hinoyossa intended to establish for commerce with the English, the Minquas could barter more conveniently with the City's traders by reducing the length of the trade route.

There was one possible deterrent to d'Hinoyossa's plans. Lenape war parties from the Delaware had been raiding homes and plantations in Maryland, and considerable hostility had developed between the tribe and the Marylanders. On September 13, 1661 d'Hinoyossa sent the resourceful Peter Alrichs to Maryland with two Lenape chiefs to try to establish peace with the English and pave the way for an official treaty.[8] No satisfactory commercial relations between Maryland and New Amstel could be attained if the Indians were allowed to disrupt the trade. Although the chiefs deserted Alrichs enroute to Maryland, Alrichs accomplished his mission, and on September 19, Governor Philip Calvert joined d'Hinoyossa and a Lenape chief named Pinna at Appoquinimink. A treaty was signed by Calvert and Pinna, and it was agreed that peace between the Marylanders and the Lenape would be maintained.[9]

At this meeting d'Hinoyossa and Governor Calvert also discussed the conduct of business between the two colonies. Calvert agreed that Maryland would supply d'Hinoyossa with 2,000 to 3,000 hogsheads of tobacco per year in exchange for Negroes, beer, and other merchandise.[10] D'Hinoyossa doubtless believed that, once the commerce was under way, additional Maryland planters would willingly participate in a highly profitable business by evading English customs duties and dealing directly with the Dutch.

D'Hinoyossa's letters and reports to Amsterdam citing the progress being made in the colony came at an opportune time. Amsterdam's trade was suffering as a result of increased competition from France, England, and Denmark, and despite the misfortunes in the City's colony during Jacob Alrichs's administration, it seemed that America still held the best business opportunities. Although the burgomasters were paying 3½% interest per annum on 132,000 florins they had borrowed on behalf of New Amstel, and additional expenditures would be required, it was decided "to push said Colonie forward with greater zeal than has hitherto been done."[11]

While the burgomasters were still debating over the recommendations made from several sources, d'Hinoyossa arrived in Amsterdam in June of 1663. From his experience in the colony and his knowledge of the friction with the Company's representatives in America, d'Hinoyossa could speak with confidence and authority. Having worked out a trade agreement with the English in Maryland, he was able to make positive recommendations about a plan of action. Peter Alrichs was also in Holland at the time, and he was no less determined than d'Hinoyossa to gain support for a program to put the colony on a paying basis.

There were many discussions, and it is uncertain who the participants were or how the differences were compromised, but what was finally resolved is implicit in the subsequent action that was taken after d'Hinoyossa and Alrichs returned to New Amstel. Doubtless the commissioners made certain suggestions, but one assumes that d'Hinoyossa's recommendations were the central elements in the new policy.

D'Hinoyossa and Alrichs left Holland in the fall of 1663 on *de Purmerlander Kerck* (*the Church of Purmerland*) and arrived in New Amstel on December 3, 1663. Alrichs was accompanied by ten farmers he had employed as servants to work his lands in the City's colony for a period of four years. Two of these were recruited from Groningen, his home, but others were from Bremen, Schleswig-Holstein, and Saxony, as well as Holland.[12] D'Hinoyossa also enlisted a number of farm families, including Swedes and Finns, to return with him on *de Purmerlander Kerck*, which also brought a large cargo of needed supplies as well as trade goods for use in the Indian trade.

When d'Hinoyossa disembarked at New Amstel he broke the happy news to van Sweringen, who was in charge during his absence, that the West India Company had agreed to convey all of its remaining lands on the Delaware to the City. The deed of transfer described the land "from the sea upwards as far as the river reaches, on the east-side inland three leagues from the bank of the river, on the west-side as far as the territory reaches to the English colony, with all streams, kills, creeks, ports, bays, and outlines belonging thereto."[13] The Company would have to vacate Fort Altena, and the Swedish-Finnish communities at Upland, Tinicum Island, Kingsessing, etc., with an estimated 110 boweries, 2,000 cows and oxen, twenty horses, eighty sheep, and several thousand swine who would all be under the supervision of d'Hinoyossa and his council.[14] The Swedes and Finns, of course, were expected to sell their surplus corn, wheat, barley, rye, and buckwheat to the City, not to other buyers. Some of the grains would be used for making beer in the brew kettles at New Amstel for sale to the English, and others would be exported to Amsterdam. D'Hinoyossa also planned that farmers from foreign countries could be induced to migrate to the City's colony because of the opportunities offered under his new policy. He was particularly eager to increase the Swedish and Finnish population because of their adaptability to agriculture.

A good start was made when the vessel *St. Jacob* arrived in Delaware Bay landing forty-one people with tools and supplies at present Lewes, where a semi-socialistic Mennonite settlement was formed under the leadership of a zealot named Cornelis Pietersz Plockhoy. The *St. Jacob* continued up the river and landed fifty farm laborers and about ten unmarried women at New Amstel, along with a supply of farm implements.[15]

Among the other items of news that d'Hinoyossa brought with him from Holland was the surprising but welcome information that the City's colony would be operated independently, and all ties with the West India Company reduced to a bare minimum. The import and export duties at New Amstel would thereafter be collected by the City, not the Company, and the duties would be shared 50-50 by the Company and the City, not by the Company alone as heretofore. That meant that Willem Beeckman lost his job, and a City employe named Gerrit Cock from Gouda, who came from Holland with d'Hinoyossa, became the new inspector and customs collector.

Appellants from the decisions made by d'Hinoyossa's council would no longer make their appeals to Stuyvesant, but could bring their cases to the supreme court in Holland, if the issue so warranted.

Private fur traders were to be excluded from bartering with the Indians, and the City would exclusively control the fur trade on the Delaware to maximize its profits. Peter Alrichs made an arrangement with the commissioners before leaving Holland that he would be their agent in conducting the fur trade with the Indians. He was not supposed to trade for his own account, but would receive a commission of one-fourth of the profits on all the pelts he obtained for the City.[16] He brought with him a good supply of duffel cloth, blankets, and other trade merchandise provided by the City. Following Alrichs's arrival at New Amstel, Beeckman wrote to Stuyvesant confirming that Alrichs would personally handle the trade at New Amstel, and that two other traders, apparently employed by Alrichs, would barter with the Indians at Passyunk and at the Hoerekil. He also stated that one year and six weeks later no private persons would be allowed to trade in furs or engage in the tobacco traffic.[17]

In his last letter written to Stuyvesant from Fort Altena on January 12, 1664, Beeckman said that d'Hinoyossa had orders from his superiors to persuade him to remain as a freeman, and in a conciliatory gesture offered him lodgings as a gift. Beeckman declined. He did not trust d'Hinoyossa and wanted nothing to do with him. Beeckman withdrew the Company's small garrison at Fort Altena and returned to New Amsterdam with his family. He continued in the Company's employ and later was given the position of commissary at a post at Esopus (present Kingston, N.Y.).[18]

Beeckman's "Clerk and Reader," old Andries Hudde, who was robbed by the Indians and practically impoverished, left the Company's employ with the intention of settling on the Sassafras River in Maryland. Among his other talents he claimed to know how to brew beer, and he and an Englishman named Henry Coursey decided to build a brewery in Maryland. Beeckman was reluctant to release him, but Hudde was so insistent that Beeckman allowed him to leave Fort Altena with his family on November 1, 1663. They got as far as Appoquinimink where he fell ill with a high fever and died there on November 4.[19] His sudden death brought an end to the life of one of the Delaware Valley's most unforgettable characters.

One might expect Peter Stuyvesant to have resented the City taking over all of the territory on the Delaware River, but this was not the case. In 1660, when the City was giving serious thought to returning the colony to the Company, Stuyvesant wrote the directors "we would wish and prefer for the best of the Company that the City should keep it in its possession."[20] The City's colony had always been a nuisance to him, and he had no regrets about vacating Fort Altena or allowing d'Hinoyossa to take over the problems, including the placating of the Swedes and Finns in the area north of Fort Altena.

In the months that followed, quantities of tobacco, furs, grains, timber, and other products were shipped to Amsterdam from New Amstel. The population increased to more than 1,000, and there was a good rapport with Lord Baltimore's government and the Maryland merchants and planters. At long last the City's venture was starting to pay off and the future looked bright. D'Hinoyossa has been accused of seeking personal gain in the commercial expansion of the colony, and it is true that he built a fine house for himself and his family on Burlington Island where he had gardens, cultivated fields, livestock, and servants. He was also planning to build a residence on the Appoquinimink Kill where he intended to found "his major city."[21]

D'Hinoyossa was not the only City official to taste prosperity at this time; Gerrit van Sweringen, Peter Alrichs, and Joost de La Grange also acquired land and property. In Holland a number of the burgomasters, having "inside" information, invested their own private funds in cargoes and chartered vessels. In the latter days of the d'Hinoyossa administration, the City itself handled only one-quarter of the shipments from the Delaware, whereas the majority of the business was conducted by individual burgomasters on a private basis for their own personal profit.[22] At long last, New Amstel proved to be a successful venture with more prosperous days expected in the near future.

But all hope for the continued success of the City's colony came to a sudden and disappointing halt. Charles II, urged by Parliament, concluded it was to England's best economic interests to possess the New Netherland and eliminate Dutch competition. To achieve that objective the King granted his brother James Stuart, Duke of York (later to become James II) a patent that included all of the New Netherland except the territory on the western shore of the Delaware River where the City's colony was flourishing. As explained earlier, Lord Baltimore considered New Amstel and all of present Delaware as part of Maryland according to his proprietary grant from Charles I, father of Charles II. Charles II couldn't legally give his brother

James land their father had patented to Lord Baltimore even though the Dutch were seated on part of it.

Although England and Holland were then at peace, the Duke of York sent an expedition of warships and troops under command of a commission headed by Colonel Richard Nicolls to seize the land his brother had patented to him. Stuyvesant was forced to surrender Fort Amsterdam and Manhattan Island, which gave the English control of the heart of New Netherland. Although the Duke's instructions to his officers said nothing about Maryland or New Amstel, it was immediately apparent to Colonel Nicolls and his associates that their mission would be incomplete unless they halted the illicit commerce between Maryland and the Dutch in the City's colony. Nicolls was well aware that the Maryland government chose not to disturb this profitable commerce by challenging the Dutch, but as a loyal subject of the Stuarts who had served the Duke with untiring energy, Nicolls did not hesitate to act in what he believed was in the Duke's best interests. He agreed that one of his associates, Sir Robert Carr, should move against New Amstel while he organized a new government in New Amsterdam. The flotilla, which conveyed a total of 400 or 500 soldiers, was divided, and Sir Robert took two of the vessels, a formidable warship, the *Guinea*, with forty cannon, an armed merchant ship, the *William Nicholas*, and approximately 100 foot soldiers. The other troops and vessels remained in New York with Colonel Nicolls, to support him in setting up the Duke of York's new government.

Nicolls recognized that Carr had a ticklish assignment because the Duke's patent did not give him any authority in the province where Lord Baltimore was the proprietor. Knowing that Charles Calvert had succeeded Philip as governor of Maryland, Nicolls instructed Carr that should the new Lord Baltimore offer any objections to his invasion of New Amstel, "you are to say that you only keep possession till his Majesty is informed and satisfied otherwise. In other things I must leave to your discreccon, and the best Advice you can get upon the place."[23]

Sir Robert Carr's forces arrived off New Amstel on October 1, 1664, with troops who had long awaited action. They had crossed an ocean to fight for their monarch, but Stuyvesant had surrendered peacefully without putting up any military resistance. New Amstel was their last chance to do battle and they were eager to charge the Dutch fort. No description of the condition of the much-repaired fort at New Amstel was recorded except that Nicolls referred to it as "inconsiderable" and Carr wrote that although it had fourteen cannon it was "not tenable." D'Hinoyossa had constructed a brewery within the fort, and it was also used for the storage of large quantities of the City's supplies, and several of the houses occupied by soldiers were full of linens, wine, brandy, stockings, shoes, shirts, and tools. The probability is that the defenses had deteriorated, because d'Hinoyossa no longer had any fear of an attack by the Marylanders who were cooperating with him, and there seemed little likelihood of a coup d'etat on the part of Swedes and Finns busy on their farms.

The events preceding the attack and the attack itself are well described in contemporary records, and one of the detailed accounts is found in a deposition of a Dutch sergeant, Godefro Meyer van Cloppenburgh, and two farm hands who were present at New Amstel.[24] When the *Guinea* dropped anchor, three members of the council, Peter Alrichs, Gerrit van Sweringen, and Joost de La Grange went on board demanding an explanation. Sir Robert Carr showed them some documents and said they had come to take possession of the country for the King of England either by agreement or force. The councilmen returned to the fort and reported to d'Hinoyossa. Evidently by prearrangement, d'Hinoyossa and Carr met on the land outside the fort the next morning, each accompanied by four soldiers. Carr was unaware that the Dutch army consisted of only thirty men!

Carr and d'Hinoyossa withdrew from the group for a discussion after which Carr returned to the vessel with his party and d'Hinoyossa ordered Sergeant van Cloppenburgh to load the

cannon with shrapnel and supply the Dutch soldiers with muskets and sidearms. D'Hinoyossa asked if they were resolved to
fight, and they all replied affirmatively "as long as they could
stand up."

Early the next morning about 130 soldiers and sailors from
the two English vessels landed and marched around the rear of
the fort. At about three o'clock in the afternoon the English
fired their cannon from the ships, striking the roofs of the
houses in the fort. The Dutch soldiers in the fort, including van
Sweringen and Peter Alrichs, fled over the walls pursued by
English soldiers firing at them. Sergeant van Cloppenburgh said
he asked d'Hinoyossa whether he should fire the cannon at the
ship, but "the governor forbade him to do so and ordered him
not to shoot." D'Hinoyossa's motive for not firing the cannon
has never been explained.

In his report to Colonel Nicolls, Sir Robert Carr stated that
before launching the attack he conferred with d'Hinoyossa, as
well as the burghers and townsmen. The latter consented to his
demands, but d'Hinoyossa and the soldiers refused to surrender.
Carr indicated that after landing his men he fired two broadsides
from each of the two vessels, after which the soldiers and
seamen stormed the fort and plundered the stores of supplies.[25]
Carr minimized the extent of the looting and the property he
personally seized after the attack, but it was a matter of "to the
victor belongs the spoils" and the soldiers and sailors apparently ran amuck in releasing their pent up energy. There were
no English casualties, but three Dutch were killed and ten
wounded.

Van Sweringen itemized some of the property that was taken
in the attack: 100 sheep, thirty or forty horses, fifty or sixty
cows and oxen, sixty or seventy Negro slaves, corn and hay
recently harvested, cloth, linens, shoes, brandy, wine, tools, a
sawmill, a brewhouse, nine sea buoys with their chains, arms,
powder, shot, tools, plows, and the twenty-four cannon, which
were transported to New York.[26]

Sir Robert generously divided among his staff officers the property belonging to the administrative officers in the City's employ. He gave his relative Lieutenant John Carr the house, servants, lands, and personal possessions owned by van Sweringen. He rewarded Ensign Arthur Stock with houses, lands, certain personal possessions, and eleven Negro slaves belonging to Peter Alrichs. He also gave lands to a number of the English soldiers for their services in the campaign, and he kept the richest prize for himself—d'Hinoyossa's estate on Burlington Island. He sold a number of d'Hinoyossa's black slaves to Maryland planters for beef, pork, corn, salt, and other commodities.

Sir Robert was very lenient in his surrender terms to the burghers, townsmen, and farmers. He permitted all of them to retain their homes and personal property. Any resident who did not want to live under English rule was free to depart unmolested within six months. Everyone was guaranteed freedom of conscience in church disciplines. All the inhabitants, Swedes, Finns, and Dutch alike, were required to take an oath of allegiance and submit to the King of England, after which they were as free as Englishmen to enjoy the privileges of the Duke of York's colony. The Dutch schepens were permitted to continue to administer justice for six months.

When Colonel Nicolls eventually learned of the booty taken at New Amstel he reported to London that Sir Robert claimed that what he had ''Tis his owne, being wonn by the sword.'' Sir Robert did not remain very long on the Delaware, and he eventually returned to England lamenting that he suffered a leg injury on the Delaware and had nothing to show for a battle in which he hazarded his life. John Carr took temporary possession of Burlington Island. Colonel Nicolls also complained that he had spent his own money in the Duke's interest for which he had not been properly compensated. Details of how the English soldiers disposed of the land acquired in the attack at New Amstel is another story not relevant here.

Both Gerrit van Sweringen and d'Hinoyossa and their families moved to Maryland after the attack. Van Sweringen, his wife Barbara, and his children Elizabeth and Zacharias were naturalized as Maryland citizens in May, 1669.[27]

D'Hinoyossa remained for several months in the home of one "Capt. Thomas Houwel" in St. Marys, as he spelled his host's name in an undated letter to Colonel Nicolls. In this letter he asked for the restitution of his estate in return for which "I am resolved to live under Your Honor's Government; yea, on the same conditions that I had from the city of Amsterdam—to cultivate the land in company for our mutual profit . . ."[28] Nothing came from this offer, and d'Hinoyossa returned to Holland in 1665, but he later returned to Maryland. In 1671 he was living on Foster's Island in Talbot County, and in April of that year he, his wife, whose name is given as "Margaretta" (de Haes?) and his children, Alexander, Johannes, Peter, Maria, Johanna, Christina, and Barbara, became naturalized citizens of Maryland.[29]

D'Hinoyossa again returned to Holland shortly thereafter. In the war between France and Holland he obtained a captain's commission and was sent to hold Wesel, across the Dutch border. Town after town surrendered to the invading French armies, including Wesel. After the surrender the Dutch officers were summoned to appear before a court martial at Bodegraven to account for their actions. D'Hinoyossa was accused of "having left his post, of faintheartedness, of unwillingness to fight and of mutiny to which he had also incited others." He was sentenced to be beheaded, and was executed on August 8, 1672.[30] An inglorious end to "the little Prince."

New Amstel underwent another name change after Sir Robert Carr's victory. In one of his messages to Colonel Nicolls on October 13, 1664, he indicated he was writing from "Dellawarr Fort," which was the first English name applied to New Amstel. But the town did not yet have an official name on October 24 when the other commissioners agreed that Colonel Nicolls should "repaire to Delaware Bay" and look the situation over. The records are not clear whether Nicolls made the trip or not, but it seems likely that he was responsible for the official name change. Not only was he in command, but in a fragmentary undated letter to the Duke of York he indicated he had given the name New York to Manhattan Island, Albania to land west of the Hudson River, and he named Long Island, Yorkshire, to honor the Duke's titles; he also applied the Duke's Scottish title, Duke of Albany, to the Dutch town of Beverwyck on the Hudson.

The first documentary reference the writer has found to the name New Castle as a replacement for New Amstel occurs in a "visa" dated April 22, 1665 wherein Nicolls, writing from New York, granted permission to Martin Crieger "to Passe from hence to New Castle in Delaware Bay."[31] Crieger wanted to trade with the Indians for furs and a pass signed by Nicolls was necessary for him to get clearance at "Dellawarr Fort" where Sir Robert Carr was still in command.

Nicolls did not explain why he selected the name, but the reason seems obvious. William Cavendish, a friend of the Duke of York's, was created Earl of New Castle in 1628, Marquess of New Castle in 1643, and Duke of New Castle in 1665, successive ranks in the peerage. During the Civil Wars in England which occurred when Charles I (the Duke of York's father) was on the throne, Cavendish remained loyal to the Crown and won renown as a cavalier general. There was no doubt in Nicoll's mind that the Duke of York would have approved the name. Now in use for over 300 years, New Castle is well established on countless maps, atlases, and land titles. The likelihood is that it will not readily yield to another change.

New Amstel lost its official political identity with the English conquest of 1664, and except for one brief interlude the new municipality known as New Castle was no longer in Dutch control. War broke out between Holland and England, and in 1673 a powerful Dutch fleet, fresh from victory over the English and their French allies, crossed the Atlantic and in a bold stroke seized Fort James at New York. The English were forced to give up their rule of the former New Netherland, and the Duke of York's province was placed under the command of Captain Anthony Colve who was named the Dutch governor-general. On September 19, 1673, Colve put Peter Alrichs in charge of the settlements on both sides of the Delaware River where Dutch suzerainty was temporarily restored. The majority of the magistrates and constables remained in office but swore allegiance to the States General and the Prince of Orange. There was no resistance on the Delaware, no military action at New Castle, and no bloodshed.

An important political change occurred during this interval when Peter Alrichs held office as the "Schout and Commander." Three courts of justice were established, one at New Castle, a second at Upland (Chester), and a third at the Hoerekill. The inhabitants of each jurisdiction, which was formally bounded, were directed to nominate candidates for the positions of justices, and the Dutch officials made their selections from the nominees. This concept of judicial districts was the forerunner of the counties of New Castle, Sussex, and Chester, which were outgrowths of the courts. (Another county, St. Jones, created in 1680 by the Duke of York government, was later named Kent.)

The provisional Dutch government on the Delaware under Peter Alrichs's direction did not last very long through no fault of its own. When the Treaty of Westminster was signed on February 19, 1674 the war ended, and by the terms of the peace treaty the Dutch returned all of the New Netherland to the English. The Duke of York's government was reinstated at New Castle on November 2, 1674, but by no means did the non-English officials suddenly disappear. Governor Andros reinstated all the magistrates and other officials who were then in office with he exception of Peter Alrichs who was replaced by two Englishmen, Captain Edmond Cantwell and William Tom.

In due time, Peter Alrichs was again in good graces, and on September 23, 1677 Governor Andros named him, Gerrit Otto, John Moll, Fopp Outhout, Jean Paul Jacquet, William Tom, and Walter Wharton as the justices of the New Castle court where they performed judicial functions and also acted as a town council in legislative matters.[32] All of them pledged their allegiance to England and the Duke of York's government, but only Tom and Wharton were Englishmen.

The complete story of New Castle during the administration of the Duke of York still remains to be published.* The period ended when William Penn took over in 1682 as the Proprietor of Pennsylvania and the "Three Lower Counties," i.e., New Castle, Kent, Sussex, which were destined to become the state of Delaware. A new kind of representative government introduced by Penn brought a number of non-English officials to the General Assembly and the Provincial Council of Pennsylvania. Peter Alrichs was among these along with Lasse Cock, John Moll, Andros Binckson, Swan Swanson, John Kipshaven, Albertus Jacobs, Johannes D'Haes, and others. The influence of the Dutch, Swedes, and Finns continued to be felt in the changing culture as the Delaware River valley was exposed to anglicizing pressures.

---

* I am not unmindful of a thesis by Louise B. Heite, "New Castle Under the Duke of York: A Stable Community" (1978), and a dissertation by Dr. Constance J. Cooper, "A Town Among Cities: New Castle, Delaware, 1780-1840" (1983), both submitted to the faculty of the University of Delaware in partial fulfillment of advanced degrees.

ABBREVIATIONS USED IN THE NOTES

BASD
: *Bulletins*, Archeological Society of Delaware, published irregularly from May 1933 to the present, Wilmington.

Bachman
: Van Cleaf Bachman. *Peltries or Plantations, The Economic Policies of the Dutch West India Company in New Netherland 1623-1639.* (Baltimore: The Johns Hopkins Press, 1969).

Eckman, 1950
: Jeannette Eckman. *New Castle on the Delaware*. (Wilmington: New Castle Historical Society, 1950).

Gehring
: Charles T. Gehring, ed. and trans. *New York Historical Manuscripts Dutch*, vols. XVIII-XIX. Delaware Papers. (Baltimore: Genealogical Publishing Co., Inc., 1981).

Instruction
: Amandus Johnson, ed. and trans. *The Instruction for Johan Printz*. (Philadelphia: Swedish Colonial Society, 1930).

Lindeström   Peter Lindeström. *Geographia Americae*. ed.
                 and trans. Amandus Johnson. (Philadelphia:
                 Swedish Colonial Society, 1925).

NYCD   *Documents Relative to the Colonial History of
                 the State of New York*. E.B. O'Callaghan ed.
                 and trans. vols. I-IX. Berthold Fernow ed. and
                 trans. vols XII-XIV (Albany, 1856-1887).

Narratives   Albert Cook Myers, ed. *Narratives of Early
                 Pennsylvania, West New Jersey and Delaware*.
                 (New York: Charles Scribner's Sons, 1912).

SS   Amandus Johnson. *The Swedish Settlements
                 on the Delaware*, 2 vols. (Philadelphia: Uni-
                 versity of Pennsylvania, 1911).

Weslager, 1961   C.A. Weslager. *Dutch Explorers, Traders and
                 Settlers in the Delaware Valley*. (Philadelphia:
                 University of Pennsylvania Press, 1961).

NOTES

Chapter 1

1. C.A. Weslager, *The Delaware Indians, a History* (New Brunswick, N.J.: Rutgers University Press, 1972), p. 208.
2. *Lindeström*, Map "B," which also shows a creek north of the fort without a name. The latter stream is shown as "The Town Creeke" on a surveyor's drawing made November 23, 1681 for Arnoldus de la Grange. The drawing shows the stream crossed by a "foott dyke," a walkway used by pedestrians to cross the stream, *Survey Book of New Castle County, 1806* (Delaware State Archives), pp. 338-39.
3. A.R. Dunlap, "Dutch and Swedish Land Records Relating to Delaware," *Delaware History* 6 (March 1954):29.
4. A.R. Dunlap, *Dutch and Swedish Place-Names in Delaware* (Newark: University of Delaware Press, 1956), p. 50.
5. Alexander B. Cooper, "Fort Casimir," *Papers*, Historical Society of Delaware 43 (1905):16.

6. De Vries, "Kort Historiael, etc.," *Narratives*, p. 25.

7. Jasper Dankers and Peter Sluyter, *Journal of a Voyage to New York* (Brooklyn: *Memoirs*, Long Island Historical Society, 1867) 1:227-28.

8. *Weslager, 1961*, p. 33.

9. NYCD 113-14. The map faces p. 11. Lindeström's Map "A" is probably the first map to show the Santhoeck, which he identifies as "Tamakonck, de Santhoeck nu kallas Treefaldigheets Fort" (Tamakonck, the Santhoeck, now called Trinity Fort), *Lindeström* Map "A" insert.

10. Simon Hart, *The Prehistory of the New Netherland Company* (Amsterdam: City of Amsterdam Press, 1959).

11. Thomas J. Condon, *New York Beginnings—the Commercial Origins of New Netherland* (New York: New York University Press, 1968), p. 120. Referred to hereafter as *Condon*.

12. *Bachman*, pp. 54-55. For the number of the Company's employes and ships c. 1633-34 see NYCD 1:62-63.

13. *Van Rensselaer Bowier Manuscripts,* trans. and ed. A.J.F. van Laer (Albany: University of the State of New York, 1908), p. 247.

14. "Instructions for Willem Verhulst," *Documents Relating to New Netherland 1624-1626*, trans. and ed. A.J.F. van Laer. (San Marino, Cal.: Henry E. Huntington Library and Art Gallery, 1924), pp. 59, 71, 76. Referred to hereafter as *Van Rappard Docs*.

15. From Nicolaes Wassenaer's "Historisch Verhael," *Narratives of New Netherland 1609-1664*, ed. J. Franklin Jameson. (New York: Charles Scribner's Sons, 1909), pp. 63-96.

16. *Condon*, p. 93, speculates that the Walloons went as Company employes not free colonists, which is incorrect. "The Provisional Regulations for the Colonists" adopted by the Assembly of XIX on March 28, 1624 makes this clear, *Van Rappard Docs.*, pp. 2-18. Wassenaer's "Historisch Verhael," p. 76 also explains they went as free agents.

17. *Van Rappard Docs.*, p. 9.

18. *Weslager, 1961*, chapter 3.
19. NYCD 1:xxv-xxvi.
20. Wassenaer's "Historisch Verhael," p. 79.
21. *Van Rappard Docs.*, p. 40.
22. *Bachman*, p. 20, n. 63.
23. *Van Rappard Docs.*, p. 51.
24. Burlington Island's early history is covered in *Weslager, 1961*, pp. 75-81. In modern times it was the site of an amusement park destroyed by fire in 1928. Today, the island is a source of water for the city of Burlington, Henry H. Bisbee, *Burlington Island, the Best and Largest on the South River* (Burlington: Heidelberg Press, 1972).
25. C.A. Weslager, "The Minquas and Their Early Relations With the Delaware Indians," BASD 4 (May 1943):14-23.
26. De Vries, *Narratives*, p. 7.
27. *Weslager, 1961*, chapter 4. The creek was not named for the city of Hoorn and the contemporary Dutch never called it the Hoorn Kill as erroneously stated in *The Papers of William Penn*, eds. Mary Maples Dunn and Richard S. Dunn (Philadelphia: University of Pennsylvania Press, 1981):1:310, n. 3.
28. *Weslager, 1961*, ibid.
29. De Vries, *Narratives*, pp. 18, 21.

Chapter 2

1. SS 1:12-13.
2. *Van Rappard Docs.*, p. 75.
3. *Collections of the New York Historical Society*, 2nd series (New York: H. Ludwig, 1841):1:385.
4. *Bachman*, p. 90.
5. *Ibid.*, p. 155.
6. Penn's letter, *Narratives*, p. 260.

7. SS 1:chapter 12.

8. "Instructions to Minuit," *Weslager, 1961*, pp. 169-81.

9. Anna T. Lincoln, *Wilmington, Delaware, Three Centuries Under Four Flags* (Rutland, Vermont: Tuttle Publishing Co., 1937), p. 27.

10. I am indebted to the late Mrs. Nora Thompson Dean (Touching Leaves), a fluent Lenape speaker, for these translations, which update the speculative translations made by A.R. Dunlap and myself in our *Indian Place-Names in Delaware* (Wilmington: Archeological Society of Delaware, 1950), p. 17.

11. *Narratives*, p. 87.

12. *Ibid*.

13. NYCD 1:598.

14. Johnson concurs with this opinion, SS 1:184.

15. NYCD 12:19.

16. SS 1:197.

17. *Ibid*., pp. 200-01.

18. *Van Rappard Docs*., pp. 51-52.

19. *Weslager, 1961*, pp. 268-69.

20. NYCD 1:542.

21. *Condon*, pp. 67-68.

22. *Bachman*, p. 147.

23. *Pennsylvania Archives*, 2nd series (Harrisburg: E.K. Meyers, 1890):5:58. The Company suffered a net loss in the New Netherland of 550,000 guilders between 1626 and 1644, *Condon*, p. 145.

24. *Bachman*, p. 151. At first the States General objected to approving the new policy, see NYCD 1:110-115, but finally agreed to try it out provisionally, *Cf. ibid*., pp. 160-62. During Stuyvesant's administration it was necessary to apply to him for a license to trade, thus enabling him to impose restraints on unwelcome English traders, NYCD 12:68.

25. SS 1:19. Minuit never returned to Sweden. He met an untimely death at the island of St. Christopher, *Weslager, 1961*, pp. 182-83.

26. Thomas Campanius Holm, *A Short Description of the Province of New Sweden*, trans. Peter S. Du Ponceau (Philadelphia: Memoirs of the Historical Society of Pennsylvania, 1834):3:157.

27. Francis Jennings, *The Ambiguous Iroquois Empire* (New York: W.W. Norton Co., 1984), p. 52.

28. SS 1:158-59.

29. C.A. Weslager, *The English on the Delaware* (New Brunswick: Rutgers University Press, 1967), pp. 96-97. *Cf. Instruction*, p. 232, n. 14b.

30. *Ibid.*, pp. 104-05. James Waye's deposition, one of the settlers, is given in *Weslager, 1961*, pp. 300-01.

31. Christopher Ward, *The Dutch and Swedes on the Delaware 1609-1664* (Philadelphia: University of Pennsylvania Press, 1930), p. 108.

32. *Instruction*, p. 82.

33. *Ibid.*, pp. 107-08.

34. *Ibid.*, pp. 111, 113.

Chapter 3

1. *Weslager, 1961*, p. 144; see also pp. 307-08 for a transcript of the Indian deed to Hudde dated September 25, 1646. See also NYCD 12:27, 44-47 for the names of Dutch colonists who attempted to build on the land.

2. *Gehring*, pp. 6-7.

3. His commission appears in NYCD 1:178.

4. Christopher Ward, *New Sweden on the Delaware* (Philadelphia: University of Pennsylvania Press, 1938), p. 92.

5. *Instruction*, pp. 32, 130; *Gehring*, p. 2.

6. *Instruction*, p. 125.
7. *Ibid.*, pp. 68-70.
8. *Ibid.*, p. 74.
9. *Ibid.*, pp. 133-34.
10. *Weslager, 1961*, p. 146. For a discussion of the probable location of Beversreede, see Henry D. Paxson, *Where Pennsylvania History Began* (Philadelphia: privately printed, 1926), pp. 64-69.
11. NYCD 1:588, 593.
12. *Instruction*, p. 277. *Cf.* Peter Stebbins Craig and Henry Wesley Yocom, "The Yocums of Aronameck in Philadelphia, 1648-1702," *National Genealogical Society Quarterly* 71 (December 1983):243-79.
13. Information about the size of Stuyvesant's forces taken from Printz's letter of August 1, 1651, *Instruction*, p. 180.
14. *Instruction*, pp. 180-81; SS 1:435-36.
15. NYCD 1:564.
16. *Narratives*, p. 235.
17. NYCD 1:597-99.
18. *Narratives*, p. 88. *Cf.* SS 1:183-84 for reference to the two lost deeds.
19. NYCD 1:599.
20. A.R. Dunlap, "Dutch and Swedish Land Records Relating to Delaware," *Delaware History* 6 (March 1954):29. A facsimile of this document appears in SS 1: facing p. 440, although Johnson did not translate it.
21. Printz evidently had a second meeting with Notike and Kiapes; see SS 2:757 for a transcript of a covering document dated July 3 wherein Metatsimint's ownership is again confirmed. It is difficult to reconcile the dates of these conferences; Johnson attempted clarification in SS 1:445, n. 102, but Dunlap's translation of the July 13, 1651 document had not yet been published.
22. NYCD 1:599-600. The transcript is erroneously dated 1655.

23. *Ibid.*, p. 590. In SS 1:446 Johnson expresses doubt that Printz made such an agreement.
24. *Instruction*, pp. 182-83.
25. NYCD 12:72.
26. *Weslager, 1961,* op. p. 60.
27. The origin of the name was first suggested by *Eckman, 1950*, pp. 24-25.

Chapter 4

1. *Instruction*, p. 181.
2. *Ibid.*, p. 188.
3. SS 1:462-63.
4. *Instruction*, p. 188.
5. NYCD 12:75. The directors also complained about the Company's financial condition and how difficult it was to meet expenses, p. 74.
6. *Ibid.*, p. 73.
7. *Ibid.*, p. 75.
8. *Instruction*, p. 96.
9. *Narratives*, p. 149.
10. SS 2:chapter 39 for a discussion of the expedition.
11. *Lindeström*, pp. 25-26.
12. *Instruction*, pp. 179-84.
13. SS 2:581.
14. *Ibid.*, p. 479.
15. *Lindeström*, p. 85.
16. *Ibid.*, pp. 86-87. Acrelius refers to the fort being abandoned "on account of gnats," *Narratives*, p. 68, but Lindeström specifically refers to mosquitoes. Benjamin Ferris, *A History of the Original Settlements on the Delaware* (Wilmington: Wilson & Heald, 1846), p. 79 says the building of Fort Casimir permitted the Dutch to enforce *lex*

talionis (law of retaliation), which is why the Swedes abandoned Elfsborg, and he maintains the tale about the mosquitoes is ridiculous.

17. NYCD 1:602.
18. *Ibid.*, pp. 603-06.
19. *Ibid.*, p. 602. For Rising's statement to van Tienhoven and Bicker's report see *Ibid.*, pp. 601, 604.
20. *Rising's Journal.*
21. SS 2:498.
22. *Narratives*, p. 136.
23. *Ibid.*, p. 149.
24. *Rising's Journal.*
25. See Orders of the Commercial College, December 1653, *Pa. Archives*, 2nd series 5:813-14. *Cf.* Queen Christina's proclamation of March 16, 1654, NYCD 12:73-74.
26. *Lindeström*, p. 173.
27. Thomas Campanius Holm, *A Short Description of the Province of New Sweden*, trans. and ed. by Peter S. Du Ponceau, Memoirs of the Historical Society of Pennsylvania, 1834, 3: op. p. 82. Gregory B. Keen reproduced this drawing in his "New Sweden on the Delaware." *Narrative and Critical History of America*, ed. Justin Winsor (New York: Houghton, Mifflin & Co. 1884), 4 p. 473.
28. SS 2:522-25.
29. See Maps "A" and "B" in *Geographia Americae.*
30. Rising's 1655 Report in *Narratives*, pp. 156-58.
31. *Ibid.*, p. 164.

Chapter 5

1. SS 2:479, 500 n. 6; 741-46.
2. A typed translation of Rising's Journal is among the Amandus Johnson papers in the Balch Institute, Philadelphia, Box 56,

Folder 7. This translation was not made by Johnson because in his published works Johnson quotes translations of excerpts from the journal that differ in phraseology from the translation at the Balch. The likelihood is that Johnson's friend and colleague, Baron Johan Liljencrants is responsible for this translation from the original Swedish journal in possession of the University of Uppsala in Sweden. The writer does not feel competent to evaluate the quality of the translation at the Balch, but he is reluctant to quote verbatim from it although the substance seems to be reflected in the translation. Drs. Dahlgren and Norman of Uppsala University are currently working on a new translation.

3. NYCD 12:85-86; 90.
4. SS 2:596.
5. NYCD 12:88-89.
6. *Ibid.*, p. 92.
7. "Two Original Letters [by Johannes Bogaert] Relating to the Expedition of Governor Stuyvesant Against Fort Casimir on the Delaware." trans. Henry C. Murphy, *The Historical Magazine* 2 (Sept. 1858):257-59.
8. *Lindeström*, p. 259 gave 1500 as the number of attackers and Rising gave 600 to 700, *Narratives*, p. 170.
9. NYCD 12:97.
10. SS 2:596.
11. *Narratives*, pp. 170-71.
12. *Ibid.*, p. 171; *Lindeström*, chapter 29.
13. Amandus Johnson, *The Swedes on the Delaware 1638-1654* (Philadelphia: International Printing Co., 1927), p. 316.
14. *Gehring*, pp. 38-39.
15. *Bogaert, ibid.*, p. 258. *Cf.* three other translations, NYCD 12:102, *Gehring*, 39-40; Samuel Hazard, *Annals of Pennsylvania* (Philadelphia: Hazard and Mitchell, 1850), pp. 185-86.
16. *Narratives*, p. 171.
17. *Ibid.*

18. *Gehring*, p. 39.
19. *Narratives*, p. 173.
20. *Ibid.*, p. 174; NYCD 12:109; *Acrelius*, pp. 79-80.
21. *Gehring*, p. 35; Jennings, *The Ambiguous Iroquois Empire*, p. 53.
22. *Gehring*, p. 36.
23. *Ibid.*, p. 37.
24. *Lindeström*, p. 271. The full surrender terms are given in *Gehring* pp. 42-44; also NYCD 12:104-05.
25. Paraphrased from pp. 11-12 of the Rising Journal at the Balch Institute.
26. *Lindeström*, pp. 271-72; *Narratives*, p. 176.
27. SS 2:614.
28. *Gehring*, pp. 46-47.
29. NYCD 12:119.
30. *Narratives*, p. 174.

Chapter 6

1. NYCD 12:87.
2. *Ibid.*, pp. 114-17.
3. *Ibid.*, p. 116.
4. Jeannette Eckman, "Life Among the Early Dutch at New Castle," *Delaware History* 4 (June 1951):266.
5. Eckman produced Map "B" as the frontispiece in her *Crane Hook on the Delaware* (Wilmington: Swedish Colonial Society, 1958).
6. *Gehring*, pp. 50-51.
7. *Ibid.*, pp. 51-52.
8. *Ibid.*, p. 77.
9. *Ibid.*, pp. 78-79.
10. *Ibid.*, p. 78.
11. *Ibid.*, pp. 71, 72, 52.

12. *Narratives*, p. 45 n.
13. *Gehring*, p. 81.
14. Peter S. Craig, an attorney who lives at present at 3406 Macomb St. N.W., Washington, DC 20016, has given deep study to the history and genealogy of a number of the early Swedish settlers on the Delaware, and has compiled the pedigrees of many of the families.
15. NYCD 12:119; *Gehring*, p. 65.
16. The names cited are all found in *Gehring*, pp. 48, 49, 52, 53, 81, *passim*.
17. This incident and the others cited in this chapter that occurred at Fort Casimir during the Jacquet administration are all found in Hudde's minutes as transcribed and translated by *Gehring*, pp. 48-83. To avoid burdening these notes with a series of *ibids.*, the author has not given page numbers, but Gehring's excellent index provides information on the individuals named.
18. Dunlap, *Dutch and Swedish Place-Names*, p. 28.
19. NYCD 12:177-83; *The Duke of York Record* (Wilmington: Sunday Star, 1903):6-17. See also Jeannette Eckman's notes on file at the Historical Society of Delaware.
20. *Gehring*, p. 59.
21. *Ibid.*, p. 60; see also Eckman, "Life Among the Early Dutch," p. 258 where she refers to Jan Roeloff de Haes as a native of Holland, partly of French descent, but he was more likely Norwegian, see John D. Evjen, *Scandinavian Immigrants in New York*, etc. (Minneapolis 1916):61-64.
22. Kenneth Scott, "New Amsterdam Taverns and Tavern Keepers:I," *de Halve Maen* 39 (April 1964):1 ff.
23. *Gehring*, pp. 50, 73-74.
24. *Weslager, 1961*, p. 195.
25. *Gehring*, p. 54.
26. *Ibid.*, p. 80.
27. NYCD 12:167-71.

28. *Ibid.*, p. 173.
29. Eckman, *Crane Hook*, pp. 20-21, n. 10.

Chapter 7

1. Many of the details that follow were abstracted from part one of the writer's two-part paper, "The City of Amsterdam's Colony on the Delaware, 1656-1664; With Unpublished Dutch Notarial Abstracts," *Delaware History* 20 (Spring-Summer 1982):1-26.
2. NYCD 2:17; Eckman's "Life Among the Early Dutch," pp. 280-81 for Pietersen's second letter.
3. *Gehring*, pp. 324, 337.
4. NYCD 12:225, 369.
5. C.A. Weslager, "Watermills, Windmills, Horsemills—and a Tidemill: Early Colonial Grain Mills in Delaware," *Delaware History* 15 (April 1970):52-60.
6. NYCD 2:64.
7. For amounts of duties see NYCD 1:625-26.
8. NYCD 12:186.
9. *Hazard's Annals*, 242-44; NYCD 12:211, 213, 271.
10. NYCD 12:233.
11. *Ibid.*, pp. 220-22.
12. *Ibid.*, 12:215, 221.
13. *Gehring*, pp. 121-23.
14. A transcript of the deed was published for the first time in *Weslager, 1961*, p. 289.
15. The site of the "Company's Fort" on Pilot Town Road in Lewes is located by David Marine, "Duke of York Patents on Pilot Town Road," *The Archeolog* 7 (September 1955):2-3.
16. NYCD 12:249-50.
17. *Gehring*, p. 159.

18. Weslager, *English on the Delaware*, pp. 162-75.
19. *Gehring*, pp. 135-36.

Chapter 8

1. *Gehring*, p. 187. For more on the van Gezel matter see Weslager, "City of Amsterdam's Colony," and Eckman, "Life Among the Early Dutch," pp. 289-91.
2. *Gehring*, pp. 223-24; 229-30; 184.
3. *Ibid.*, p. 225.
4. *Ibid.*, p. 274.
5. NYCD 12:313-14.
6. *Gehring*, p. 187.
7. *Ibid.*, p. 269.
8. *Ibid.*, p. 240.
9. See treaty in Weslager, *Delaware Indians*, p. 142.
10. *Gehring*, p. 243.
11. NYCD 2:197, 198.
12. Weslager, "City of Amsterdam's Colony," part 2, p. 85.
13. NYCD 12:449.
14. NYCD 2:210.
15. Leland Harder, "Plockhoy and His Settlement at Zwanendael, 1663," *Delaware History* 3 (March 1948):38-154; *Gehring*, pp. 327, 340.
16. Weslager, "City of Amsterdam's Colony," pp. 86-87.
17. *Gehring*, pp. 340-41.
18. *Ibid.*, p. 342.
19. *Ibid.*, p. 192; 325, 335, 337.
20. NYCD 12:327.
21. *Gehring*, p. 340. There is no evidence that d'Hinoyossa ever settled at Odessa as stated in Scharf's *History* 2:1005.
22. Simon Hart, "The City Colony of New Amstel on the Delaware II," *de Halve Maen* 40 (April 1965), p. 7.

23. Discussed in Weslager, *English on the Delaware*, chapter 12, with complete documentation.
24. See their deposition, *Weslager, 1961*, pp. 240-43.
25. *Pennsylvania Archives*, 2nd series 5:577-78.
26. NYCD 3:345-46.
27. *Md. Archives* 2:205-06.
28. *Pennsylvania Archives*, 2nd series, 5:587.
29. *Md. Archives* 2:282-83.
30. William J. Hoffman, "Alexander D'Hiniossa, the Last Dutch Governor on the Delaware," *New York Genealogical and Biographical Review* (Oct. 1942):250.
31. NYCD 12:459. Cf. C.A. Weslager, "New Castle, Delaware and its Former Names," *Names* 24 (June 1976):101-05.
32. *Records of the Court of New Castle, 1676-1681* (Lancaster: Colonial Society of Pennsylvania, 1904), pp. 144-45.

APPENDIX

1. The Location of Fort Casimir

The following entries referring to the fort are found in the *Records of the Court of New Castle on Delaware, 1676-1681* (Lancaster: Colonial Society of Pennsylvania, 1904). I have normalized the spelling, added punctuation, and spelled out the abbreviations for the reader's convenience:

Engelbert Lott proffered in court a petition desiring a grant from this worshipful court to take up the lot at the east end of this town *where the old fort formerly stood*. The court granted the petitioner his said request, he levelling the old walls and building upon the same according to his honor the said Governor's regulations (pp. 147-48).

The governor referred to was Edmond Andros, and Englebert Lott's petition was approved by the court in the session of

November 7-8, 1677. Note that he was obliged to level what remained of the old fort, and then erect a house on the site. Lott was a tydable person (over sixteen years of age) living in the court's jurisdiction (p. 160). He was elected one of the church wardens the same year (p. 264).

The land immediately north of the old fort property purchased by Englebert Lott was also vacant, and:

> Upon the request of Abram Mann, the court granted him a lot within the town of New Castle *next to the old fort*, that is to say on the east side thereof, the building and fencing the same according to orders (p. 264).

Mann's lot was actually not adjacent to the fort, but was separated from Engelbert Lott's property by another piece of land as indicated below:

> Upon the petition of Abram Mann the court does grant him a lot of ground 60 feet broad next to the lot of Engelbert Lott *or the old fort* provided the said petitioner makes improvements thereon according to law (p. 406).

Another town resident Hans Coderus, a cooper, also wanted one of the riverfront lots north of the fort, and:

> Upon the petition of Hans Coderus, a cooper, the court does grant him to take up within this town of New Castle one lot of land which heretofore is not granted to others, provided he the petitioner himself settles the same and follows the cooper's trade for encouragement and the convenience of the inhabitants (pp. 412-13).

The court obviously didn't want any of these lots to remain unoccupied, and by the fall of 1681, Hans Coderus had not erected a house on his lot. Therefore:

Upon the motion of Justice William Semphill [one of the judges or magistrates in the court] ordered that if cooper Hans Coderus doth not settle his lot granted him by this court lying next to Engelbert Lott within one year after the date of the grant, then to forfeit the same and Mr. Semphill to have preference to take it up before any others (p. 488).

The above entries leave no doubt that the old fort was situated on land purchased by Engelbert Lott, and as further clues to locate his property we have the names of Hans Coderus, the cooper, and Abram Mann who were granted land adjacent to Lott's riverfront property.

An article by Alexander B. Cooper entitled "Fort Casimir," *Papers of the Historical Society of Delaware* (1905), 43:5-39, cites the following deed reference to the property laid out for Engelbert Lott. I have used the same spelling given by Cooper:

By virtue of a warrant from the court of New Castle bearing date the eight day of November, 1678.

Laid out for Engelbert Lott, two lotts of Ground situated in the towne of New Castle att the North east end thereof, one of which lotts being the same *whereon the Old Forte stood*, the other being a lott formerly laid out for Hendrick Vander Burch, being bounded as followeth,—To the South West with the Highway or street which leadeth to the woods [Thwart Street now Chestnut Street],—To the North East with the common not yet taken up,—to the South East with ye street by ye water side,—to the North West by Land Street. Being long to the South West next the Highway 277 ft. to the north east 268 ft. being broad behind and before 220 feet, with express condition that the said Lott *shall and will make even the Old Forte* and have sufficient street or Highway at the Water side laid out, the 24th of May 1679.

was signed
Ed. Cantwell [Sheriff]

The above document makes clear that not only was Engelbert Lott obliged to make the fort site level by removing the debris, but he was required to extend the street, which terminated at the fort, through the site to the river bank.

Another reference to the old fort is found in the old resurvey book of New Castle County (1806), pp. 338-39, in the Delaware Hall of Records. It also includes a surveyor's drawing of the property. I published the description of the lot, and a photocopy of the drawing in "Watermills, Windmills, Horsemills and a Tidemill: Early Colonial Grain Mills in Delaware," *Delaware History* (April 1970), 14:57-58.

For the reader's convenience I have also normalized the spelling in this document as follows, with italic added:

New Castle, November 23, 1681,

By virtue of an order of the commissioners of New Castle bearing the date the 1st November 1681, laid out for Mr. Arnoldus De Lagrange a vacant piece of land with a small piece of marsh to it granted him by the commissioners for the erecting of a windmill upon it for the common good of the inhabitants. Including in this survey a lot formerly belonging to Richard Kittle and since purchased by said De Lagrange adjoining to the tract granted him by the commissioners. The said land being situated and lying at the northeast end of this town of New Castle next to the foot dyke and from thence southwest along the said Dyke Street leading towards Land Street 598 feet to *the corner of the Thwart Street by the old fort* then north northwest along the street or way which goes over the great dyke 400 feet to the corner of a little ditch which parts this from a piece of marsh belonging to Mr. [John] Moll, then east and by north along the said little ditch 200 feet to another stake standing near the creek from thence southeast by south eighty-eight feet to the first mentioned stake. Surveyed by me

Ephraim Herman, Surveyor

The surveyor's drawing shows not only the land laid out for Arnoldus De Lagrange, but "the Thwart Street to the river side" and the lots owned by Engelbert Lotts, Abram Mann, and the cooper, Hans Coderus. The documents herein quoted, supported by the surveyor's drawing, leave no doubt that Fort Casimir stood at the north end of present Chestnut Street near or at the former ferry slip. The east, or river side of the fort, was certainly washed away before Engelbert Lott acquired the property, and whatever debris remained of the west side of the fort in 1679 was hauled away by the new owner. This does not rule out the possibility that subsurface evidence of the fort or structures appertaining to it on the west side might still be uncovered by archeological work.

2. The Later Blockhouse and Fort

Almost ten years before Engelbert Lott acquired the site of the old fort, the English authorities at New Castle realized that what remained of Fort Casimir was worthless for defense purposes. Relations with the Delaware Indians had deteriorated under the English administration and two of the town's residents William Tom and Peter Alrichs wrote a letter to Governor Francis Lovelace (Governor Andros's predecessor) recommending that measures be taken to prepare for a possible Indian attack. The following passage is from their letter dated March 9, 1670 written at New Castle:

. . . . our intencion here is to build a blocke house 40 foote square with 4 at every end for Flanckers [bastions] in the middle of the Towne[,] the fort not being fitt to be repaired and if repaired of noe defence lying att the extreame end of the towne and no garrison[;] therefore we begg that wee may have the liberty to pull itt downe and make use of the tiles[,] bricks and other material for the use of our new intended fortificacion which if wee have no occasion for as wee feare wee shall will be convenient for a Court house notwithstanding. [*N.Y. Historical Manuscripts: Dutch, Delaware Papers (English Period)*, ed. Charles T. Gehring, (Baltimore: Genealogical Publishing Co., Inc., 1977, p. 11).]

C.H.B. Turner made a grievous error in *Some Records of Sussex County, Delaware* (Philadelphia: Allen, Lane & Scott, 1909), p. 7 in which he quotes this letter and indicates it had reference to building a blockhouse at Lewes, Delaware. He goes on further to say the blockhouse was subsequently built, but destroyed before 1773 when a bridge was erected over Lewes Creek "to begin at or near the place where the fort in the said town stood."

If Turner had gone more deeply into the records he would have found the following resolution approved October 6, 1670, signed by Captain John Carr, who was in command, and the council then consisting of William Tom, Hans Block, Israel Helm, Peter Rambo, and Peter Kock:

1. That it was thought the market place where the bell hangs, was *the most convenient place in New-Castle* to erect block-houses for defensive purposes and it was resolved to give the order accordingly, provided that his Honor Captain Carr shall cede forever the necessary ground thereto, without retaining any claim on it. As to the expenses and labor required for the aforesaid fortifications and blockhouses, the citizens of New-Castle are first to advance money, each according to his means and position, to pay the laborers, provided that the inhabitants of this

district, able to do all such work, shall be held to assist in the work, as occasion may require.

2. Concerning the fortifications above, the matter is left to the discretion of the people there, to choose the most convenient place or places for the defense.

3. All however with this understanding, that, if no war breaks out with the natives, which God may prevent, the said houses shall be used for the public service, as Council house, prison and for other public purposes, while they may be used as such by the whole river for a general and public account and expenses.

4. This resolution shall not be carried into effect without order of his Honor the General [Governor Lovelace], but preparations may be made in secret without arousing suspicion among the natives (NYCD 12:474-75).

A blockhouse was usually built of logs hewn square, placed horizontally one on top of the other to form the walls, and dovetailed at the corners. In some blockhouses, instead of dovetailing, the corners were formed by vertical posts into which the wall timbers were mortised. All blockhouses had embrasures or loopholes to accomodate muskets or small cannon. Although the above petition uses the plural, Governor Lovelace and his council approved the building of only one "New fforte or Block House," and he authorized Captain Carr to erect the structure at once. As a fund to help pay for the work, Lovelace levied a tax of "one guilder per can" on "strong liquor" to be paid by distillers at New Castle. He also approved salvaging any material from the old fort, i.e., Fort Casimir, that could be used in building the "new fort" (NYCD 12:482-83).

Construction on the new fort was delayed, and other events occurred, which caused Governor Lovelace to discharge the former Dutch magistrates and set up New Castle as a corporate bailiwick with Peter Alrichs as the bailiff, or principal civil magistrate, and Captain Edmond Cantwell as the high sheriff to replace the former schepens. One of the first things Cantwell did was to write Lovelace and tell him that no progress had been made by his predecessors in finishing the blockhouse, and he asked for further instructions.

Governor Lovelace replied promptly. He was angry that his former orders "have been noe better observed," and he wanted the blockhouse completed before November 1, 1672 under the penalty of 1,000 guilders in sewant to be raised by the English officers (NYCD 12:501). The political situation had worsened because the Marylanders were threatening to invade New Castle, which aggravated the Indian threats.

At this point the war between Holland and England temporarily interrupted the political situation in America as discussed in Chapter 8. If the blockhouse was completed prior to the signing of the Treaty of Westminster on February 19, 1674, it was temporarily taken over by the Dutch, but on November 6, 1674, the new English governor who replaced Lovelace, Sir Edmond Andros, authorized Captain Edmond Cantwell and William Tom "to take possession of the fort at New Castle in Delaware, as also the Cannon and all other Stores of Warre there . . ." (NYCD 12:515). Cantwell replied promptly and said he had the fort in his possession. This structure seems to have been located near the site of present Immanuel Church before the church was built. No plans or drawing are known to exist, but it seems to have served more as a municipal building than a fortress, having been used as a town hall, jail, and the upper story as a court-room. This phase of New Castle's history goes well beyond the Dutch period and still remains to be thoroughly studied.

3. Henri Couturier of New Castle—
Delaware's First Portrait Painter

A number of Dutch artists came to the New Netherland in the seventeenth century, and although painting in oils was among Holland's esthetic traditions, it was secondary to the trades or professions they followed in America. It was as difficult then for an artist to make a living in Delaware as it is today. Henri, or Hendrick, Couturier was one of these early native Dutch artists. No biography of him has yet been written although brief background information is given in an article by Charles X. Harris entitled "Henri Couturier An Artist of New Netherland," *New York Historical Society Quarterly* 11 (July 1927):45-52.

Couturier was born in Leyden, Rembrandt's birthplace. His father was a burgher whose occupation was a linendraper, i.e., a merchant who deals in buying and selling linens. Couturier's birthdate is not known, but he married Lysbeth (Elizabeth) Coppyn in Leyden in 1648 where their marriage record refers to him as a schilder ("painter"). He had apparently been an art student, and when the St. Luke's Art Guild was founded in Leyden the year of his marriage he was enrolled as one of the "original members."

A few months after Couturier's marriage he signed a notary record as a groff greynreder ("grossgrain cloth manufacturer"), a specialized fabric having heavy cross-wide cords. Like other Dutch painters of his time, he needed income from a vocation while he pursued his avocation as a painter. Children were born to the Couturiers, and about 1656 or 1657 he came to the New Netherland presumably accompanied by his family although these details are uncertain.

The writer has found Henri Couturier's name in the New Amstel records on June 30, 1660, and the entry indicates he then had a house in the town (*Gehring, Dutch Period*, 1981, p. 204). Thereafter, his name is briefly mentioned with such spellings as Cousturier, Coururie, Coustrien, Casturier, Coutrie, and in other variants. Although he was a Dutch citizen, his name is obviously of French or Walloon origin, and Dutch scribes had difficulty with the spelling, and doubtless with the pronunciation.

On July 3, 1663, Couturier's wife's name is cited in the New Amstel records, which suggests she was then living in the town with him (*Ibid.*, p. 324). These references are tantalizingly brief, although it is known that she conducted her own mercantile business. This may have been an unusual activity for a female in the seventeenth century in New Amstel, but Mrs. Couturier seems to have been an unusual person. Harris states that the records of the Dutch Reformed Church in New Amsterdam indicate that three of her children were baptized there on November 22, 1662 (*Harris*, p. 46). Since the Couturiers were then residents of New Amstel and the records are clear that there was no Dutch Reformed minister there at the time, it is possible that baptism was delayed until a propitious time when newly-born members of the family could accompany their parents to New Amsterdam. Harris also states that two sons were born to the couple in Leyden before they came to America and were baptized there, and twin daughters and another son were baptized in old Amsterdam. If this information is correct Mrs. Couturier by 1662 was the mother of eight children, but there is no supportive documentation in the New Amstel records. On the other hand there is no evidence to negate this information.

What can be corroborated by the author's research is that Couturier was a merchant in New Amstel for ten years, or longer, and that he imported and sold cloth, shoes, and other merchandise. But he was not an ordinary merchant; he also became a leading political figure as a burgomaster and a member of Alexander d'Hinoyossa's council during the period when the City of Amsterdam owned the colony. After the Duke of

York's forces seized the town, as discussed in Chapter 8 above, he was one of the six burgomasters who signed the oath of allegiance to England on October 1, 1664 "on behalfe of themselves and all the Dutch and Swedes inhabiting the Delaware Bay and River" (*Pennsylvania Archives*, 2nd series 5:574-75).

On October 26, 1664, Colonel Richard Nicolls, the Duke of York's ranking officer at New Amsterdam (renamed New York) issued a permit to "Elizabeth Consturier wife of Henry Consturier of Delaware Bay" to "Transfer herself and Goods to Delaware . . . and there to Trade or Traffique" (*Ibid.*, p. 579). This can be interpreted to mean that the change from the Dutch to the English government did not interrupt the Couturier's business activity. Having already pledged his loyalty to the English government Couturier did not require a special permit to continue his business, but his wife was apparently in New Amsterdam at the time the oath was signed at New Amstel. The records indicate that the couple did business both in New Amstel and New Amsterdam during the Stuyvesant administration.

On January 23, 1657, Governor Stuyvesant, at the behest of his council, ordered that thereafter all merchants desirous of doing business in New Netherland were required to purchase a Burgherright and to keep a shop in New Amsterdam in "their own or a leased house or room" and only those possessing the Burgherright "may keep open shops or trade elsewhere in the province." This explains why the Couturiers had stores and residences in both towns. During the English administration, Couturier bought a house and lot on High Street in New York on December 9, 1669 ("Original Book of New York Deeds, Jan. 1, 1672 to Oct. 19, 1675" *Collections of the New York Historical Society for the Year 1913* New York, 1914, 46:36-37). The same year, he was elected a deacon of the Dutch Reformed Church in New York (*Harris*, p. 46). But we know he was still doing business in New Amstel as late as May 30, 1671 when he was the highest bidder on goods salvaged from a sloop wrecked in Delaware Bay (*Gehring, English Period*, 1977, p. 22).

On April 15, 1675, a Dutch official named John Moll took possession of a house in New Amstel, which he noted in his flawed English was "whare Mrs. Coutrie Leved in Laest heer" (*Ibid.*, p. 59). Whether this was a rented dwelling or one owned by her husband or herself is not stated.

Apparently Couturier prospered in business, and Harris states he went to England in 1674 where he died in 1683 or 1684; on July 6, 1684 his wife is referred to in an English record as Elizabeth, widow of Henry Couturier (*Harris*, p. 48). Evidently Couturier went to England ahead of his wife, because on June 30, 1674, having her husband's power of attorney, she sold his house and lot on High Street in New York, and possibly any property he may have owned in New Amstel ("Original Book of New York Deeds," *Ibid.*, pp. 36-37).

Couturier's authorship of Peter Stuyvesant's portrait, and the picture of his fifteen-year-old son Nicholas William, is corroborated in a citation quoted from the Executive Board of Burgomasters of New Amsterdam reading as follows:

Friday, June 12, 1663, at the City Hall[,] present Messrs. Marten Cregier, Olof Stevenzen van Cortlant and the Officer Pieter Tonneman.
The wife of Hendrick Coutrie appearing, she is told, the Burgomasters had learned, that she sold in retail; therefore she is bound to purchase the Burgherright. She answers it was given to her husband by the Director General [Stuyvesant]: asked whether she had not given something for it to the General, she says, her husband has painted the portrait of his Honour and drawn pictures of his sons (*Minutes of the Orphanmasters Court of New Amsterdam, 1655-1663*, vol. 2 entitled *Minutes of the Executive Boards of the Burgomasters of New Amsterdam, etc.*, trans. Berthold Fernow (New York: Colonial Dames, the State of New York, 1907), pp. 176-77).

According to two ordinances passed by Governor Stuyvesant and his council in 1657, an applicant paid twenty guilders Dutch money for a "small" Burgherright and fifty guilders for a "great" Burgherright. Those who did not possess a Burgherright could not do business. The fees were to be used in "the strengthening and circumvallation of this City," which simply means the money was intended to keep the city wall in repair (*Laws and Ordinances of New Netherland 1638-1674*, trans. E.B. O'Callaghan (Albany:1868), pp. 298-303).

In lieu of paying cash to obtain the Burgherright for his wife and himself, Couturier made a special arrangement with Stuyvesant to paint his portrait and pictures of his two sons, Balthazar Lazar (1647-1678) and Nicholas William (1648-1698), a year younger than his brother. The paintings of Governor Stuyvesant and his son Nicholas William have been accounted for and are in the collections of the New York Historical Society along with paintings of other members of the Stuyvesant family, but the whereabouts of the picture of Balthazar Lazar is unknown (A.J. Wall, "New York City's Tercentenary and the Stuyvesant Family Portraits," *New York Historical Society Quarterly* 10 (April 1926):14-16).

Mrs. Couturier used the past tense in referring to the three paintings, which means they had all been executed prior to June 12, 1663, but not earlier than 1657 when Stuyvesant ordered merchants to obtain the Burgherright. There is little reason to question her veracity. A respectable businesswoman, the wife of a New Amstel official and a prominent merchant, would scarcely perjure herself before an important body like the Burgomasters of New Amsterdam who could readily check the facts. These officials were doubtless personally acquainted with her and her husband, and an extant portrait of one of them, Olof Stevenzen van Cortlant (1618-1684), is believed to have been painted by Couturier (*Harris*, p. 48).

A foremost contemporary authority on early New York portraiture, Mary Childs Black, is of the opinion that the portraits of Peter Stuyvesant and his son Nicholas William, both executed in a similar crude, harsh style on wood panels of similar size, were painted by Couturier. She also believes that a portrait of Cornelis Steenwyck, New York's third mayor, and a member of Governor Lovelace's council, may also be the work of Couturier (Personal correspondence, Dec. 5, 1986; Dec. 15, 1986).

One of the problems of identification is that Couturier's paintings did not bear a personal signature, which was not unusual among many early painters. There is, however, one clue that may identify some of his works. Couturier, and other contemporary merchants doing business in New Amstel, used a distinctive personal mark on their invoices and on the actual shipments of merchandise. No doubt the collectors of custom duties also found the identifying marks useful. It is fortuitous that Couturier's mark was preserved on an invoice for duffel cloth shipped to him from Holland to New Amstel in 1663 on the vessel *St. Jacob* (NYCD 12:429). A copy of the mark is shown as Fig. 1, at right.

The portrait of Olof Stevenzen van Cortland mentioned above bears what is essentially the same inscription with a second "c" added. See Fig. 2. A portrait of Frederick Philipse, first Lord of the Manor of Philipsborough at Tarrytown, New York, dated 1674, owned by the National Gallery of Art in Washington, D.C. bears a similar mark. Doubt has been expressed by some critics about the attribution of certain works to Couturier, but questions are invariably raised about unsigned art works, and even the authorship of many that bear marks or signatures is questioned (see *American Paintings, An Illustrated Catalog*, Washington, D.C., National Gallery of Art, 1980, pp. 307-09; E.P. Richardson, *A Short History of Painting in America*, New York: Thomas Y. Crowell Co., 1963, pp. 22-23).

Entirely apart from the question of whether Couturier painted this or that portrait, which we will leave to the art critics to resolve, the fact remains that he was Delaware's first resident portrait painter, and the first professional artist in the Delaware Valley. Thus, he was the predecessor of Gustavus Hesselius (1682-1755) a native of Sweden who settled in Philadelphia in 1711 and won renown for his attainments as a pioneer artist in the middle colonies.

What paintings Couturier executed during the time he lived in New Amstel is a question that cannot now be answered, but it goes without saying that an artist with his talents would not have lived at New Amstel as long as he did without practicing his craft. One cannot rule out the possibility that one or more of New Amstel's prominent officials may have sat for his portraits. Would it not be a thrilling experience to find in the cobwebs of an attic an old painting bearing his initialed trademark which had two variations:

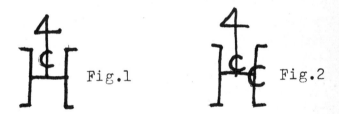

Fig.1   Fig.2

Figure 1 appears on the invoice received at New Amstel for merchandise shipped to Couturier on May 5, 1663. The design element at the top is not the numeral four, because the identical paraph occurs in the marks made by a number of other contemporary merchants. Dr. Charles T. Gehring suggests it may be "a case of function deterring form if you consider the 45 degree bar as the strengthening element in a branding iron used to identify the personal consignments aboard ship" (Personal correspondence, December 29, 1986). In other words, the mark could be applied by ink or paint to a document, bill of lading, or painting, but it may have also been used as a brand stamped by heat on a wooden shipping case or barrel.

Figure 2 is the mark appearing on two paintings, which some art experts, but not all, believe are genuine works by Couturier. One may well ask: why doesn't the mark appear on all Couturier's paintings? The answer is that no one knows. It is no more unusual than the omission of his signature from the paintings attributed to him. He had his own reasons just as Rembrandt did for executing dozens of unsigned paintings. Van Gogh, we may recall, did not sign many of his paintings executed in France because he said the French could not properly pronounce his surname.

INDEX